RAZOR
POCO

Also available at all good book stores

9781785315282

9781785315077

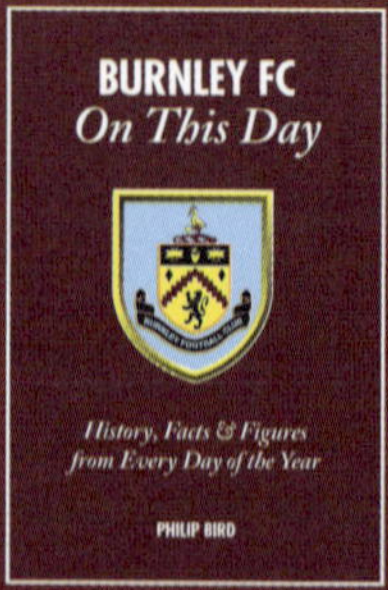

9781785314254

9781785317682

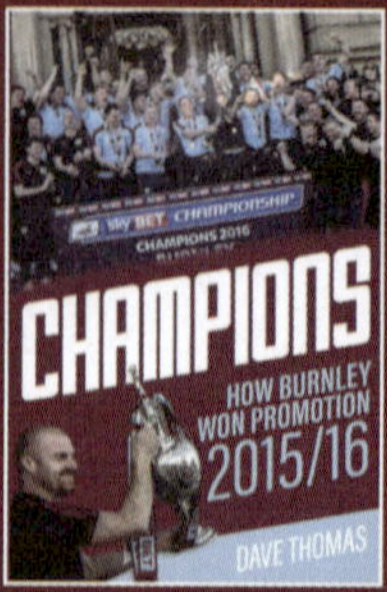

9781785312274

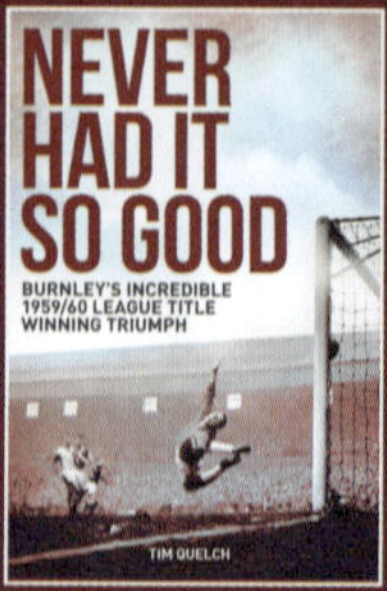

9781909626546

9781909626690

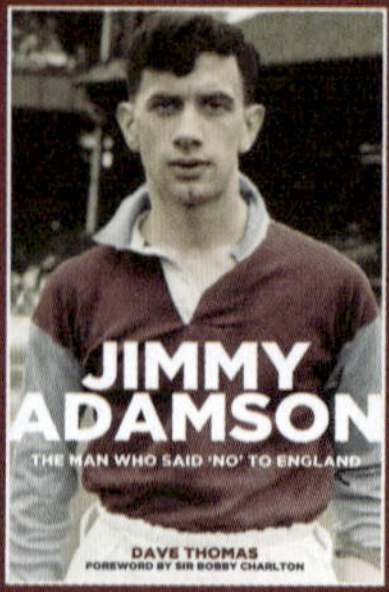

9781785314032

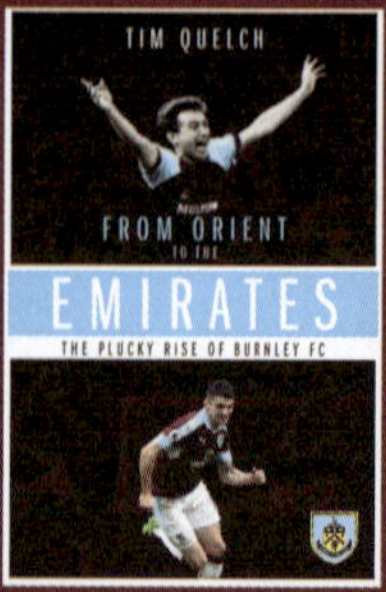

9781785313127

A Director's Tale

Dave Thomas

A Director's Tale

John Bond, Burnley, and the Diaries of Director Derek Gill

Foreword by John Helm

pitch

First published by Pitch Publishing, 2022

Pitch Publishing
A2 Yeoman Gate
Yeoman Way
Worthing
Sussex
BN13 3QZ
www.pitchpublishing.co.uk
info@pitchpublishing.co.uk

A CIP catalogue record is available for this book from the British Library.

ISBN 978 1 80150 072 2

Typesetting and origination by Pitch Publishing

Printed and bound in India by Replika Press Pvt. Ltd.

Contents

Acknowledgements

IN TELLING this story I have been able to dip into various books, including:

- *No Nay Never Volumes One and Two*, Dave Thomas
- *Bob Lord of Burnley*, Dave Thomas and Mike Smith
- *Mud, Sweat and Shears*, groundsman Roy Oldfield's revealing book

From Roy's story I confess I have taken much of his account of the 1984/85 season verbatim. That seems reasonable since we wrote the book together and there seemed little point in simply re-arranging the words.

I have also consulted the following:

- *BFC and Me*, Paul Fletcher
- *Clarets Chronicles*, Ray Simpson
- *Forever and Ever*, Tim Quelch
- *The Forgotten Fifteen*, James Bentley
- *He's Here, He's There: The Gerry Gow Story*, Neil Palmer
- *Got to be There*, Dave Burnley

Local reporter Peter Higgs of the *Burnley Express* and *Evening Star* wrote several of the articles used. I have also reproduced an article from the *Lancashire Telegraph* setting out Martin Dobson's thoughts.

Edward Walton of Burnley Civic Trust helped enormously with photographs.

The extensive personal diaries of director Derek Gill give immense details of the period and are crucial to this book. Gill wrote his recollections of his time at the club in 1987, in longhand, then committed them to print on his personal computer during his Tenerife holidays. He inserted more comments in 2005 prompted by the publication of *No Nay Never Volume One*. They are what they are, personal diaries, and as such give what some might feel is a one-sided view of things. It has to be noted that chairman John Jackson, so often mentioned, is no longer here to give his responses. I was, however, in touch several times with his daughter Rebekah.

I write detailed diaries myself and have done so for many years. I know full well that what you write down is very much geared to yourself and your own interpretation of things. If we write our opinions of other people, they can be none too flattering. If only John Jackson had kept a diary; that too would have been fascinating.

Club programmes from the John Bond season were invaluable. His candid and blunt programme notes tell his story and express his thoughts perfectly.

It surprises me that there is no existing biography of John Bond. This book does not give the complete picture but at least gives some insight into him and his career. The general picture of him at Burnley is not too favourable; he is seen by many as a disaster. And yet that is not the complete picture, as this book will show. He was only part of the problem. A substantial one, it's true, a square peg in a round hole, but as his tenure progressed the boardroom became more and more toxic as the blame game began. Dante's *Inferno* comes to mind, where the sign over the gates to Hell reads 'Abandon Hope All Ye Who Enter Here'. Much the same could be said of the doorway into the Burnley boardroom.

'Why did I ever come to Burnley?' Bond once said in a TV interview.

Several players contributed to this story, including Martin Dobson, Joe Gallagher, Derek Scott and Vince Overson. Former manager Frank Casper was always on hand to give his side of what went on. Like Brian Miller, Casper had no great affection for John Jackson. Again, that does not suggest that Jackson was the villain of the piece, far from it. But neither Miller nor Casper got on with him. Chalk and cheese, you might say.

Sadly, the people who could have given more insights are all gone: John Jackson, Frank Teasdale, Brian Miller, John Bond and Derek Gill. But I am grateful to Derek's sons David and Stephen for their help and support, plus John Jackson's daughter Rebekah Hipkiss, and the family of Brian Miller.

Cover design is by Duncan Olner with thanks to Mike Procter for his permission to use the painting of Turf Moor.

I am grateful to journalist and broadcaster John Helm for the foreword.

Thanks also to Phil Whalley for his contributions including: the John Jackson article in the *London Clarets* magazine, issue 180, April 2008; his Derek Gill interview in the same magazine, issue 165, June 2005; his John Bond interview, again in that publication, issue 159, June 2004.

Robert Smith responded to the request for help by immediately heading for his loft where he has a lifetime's collection of Burnley memorabilia, programmes and local newspapers. I collected a box full of resource material from him.

John Gibaut over in Seattle did the preliminary proofing and read-through.

My computer/technical skills are minimal. A thousand thanks to Mrs T for her knowledge.

Foreword by John Helm

I AM often asked by football fans to nominate my most memorable match; not an easy task as I have been able to attend more than 5,000 over the past 70-odd years. The quick and easy answer is Brazil versus Italy at the 1982 World Cup finals where Paolo Rossi's breathtaking hat-trick knocked out the most exciting team it has been my privilege to see. Even as a neutral observer and commentator I desperately wanted to see Zico, Sócrates, Falcão, Éder et al lift the trophy.

Yet that is not the only answer I give to the question. Saturday, 9 May 1987 still ranks as the most emotional footballing day I can recall.

I had been to Turf Moor on many occasions. My school, Salt Grammar in Shipley, used to play Burnley Grammar School annually. It was always fixed to coincide with a match at Turf Moor, hence I saw Jimmy McIlroy and Albert Cheesebrough score hat-tricks in an extraordinary 7-3 victory over Leicester City in 1957.

That was nothing compared to the drama and emotion that enveloped Turf Moor on the final day of that fateful 1986/87 season. At that time, I was working for ITV and was despatched to Turf Moor to see whether Brian Miller's side could preserve the Football League status of a club formed more than a century before.

I had not, and never have since, witnessed anything quite like that day. It was as if every one of the 15,781 people present were praying for a miracle. The only exceptions would have been the odd few supporting Leyton Orient who were supposed to be the sacrificial lambs.

Burnley's very existence seemed to be at stake.

The aforementioned McIlroy, by then working as a journalist, had hinted at extinction if the worst came to the worst, and a future in non-league football was not an acceptable or appealing option. Neil Grewcock's first-half goal eased the tension a little with scores coming in from elsewhere adding to the drama.

I was sitting with a cameraman and sound recordist within touching distance of the directors' box and alerted my colleagues to the potential of unforgettable scenes at the final whistle. So, after Ian Britton's goal helped clinch the 2-1 victory, I thrust the microphone under the nose of chairman Frank Teasdale and procured one of the most emotional interviews imaginable. It was heart-wrenching, tear-jerking stuff with a background of diehard fans singing jubilantly for the first time in months.

Incredibly, my sound recordist thought we were doing a microphone test and cocked up what should have been a lead item on the evening news. Thanks pal! The following day I was interviewing disbelieving Lincoln City fans whose team had been relegated after losing to Swansea.

Well-known Burnley journalist Keith McNee sat next to me throughout the match with his back turned to the pitch. He couldn't bear to watch and tragically died soon afterwards; at least not of a broken heart which would have been the case if his beloved club had been beaten that day.

This book covers all the events during the seasons that lead up to the Orient game with the build-up involving the three key characters: John Bond, Derek Gill and John Jackson. They are events that are almost as dramatic as Ian Britton's goal and the final whistle. Had Burnley lost and been relegated that day, contrary to what Jimmy McIlroy suggested, Derek Gill would have ensured that the club continued.

I knew John Bond from his days at Manchester City and perhaps it is clear now that he was never the right man for Burnley. Overall, this is a story of club politics and failed relationships.

Dave Thomas has captured the mood of the town, researched the reasons for the demise, interviewed the men who played leading roles and covered one of the most incredible periods in the history of Burnley Football Club in an engaging and exhaustive way. This will be compulsive reading for all those of a claret persuasion.

John Helm
February 2022

1
The background

THIS IS the story of four years at Burnley Football Club, a club with a long and illustrious history. As at any club, there were good years and bad, winning years and years of turmoil, years of success and years of failure. These particular four years saw everything; glory, chaos, triumph and debacle, all condensed into one short snapshot of time when set against the long history of the club that began in 1882. A most unexpected promotion, an immediate relegation, one season with John Bond, and on his departure, relegation the next season. If drama is what you want then look no further than Turf Moor from 1981 to 1985. And then, just two years after that came the Leyton Orient season. It was a time when strong hearts were needed.

It had everything and underlying it all were the main characters: chairman John Jackson, director Derek Gill, along with managers Brian Miller, Frank Casper, John Bond and finally John Benson. The Bouncing Czech, Robert Maxwell, had what we might call a walk-on part. One of Derek Gill's sons proudly recalls the time that one Sunday morning he bluntly told Maxwell to fuck off, when Derek was out and Maxwell insisted on speaking to him.

Owld Bob Lord was dead, the great patriarch finally gone and replaced as chairman by John Jackson. Not quite a coup but almost, too ill to attend the board meeting at which he was replaced. Lord's daughters were furious, in particular Barbara. Lord had been replaced without his knowledge while he was as good as dying. 'Stabbed in the back,' she said. In truth, what else could the directors do?

'Burn everything,' Lord told her in his final days. 'Burn the lot.' And so up in smoke went all the records, letters, documents and paperwork he had accumulated at home over the last 25 years and more. It took a week to destroy them. Up in flames went the records of his time at the club, his legacy obliterated, or at least what was left of it. Had he not been ill he would have faced an FA inquiry into the club's finances and his involvement with them. His death spared him that. Perhaps that is why he ordered Barbara to burn everything. We shall never know.

As he lay dying, the team struggled in the Third Division; wins were rare and they were at the bottom end of the table. Ironically, after his death they recovered, bit by bit; it was the defeats that became rare. They clawed their way back up the table so well that under manager Brian Miller, and on the field marshalled by the incomparable Martin Dobson, by the end of the season they were the champions and returned to the Second Division, now the Championship. They were triumphant days for the team and the board of directors. The word 'preening' did not go amiss.

Beavering away behind the scenes, happy to let John Jackson take centre stage, was director Derek Gill. A quiet, family man, softly spoken, diligent, hard-working, accomplished, an accountant with a forensic mind, he ran his own engineering works and was an accomplished musician. Burnley Football Club was his love. Relations between him and the more gregarious Jackson were initially good; Jackson too was passionately in love with the club he had supported since boyhood. Directors don't fall out when things are going well.

Manager Brian Miller was one of the great rocks of the club – a player since his teenage years, first-team stalwart for years, coach, assistant manager, then manager. Miller didn't suffer fools gladly. His dislike of Jackson would eventually surface.

How many directors keep a diary of their time at a club? Precious few, but Gill was one such person. The diaries came to my attention when in a previous book, an anthology of chapters about different people and players at the club, Gill was referred to in a way that he felt did him a great injustice. Derek wrote shortly afterwards:

'To my astonishment and regret I have been made aware of a publication grandly describing itself as an anthology of my once beloved Burnley Football Club, going under the title of *No Nay Never*. Nor I must confess is it a title that would ever have attracted space on my book shelf or taken up any of my reading time, but on hearing of it from an old friend originally from Burnley, but long since emigrated to London, I have to say that I found it to be well presented with some thoroughly riveting sections.

'Unfortunately, it also contains certain references to myself from which any reader unaware of the real history of an unhappy period for the club could only conclude that the club itself was the victim of a financially reckless and devious financial director who acted against the wishes of his chairman and committed the club to unsustainable levels of expenditure, that led to the decline in the fortunes of the club.

'I was that financial director, and indeed became managing director in September 1983 until my resignation in 1985. Having kept silent on many matters for these 20 years and more and more resigned to letting sleeping dogs lie, I find myself grossly offended by distortion, and the mere half truths in the recollections. I am therefore obliged to respond. The remarks of one person in particular in *No Nay Never* go far too far to be allowed to remain unanswered.'

In this latter paragraph, Gill is referring to John Jackson, who was interviewed for *No Nay Never* and that full interview appears in this book. Gill went on to explain that had he been given an opportunity to refute the chairman's claims in the same anthology, then his ire would never have been inflamed. Thus, since then, he made his diaries available to anyone who was interested, and what an insight they provide into 'the headlines and the crazy case of Burnley Football Club from 1982 to 1985'. They present the good, the bad and the ugly of his time as managing director.

Like all diaries, they have to be treated with some caution. Many entries are factual but others are personal and judgemental. Diaries are private things where we reveal not just the good and the joyful, but angst and unhappiness. We write things that we would perhaps not say face to face. And they give our own interpretations and slant on things.

'Who cares that I was a director of Burnley Football Club?' Gill wrote. He added that he never had any desire to see his diaries, or 'book' as he called them, fully published but was simply content to print out copies whenever anyone had the interest to read them. What particularly galled him was the inference by Jackson, in the piece he wrote for *No Nay Never*, that it was the financial director who had advocated unwise financial policies, and the financial director was, in fact, Derek Gill. Jackson maintained that in allowing John Bond to spend money, he himself was merely carrying out the wishes of the board.

'Let's get stock on the shelf,' was, he insisted, the view of the board. In other words, buy players, and let's use overdrafts and other resources.

Gill's discontent was straightforward enough. Accusations of profligacy with the club's money were pointed at him. But, he argued, how could that be? The wild spending of the Bond management period took place before he became managing director.

'I disagreed with the financial director,' wrote Jackson, thereby distancing himself from Gill, and inferring that it was Gill's policy.

'We should have retained money for a rainy day. Lawyers are generally more cautious than successful businessmen, and I had seen enough rainy days at Burnley Football Club.' Herein was the suggestion that Gill was not cautious. 'What happened thereafter was a financial disaster. John Bond would ask for money. The board would authorise it. And the money was spent. I had no enthusiasm for the policies.'

All of this was part of a much longer piece that Jackson provided. On reading it, Gill was astonished. He was aggrieved when the *No Nay Never* book appeared, and to put the record straight he gave me a copy of his extensive diaries. In the local press and in the next anthology, we did indeed put the record straight. None of it was to suggest that the club's eventual woes were solely the chairman's fault, far from it. As in most things, a combination of factors came into play. If you read any Thomas Hardy novel, the characters are always at the mercy of universal elements, of fate, never in control of their own destiny. You could argue it was much the same when Bond, Jackson and Gill became entangled at Burnley Football Club.

The diaries provide a record of times that began so spectacularly well and ended four years later in acrimony and with Gill's own personal disappointment at the way things had gone against him in his final months at the club.

With wit and an erudite turn of phrase, Gill thus recorded the trials and tribulations of the comings and goings, the ins and outs, the behind-the-scenes manoeuvrings and jockeying. The way that players were signed, the mistakes that were made, the good and the bad of everything that went on, the poor treatment of Brian Miller, the poor treatment of Frank Casper, the players who were bought, and the way that John Bond swept into the club and then, having been dismissed, literally disappeared into the night.

What the diaries show initially is the way in which Gill turned around the club's financial fortunes, from the penniless shambles that Bob Lord had left behind, to money almost overflowing from the tills, as he salvaged and rescued the situation. A promotion season and money in the bank. What could possibly go wrong? Gill recorded it all.

When, only a few years ago, we referred to him in *No Nay Never Volume One*, he re-read his diaries and added to them. They evoked painful memories. They reminded him of the time he would have loved to have become chairman; and indeed, the prize was within his grasp, but at the last minute it was snatched away, he wrote. The hurt lasted for years.

Chairmen, overall, are a much-maligned breed; when things go wrong, they are, more often than not, the first target. But they are brave men who are prepared to stick their heads above the parapet. Jackson was just such a man. After that first successful promotion year, the next three were traumatic, each for different reasons, and Jackson endured some dreadful personal abuse.

Gill wrote down the bulk of his recollections in 1987, the year of the great escape, when in the last game of the season Burnley beat Orient 2-1 to avoid demotion to non-league football. It was two years after he had left the boardroom. He shed tears of relief that Orient day, a day embossed on the mind of every Burnley fan, Saturday, 9 May. Jackson undoubtedly felt the same relief and joy.

Monday, 16 May 1985 had been the day Gill walked out of the boardroom for the last time. Three and a half years earlier he had been invited to join the board, to his great surprise, and it was a prize that he felt beyond riches, such was his love for the club. In his wildest dreams and ambition, he had never expected such a position. He wrote that he would have sacrificed so much for the club and to walk out in the way that he did was the hardest and most heart-rending decision he had ever made.

'There were good reasons for it,' he wrote.

'During my years at Burnley we had four team managers,' Gill wrote in 1987, 'starting with Brian Miller, followed in extraordinary circumstances by Frank Casper, who in turn was quickly succeeded by John Bond, whose one-year tenure was ended when he was replaced by John Benson. Players, other staff and supporters did not know whether they were coming or going and it is little wonder that we suffered relegation from both the Second and Third Divisions.

'The board of which I was a member cannot possibly be exonerated from the lion's share of the responsibility, even allowing for the ludicrous shambles bequeathed to it by the previous dictatorial chairman. But as always it is necessary to look into the background to appreciate how it all came about. Even after all this time I still find it difficult to understand how supposedly professional men could have acted so stupidly over that period and somehow failed to learn from their mistakes until it was too late for the board to survive. But never, as has been asserted, would it be too late for the club to survive.

'Directors often seem unable or unwilling to differentiate between the club and their own personal interests but football clubs are not unique in that respect. Rather, it is that they are very high profile in smaller confined communities such as Burnley, beautifully dubbed "Grumpy Town" by Tommy Hutchison during his spell at the club.

'It was late October/early November 1981, when Colin Sanderson, at that time solicitor to the club, introduced me to the chairman, John Jackson, and we met at his home. Colin was to join the board sometime later, only to resign after a short period in an unhappy manner following what by then was a routine boardroom row.

'My first impression of Mr Jackson was of a man exhilarated by the prospects before him but also seemingly aware of the magnitude of the task that lay ahead, and disarmingly frank about his lack of administrative experience therein. All this had been the sole preserve of "Mr Lord" as he invariably referred to him and to Lord's trusted lieutenant, the long-serving secretary Albert Maddox.

'John did not seem to be under any illusions and made it perfectly clear that he was looking for sweeping changes in the club starting right at the top with a reconstructed board, something he confirmed to the Annual General Meeting in January 1982, when my appointment was ratified. At that first meeting with him he told me of the infighting within the board relating to the succession as chairman following the resignation[1] of the legendary Bob Lord due to what was to prove to be a terminal illness, and it was clear there were old scores to settle.

'All my life I have enjoyed a passion for music but there was never a sweeter sound to my ear than the melody that said the old regime at Burnley was on the way out and big changes were imminent. My discussions with John Jackson left me in no doubt that it would not be long before I would have a part to play.

'For years I had felt a distaste for Bob Lord and had been on the receiving end of abusive correspondence, particularly for being critical of his dismissal of team manager Jimmy Adamson. Some of his actions are related elsewhere in this book, but for now I will simply state the obvious that it is an invariable characteristic of dictators (which he most certainly was) that they fail to make any meaningful provision for their succession. The first consequence was an inevitable boardroom fight for the "chair" shortly to surface with the forcing out of Mr Jimmy Wilde, a respected solicitor and one of the consortium of four that had acquired the shareholding of Mr Lord. It was the incomparable Jimmy McIlroy who made the dry but apt comment to me when I had the privilege of inviting him back to Turf Moor, for the first time in almost 20 years that, "Even dictators are not immortal."

---

1 Bob Lord did not resign. He was simply replaced in his absence as chairman at a board meeting that he was too ill to attend. Gill did not know this at the time of writing but acknowledged it later.

'My part in the story had arrived much earlier than I had ever imagined when John Jackson asked me to examine the affairs of the club and to submit a report and with it any proposals I might have for the future. He promised me total access to any and all information and documentation within the club and access to whatever I needed to carry out the job[2].

'For me, it was the ultimate labour of love and John was totally true to his word in backing me to the hilt as I threw myself into the task. One thing has always struck me in business when dealing with consultants, which I have to say in passing is not one of my favoured pastimes, is that reports always carry that little bit of extra weight when they contain those juicy morsels which the commissioner of the report wants to hear confirmed. I was not so daft as to fail to realise the content of my report could well put me on the board, if it confirmed what the chairman wanted to hear, that is to say already knew.

'So, John got to hear what he wanted to hear and he was very close to the mark in his own assessment of the state of the club. All I needed to do was to suggest a basic standard management structure to replace the *ask the chairman everything and never use any initiative of your own.* A mentality that had been all-pervasive under Bob Lord. I thought that John was going to be a brilliant chairman and all he needed was a good organisation man and I had no doubts that I could fill that role. The reports that I submitted are reported elsewhere in this book and reflect accurately and honestly the situation that I found. A situation that could not possibly be allowed to continue without the club sinking still further into oblivion.

---

2 One does wonder if Gill knew at this point that Lord had ordered all documents and correspondence that he kept at home to be destroyed. In addition, another cache of documents went missing, no doubt incinerated, when the old Brunshaw Road Stand was demolished, and the old offices within it. Nevertheless, what he was left with enabled him to produce a damning report.

'Memory can play strange tricks and it is worth a brief summary of the legacy left by Mr Lord. Ask many, indeed most, people where Burnley were when he left and they might be surprised to learn that the position was second to last in the old THIRD DIVISION! The administration was a shambles. Suppliers were not being paid. The position with PAYE, National Insurance and the Inland Revenue was chaotic. VAT was something to ignore and hope it would go away[3].

'The chalice inherited by John Jackson, however, was not entirely poisoned. But neither did it smell of roses. But at least it was in a position where any optimist feels there is only one way to go. And that is up. We set to work with enthusiasm and I was virtually full-time in the place. There were good prospects of an early boost in income and for me, the whole place, being there doing this work, was just too good to be true. My own business was left almost unattended. And I loved every minute of it.

'Then began a run of success on the field and in the next 41 league games only two were lost. It was too easy by half.

'What clever buggers we thought we were.'

---

3 The club was, in fact, teetering on insolvency.

2

Meet the cast

TWO CHARACTERS begin this story and both are there for most of the years that this book covers: Derek Gill and John Jackson. Both, when the story begins, were individually admirable men in their own fields, capable, accomplished and respected, and this was still the case four years later. During those years, however, what might have begun as a mutual admiration society slowly changed as events unfolded. As those four years progressed, other characters came and went, each playing their part, each adding to the tale, some for the good, and others less so. By the end of the four years, Gill and Jackson were still good men, gifted and talented. It was what happened during those four years that was the problem.

John Jackson was only 68 when he died, but remained just as much a Burnley diehard as when he first fell in love with the club. His shift as chairman might have been short but it was certainly eventful. His love for the club began when he saw the triumphant team of 1947, which won promotion and reached the FA Cup Final. He was just seven years old. Ironic, of course, that his predecessor as chairman, Bob Lord, had much the same experience, but in a different era, when he saw the great team of 1914 on the Town Hall steps. Both of them experienced the thrill and delight of seeing their triumphant local team.

Jackson attended Burnley Grammar School and it was clear that he had great intellectual prowess. At 16 he was in the school football team and always remembered being sent off in a game for ungentlemanly conduct. The goalkeeper had been kicked in the head by his own defender and while he lay prostrate on the floor, Jackson slammed the ball home to score. To his final day, Jackson wondered why he was punished, since the referee had not blown his whistle to stop play.

His father was Wilfred Jackson, an Alderman of Burnley who also ran the East Lancs Platers Co on Oxford Road in Burnley. Jackson's mother, Sally, died when he was 12. Before that, she would never let him attend a game at Burnley on account of the size of the crowds. He remembered crying when, in 1947, Chris Duffy scored the goal at Wembley for Charlton that beat Burnley in the FA Cup Final.

After grammar school he went to the United States on an English-Speaking Scholarship. He loved his time there and applied for and was accepted at Harvard University, but his father wanted him to return to the UK. This he did and went to Keele University, then considered innovative and very different to the older, established centres of learning. He lasted one term there and went on to take up a management apprenticeship scheme at Marks and Spencer.

But then he did something truly out of the ordinary. He bought a betting shop that was for sale down a Burnley back street. On the spot he purchased it and reinvented himself as Johnny Edgar Bookmaker, Edgar being his middle name. The legend has it that he bought this establishment in Hereford but this is not true. The origin of this story may be to do with his wife being brought up there. The Hereford connections were, in fact, strong ones. His father-in-law had once been mayor of Hereford and was on the board of Hereford United. Jackson's wife was Miss Hereford in 1957.

So, Johnny Edgar's bookmaker business was certainly in Burnley, possibly in the Stoneyholme area. Wandering round Burnley down a back street, according to a news feature in 1983, he saw the betting shop for sale. In he went and asked how much the owner wanted.

'How much have you got?' asked the owner.

The story continues that Jackson had £300 life savings, of which £25 just happened to be in his pocket as he'd just been to the bank, so he replied that he had just £25. The bookie looked at him and took the £25, took off his linen working jacket and told him, 'Right lad, the place is yours.' Apocryphal or what? It makes a nice story at a time when Jackson's reputation was flying high at a successful and rejuvenated club. When the feature appeared in the esteemed *Daily Telegraph*, Burnley had reached the semi-final of what was then the Milk Cup, astonishingly winning at the mighty Tottenham Hotspur, and then reached the fifth round of the FA Cup.

Jackson ran the betting shop for four years, finding it 'a veritable goldmine of human behaviour'. He was successful there, made it pay, but then he took another contrasting turn. The family moved to Pasturegate Avenue and by now, having sold the business, he had chosen to attend law school in London and travelled home each weekend to be with the family. It took him just 27 months to qualify instead of the usual 36 and then he began his barrister role on the northern circuit which he continued until his death. He was acknowledged to have had one of the quickest minds on the circuit and was an extremely good orator but he never became a QC. Members of the Bar in those days looked askance at other members with connections to football clubs. He put Burnley Football Club first before progressing his career.

Serendipity or happenstance, call it what you like, but one of his heroes, the great Jimmy McIlroy, one of Burnley's finest ever players, had bought his parents' old house. A relationship grew with McIlroy who introduced him to a friend, John Cook, the son of a former Burnley director who years earlier had fallen foul of chairman Bob Lord. Jackson is thought to have paid Cook £5 each for something like 100 shares in the club and then began a campaign to get on to the board himself. In those days Lord's telephone number was no secret and, with persistent phone calls, Jackson in 1976 persuaded Lord to give him a seat on the board. For five years until Lord's death, Jackson served almost an apprenticeship but what lessons he learned were more to do with how not to run a club, since the old warhorse controlled every facet of the club and made every decision, as he gradually ran it into the ground.

'During the next few years,' Jackson wrote, 'I served an apprenticeship in every sense of the word. I learned a great deal about what to do and what not to do. On most important matters, the directors were informed rather than consulted.' It was during this time that Jackson may well have decided if the day ever came that he was chairman he would be very different.

'The financial position and the club's resources were such,' he added, 'that Mr Lord was content if the club merely stayed afloat. Consequently, and inevitably, we were close to bankruptcy and close to relegation when Mr Lord decided to retire. The harsh reality was we were close to the bottom of the Third Division, at our lowest position ever, with dwindling gates and a disenchanted public.'

Lord's shares, put up for sale in September, were sold to a consortium of four led by director Doc Iven. It is possible that Lord did not know this and thought he was selling just to Iven. Some 2,788 shares were sold for a reported £35,999.84, not the mythical £52,000 that has often been quoted.

It was October 1981 when Jackson became chairman, several weeks before Lord's death. At the October meeting Jackson stated that the first item on the agenda was the need to discuss the chairmanship of the club. He then invited the opinions of each director present, with Jackson proposing that there should be a change of chairman while the club was in such a state of inertia. Iven seconded this. Director Jimmy Wilde suggested that the matter be left in abeyance until Lord was present. This was defeated and the proposal to elect a new chairman was carried three to two. Jack Eglin was nominated. Jackson himself was nominated and became chairman by three votes to two. Wilde and Harrison, Lord's son-in-law, resigned soon after the meeting. At this point the club was £190,000 overdrawn at the bank with countless unpaid bills and debts.

Jackson's early moves as chairman were encouraging. He was under no illusions as to the task that lay ahead. The state of Denmark was indeed rotten, to paraphrase the Bard. Jackson always maintained that his position at the club was nominal, that he was head of a cabinet, not the sole decision maker. Because of the way the shares had been bought no one on the board had overriding seniority or authority to make decisions as Lord had done. And while Lord had kept fans at arm's length well away from the corridors of power, Jackson was different.

'I want fans to know,' he said, 'that I regard it as a privilege to be chairman of their club, rather than for them to feel that I consider it a privilege for them to visit this club.'

This struck an immediate chord with supporters alienated for years by Lord's arrogance. In addition, Jackson reduced admission prices, sanctioned the establishment of a supporters' club and set about improving relations with the town council. Lord had antagonised them for years; former MP Peter Pike recalled:

'The relationship with the council had completely deteriorated by the end of Bob Lord's reign as chairman. So, we had a meeting at the council offices and we tried to improve the relationship. It was the club's centenary year and the club by then were having a very hard time financially. We were anxious that the council didn't give the club a silly gift like a plaque, so after discussion with John Jackson we bought medical equipment which they felt they needed. In the end we developed a good relationship with John Jackson.'

'In a few words it is difficult to express the pleasure and deep feeling of privilege that I have in being able to write this,' Jackson wrote in the club's *Centenary Handbook*. 'It is almost ironic that the 100 years ended and an invisible chapter closed simultaneously with the death of Mr Burnley, Mr R.W. Lord. I have gathered the reins as the fortunes of Burnley Football Club are at their lowest ebb but I am determined that no stone will be left unturned in an attempt to take Burnley forward and to achieve a prominent position in the new football world. I would only add that when I say football is a team game, this is a club where I mean that literally. The team consists of directors, staff, players and most important of all, YOU the Burnley supporters.'

It is hard to imagine Lord expressing anything remotely similar to the end sentiments. All of this made Jackson's approach radically new and warmly welcomed. Jackson certainly knew that the inherited finances and systems were in a chaotic state. He moved quickly to bring some financial stability and solutions to the club, inviting local businessman Derek Gill to conduct a financial review.

In a *Sunday Express* interview on taking over, Jackson claimed his job was the easy one – it was a PR position with the commercial people having the hard time raising revenue. Burnley had always been a selling club but fans were delighted to read that it was now a club that would only sell to survive, not merely to live well, a pointed reference to the Lord regime.

'If we can keep our promising young players together with the experienced men we have, they can form a fair old side.' It turned out to be an accurate prophecy with promotion not far away.

In opting for Gill, he chose someone with an analytical and forensic mind, who was in fact a qualified accountant. The first game he ever attended was in 1942 when Burnley beat Oldham Athletic 3-0. He could even remember that Tommy Gardner scored twice. He had a ticket for the 1947 FA Cup Final but was persuaded with a bribe to give it to an uncle who told him that he could go next year. Alas, he didn't; Burnley were knocked out in the third round and his uncle was sacked for taking time off work. He loved Reg Attwell, Harry Potts and Alan Brown. Attwell could drink for England, he recalled. Gill's love of Burnley got him in trouble at school when he bunked off to watch a cup game against Middlesbrough, and when he was in the RAF, he went absent to watch them at Liverpool. They lost 4-0 and to add insult to injury he was caught sneaking back into camp and spent several days in 'jankers', as they called the punishment cells.

He was born in 1933 at his grandmother's house at Cuerden Street, which now, like many others in Burnley, is demolished. George V was on the throne, Ramsay MacDonald was prime minister and the film *King Kong* had just been released. He always said his childhood memories were happy ones with his younger brother Ken, and his parents. They even had a car in those days, which was very unusual. How his dad acquired a car is a mystery as they only had a draper's shop. The family today reckon his dad was a bit of *Dad's Army* character Private Walker, along with any other philanderer trait you could mention.

Gill's great hero was Grandad Hoyle, who had once walked to Blackburn to see Burnley play in the FA Cup, and had been to Crystal Palace to see Burnley beat Liverpool 1-0 in the FA Cup Final. It was the grandfather that started Gill's long love affair with Burnley FC.

He left school at 15, he and his brother having been brought up by their mother with no real idea what they wanted to do. Accountancy sounded all right, he remembered, when each of them were asked in class what they would like. So he went to a firm of local accountants and being a bright lad found it all quite easy and became a chartered accountant. It came in handy when he ran his own business.

Eventually, his mother could no longer put up with her husband's comings and goings, and they separated, but as she was in poor health it was down to the two boys to look after her. She died when she was only 44, and the two boys, aged 17 and 14, were basically orphaned relying on aunts and uncles to provide for them.

Racism was common throughout the land back then and when in 1956 Gill met and married an Irish girl, he was asked to leave his lodgings by the landlord. 'No blacks and no Irish' were not uncommon notices in windows.

Gill never saw his father again, until one Christmas Eve in 1964 he turned up on the doorstep at the family home at Ightenhill. He was dying and seeking reconciliation.

Gill's business career began in earnest when he remortgaged his house to purchase Lupton and Place Ltd, at the time a run-down foundry and engineering works. He transformed it and then bought another factory and consolidated the two sites to Athletic Street. He was still chairman there until 2019 having outlived and outperformed most other competitors. In so doing, he was hugely respected. He had one abiding mantra, 'We do the simple things well.'

When Gill compiled his report into the club finances, he found, 'Absolute chaos. I knew it wouldn't be good but it was chaotic beyond belief. There was no semblance of financial planning, the bank statements were the only available measure of how they stood financially; it was astonishingly amateurish. They were meticulous in the way that contracts were issued to players, because they had to be. A player couldn't get out of a contract at that time. But it was mayhem otherwise.'

The club's bank manager was also his own bank manager, and actually told him that he was just the sort of man needed to compile the report. Gill's brief was to 'review all the financing and administrative aspects of BFC with a view to identifying any areas of waste or inefficiency, recommending remedial action where necessary and making proposals for future running'. He found two posts that needed to be replaced with better-organised personnel: the secretary and commercial manager. A new management structure was essential, with directors willing to devote time to particular areas.

His full statement, finalised in November 1981, was damning. Throughout the club there was poor communication and co-ordination with too many staff taking instructions only from Bob Lord. People were afraid to make decisions. The general office and commercial departments functioned poorly. The secretarial office was poorly organised and badly run. By and large it was organisation by panic, determined by the latest crisis telephone call. There was no systematic accounting. Crucial information and documents were piled up after years of malfunction. Book-keeping methods were basic and did little more than disclose the bank balance. Staff were paid in cash weekly. Blocks of blank cheques were signed off by two directors and left on the desk. A computerised system was essential.

Perhaps the most damning part referred to Lord himself. Gill expressed the view that his expense claims were frequently unsubstantiated by proper receipts. They were often just trivial bits of notepaper; these expenses were items such as petrol and meals. Over a 12-month period that Gill examined, they amounted to around £6,000, buried in travelling and hotel expenses. He reported:

'Travelling and incidental expenses of directors must be seen to be beyond reproach and this has not been the case in the past. So far I have avoided going back very far or creating any sort of witch hunt but I regret to state that I do not believe that regular "cash expenses" claimed by Mr Lord have been adequately detailed. Nor have they been substantiated by receipts. The secretary has been placed in the invidious position of being required to pass over cash on the authority of trivial notepaper requests of the chairman. A supply of proper receipts would at least have enabled the club to reclaim VAT on the numerous meals claimed, and petrol receipts are superior evidence to "x" miles at 20p per mile. No receipts for meals have been provided. The amounts involved last year are probably around £6,000 and are submerged in the charges for travelling and hotel expenses.

'I also dislike the practice of two directors signing a block of blank cheques which are then left lying about in the secretary's office. In effect, Mr Maddox becomes the sole signatory of the club's bank account.'

The report was several pages long and looked into every corner of how the club was run except for playing staff and their management. Only a few employees came out of the report with any praise: Mrs Denwood and R. Langston in catering, groundsman Roy Oldfield, conscientious and efficient, and assistant secretary Bob Bradshaw. Gill came to the conclusion that long-time secretary Albert Maddox should be persuaded to retire. The commercial manager was inadequate, lacking initiative and imagination.

And then there was the Lowerhouse land deal. The club had bought land owned by Lord in the 1970s. He then bought a small part back. To cut a long story short, when the land assumed an increased value because it was needed by Whitehall for tipping purposes in connection with new motorway construction, Lord decided the club should sell it back to him. After much wrangling and legal threats, the club did indeed sell it back to him with the legality of how the proceeds were split being somewhat hazy. Everyone, including the club, made substantial profits out of it[4].

On the strength of his no-holds-barred report, John Jackson invited Gill to join the board as financial director. Gill was delighted.

---

4 The full story is in *Bob Lord of Burnley*, chapter 21.

The manager when this story begins is Brian Miller, eventually to be named 'Mr Burnley' on account of his years of service, his devotion, his loyalty, and because over the years he had filled every available position at the club, except for general handyman. But even there he had acted as unpaid groundsman on several occasions helping groundsman Roy Oldfield with pitch duties when Roy was under pressure.

He was born in Hapton near Burnley and joined the club as a teenager in 1952, making his debut in 1955/56. If Father Greystone, the headmaster of St Mary's College in Blackburn, had got his way, Brian would never have been a footballer. Brian took no notice of his efforts to dissuade him from joining the club he supported. In the 1950s he was one of many Burnley players who worked for the National Coal Board instead of doing national service in the army. He was at Bank Hall Pit until 4.30pm and then trained in the evenings. If there was an evening game, a sympathetic manager let him have the afternoon off. At Thorny Bank Pit another sympathetic manager and Burnley fan gave him more time off in return for tickets. How ridiculous it seems today that footballers back then could be toiling at a coal pit, and then playing First Division football in the evenings.

Miller was a regular in the title-winning team of 1959/60; the rugged half-back, strong as an ox and utterly fearless. With his superb physique and good looks, he could have doubled as James Bond. He continued playing until 1967/68 and from that point on occupied coaching positions, assistant manager and then manager. Having been made manager in 1979, he was in situ when Lord died, Jackson became chairman, and the scene was set for a totally unexpected triumphant season ending in promotion.

He played once for England and had two spells as manager at Turf Moor, the most iconic game of them all being the final day of 1986/87 when Burnley beat Orient 2-1 to stay in the Football League. An image of him sitting in the dugout, staring stony-faced and looking ahead, surrounded by a dozen photographers, is one of the great football pictures.

That great Burnley player, Jimmy McIlroy, was a huge admirer of Miller and wrote at the end of the 1981/82 promotion season, 'Brian Miller's honesty, endeavour and whole-heartedness is every bit as evident in his managerial role as it was when he was a player. Brian has one of the biggest hearts in football besides being a player of no mean skill, not at least of which was his ability to push up behind his forwards. He enjoyed every minute of his playing days and during the times we have met since he took over at Turf Moor, he has left me in no doubt that he derives a great deal of pleasure from the game. He is one of the quiet managers, who employs common sense instead of gimmicks.'

There are many over-used words in football. One of them is servant. But that is exactly what Miller was to Burnley Football Club. He served it. He never let it down. Even though he was discarded so offhandedly on his birthday by John Jackson, when he was needed again as manager by the next chairman, Frank Teasdale, he returned to support his beloved club. When he was asked to return, Burnley were in a penniless mess and total disarray, but he could not say no.

He passed away aged just 70, the first of the great championship side to go. In his own mind he was just the bloke next door, even though he was a legend and hero to so many Burnley people. He earned no great riches but left richness behind him. He played in 455 games, an FA Cup Final and all the European ties. He served Burnley through four decades. This book tells of just a couple of years in that story.

'There were no fools on the board as it quickly took shape,' wrote Derek Gill. Gill himself was accepted as board member at the AGM in January 1982. He recalled that his appointment was met with applause and complimentary remarks from Burnley fanatic and arch critic Harry Brooks, well known in the town for his outspokenness on club matters. Gill would, in fact, be on the receiving end in times to come.

'Duly elected I loved every minute of it and my own engineering business became of secondary importance,' wrote Gill.

The first board meeting he attended after his appointment was the last one for two deposed members: Jimmy Wilde, a respected solicitor, and Jeffrey Harrison, the son-in-law of Bob Lord. The meeting closed with the reconstructed gang of four – Jack Eglin, rookie Gill, chairman Jackson and vice-chairman Doc Iven. Everything began well, everyone hugely cooperative and at ease with each other. Jackson was well pleased with Gill's report, Gill revelling in his role as 'junior director' and happy that his recommendation that long-serving club secretary Albert Maddox should be encouraged to retire was accepted. His deputy Bob Bradshaw would take over the football matters with Gill taking on the more formal financial and admin work.

Financial shortfalls were still in need of correction but there was a clear bullishness about the place as the team began to stop their unfortunate habit of losing, and there was a feverish eagerness to reform the club with a new broom. All were convinced that better financial times lay ahead and soon to come was the ill-gotten money from the sale of the Lowerhouse land. One-third of the proceeds was paid into Lord's estate, one-third to the club, and one-third retained for capital gains tax which in fact was never paid.

Gill explained the transaction in his diary, 'Now Burnley is a grumpy little parochial town, ignored by government and media alike but thanks to hard work and lobbying behind the scenes, the celebrated Whitehall rubber stamp landed in the vicinity of land in Lowerhouse that had been sold by Lord to the club some years earlier. Suddenly this useless bit of land, now owned by the club, was perfect for tipping and it was decreed that a motorway would appear. Undreamed of values began to appear, in excess of £100,000 no less. Whilst Lord may or may not have been the most successful of businessmen – all contemporary records show that his business was in a difficult financial position – he had no difficulty in working out that he, and not his beloved Burnley Football Club, would be better off if he could get hold of the loot. So, in its great wisdom the board passed a resolution in or around 1977 that it would transfer the land back to Lord at the original price he had paid, £11,600.'

All came to a head after his death when the three-way split was arranged.

It was then felt that the board should be slightly bigger, six or seven members being the optimum, and the search began for suitable candidates.

The first appointee was the owner of a chain of hotels and leisure resorts, a local man and a true Burnley supporter. Thus, Alan Hutchinson joined in the capacity as commercial director and proved himself with quiet and thoughtful contributions. His sudden and untimely death robbed the club of a genuine servant. Gill, in particular, missed him and in his diaries confessed that in Hutchinson he had a true ally so that when he eventually came to think that John Jackson should be replaced as chairman, it was with Hutchinson that he discussed this.

But this was yet to come and, in the meantime, the newest director became Colin Sanderson, the former club solicitor. It was Sanderson who had once approached Lord at the time of the sale of Jimmy McIlroy in 1963 and suggested to him that he should buy a copy of the *Sunday People* for in it was the account of why Jimmy Mac had been sold. Lord had fixed him with a cold stare.

'I wouldn't waste yer money,' growled Lord. 'There's only me as knows and I won't tell, and Harry Potts and he won't tell, and Jimmy McIlroy – and he daren't.'

With Sanderson's appointment to the board, there were now six members and all seemed set fair on the good ship Turf Moor.

But then Jack Eglin prematurely passed away. So, then there were five and members could have been forgiven for thinking, 'Who's next?'

Directors in the boardroom, the manager in the office; but we must not forget the players, with one in particular integral to this story. He led the team to promotion in 1981/82 and later featured hugely in the John Bond saga. This particular player was the incomparable Martin Dobson.

'The only classical wing-half left in the country,' said the *Football Digest* in 1974. A joy to watch with his cultured stride and tall physique, instrumental in the promotion side of 1972/73, outstanding in the following season and a huge favourite until Lord sold him. His departure was inevitable. Sold to pay for the new Bob Lord Stand, folks said, but that was never the case. The old stand was in danger of collapse, as good as condemned by a surveyor's report that gave Lord sleepless nights. It would have been demolished at some stage, no matter what.

Thus, Dobson was sent to Everton, where, again, he was outstanding. It was Harry Potts who brought him back to Burnley in the summer of 1979, offering him a longer deal than Everton offered. Jimmy Adamson, by then at Leeds United, wanted him to move to Elland Road but Dobson had given his word that he would rejoin Burnley. In truth, he was shocked at the decline that he found, the state of the club a far cry from when he had last been there. Somehow, Lord had found £100,000 and hopes were high that he and Potts could inspire a return from the Second Division to the First. It was not to be and Potts left only months after Dobson had arrived; Brian Miller then took over. A season of transition in the Third Division led to 1981/82 with a truly awful start that then became something quite triumphant with Dobson at its heart, and the great Billy Hamilton at centre-forward. A new crop of youngsters emerged that they led and inspired. Derek Gill was beavering away diligently sorting out the finances and the admin. Jackson was the confident frontman, skilled at the PR that was so badly needed. It was a good time to be at Burnley Football Club.

If this story was presented as some sort of Shakespearean production, then it would be set out as a four-act tragedy. Act One, promotion. Act Two, relegation. Act Three, John Bond. Act Four, relegation again. And what would Bond be, hero or villain? Overall, it might be unfair but popular interpretation is undoubtedly that of villain, and his appearance in Act Three is a huge part of what this book is all about. But like all Shakespeare's tragedies, the hero or villain simply becomes a victim; a puppet being thrown around and buffeted, pillar to post, by forces and events surrounding him, over which he has no control. And so it was with Bond. An injury to a key player, a boardroom at war with itself, antagonistic fans; the Bond year was doomed to failure.

John Bond was a West Ham player for something like 16 years, in the side that won promotion in 1958 and reached the 1964 FA Cup Final. He became manager of Bournemouth, leading them to promotion at the end of his first season. Success there led to his appointment at Norwich City and arguably the best time of his career. A relegation and then a promotion with some top players and he kept them in the top division until he left to take over at Manchester City at a troubled time for them. He took City to Wembley for the FA Cup Final but they lost against Tottenham. He resigned in February 1983 after falling out with chairman Peter Swales. John Jackson at Burnley noted his availability and that he was an affable and courteous man, a people person, at ease in all manner of situations. Unfortunately, his ultra-fine dress sense and stylishness made him look out of place at a still working-class, drab Burnley.

He was certainly no hero there and after the traumas of his season at Burnley he famously said in an interview, 'Oh why did I ever go to Burnley?' A fitting epitaph.

3

A triumphant whirlwind season

IN 1981, *Dallas* was the big hit on TV during an age without millions of computers and mobile phones. The internet was still science fiction, as were wall-mounted flatscreen TVs. Rubik's Cubes were more common than video games. There were no microwaves in kitchens, but you might have seen a sandwich toaster. Bottled water; what was that? You kept your frozen food in a big chest freezer in the garage but there was far less choice of fresh vegetables and fruits. Australian wine was a joke; most wine still came from France. Supermarkets were on the increase, but out-of-town shopping malls hadn't been thought of. High streets and town centres were still busy and thriving places. There were Woolworths everywhere.

Sunday, and the only thing open was a church. Marriage was still the accepted norm, especially with Charles and Diana due to wed in the summer. The nation went mad about it. Single-parent families were uncommon; same-sex marriages unheard of. Divorce was far less widespread than now.

Eating out was far less common; there just wasn't the choice of restaurants. But pubs were plentiful and you could enjoy a cigarette or a pipe in there. So too at Turf Moor where the air was filled with cigarette smoke on matchday. No one had thought of passive smoking. A packet of 20 was still under £1.

In the home, a music centre might have been the centre of attraction along with the TV. The music centre played LPs, cassettes and radio stations. LPs were those round vinyl things, 12 inches wide, with grooves that the pick-up arm and needle translated into music. There were no CDs yet. We listened to Diana Ross, Lionel Ritchie, Phil Collins, the Stones, The Police, Rod Stewart, Soft Cell, Blondie, Kim Wilde, ELO, Bucks Fizz, Adam Ant, Genesis and the Commodores, among many others. Oh, and Cliff Richard.

The cinema was still the go-to place in an evening and there were plenty of them. We watched *On Golden Pond*, *Raiders of the Lost Ark*, *Mad Max 2*, *Gallipoli*, *The Cannonball Run*, *For Your Eyes Only*, *Arthur*, *Chariots of Fire*, and *The Postman Always Rings Twice*.

Believe it or not, you could still get to see the manager in the high street bank quite easily, and your doctor by just walking in. Not quite so many dentists or opticians though. Basic tax rate was only 30p, prescription charges didn't need a mortgage, pensioners got £27 a week and students didn't need to take out loans that saddled them with debt.

Maggie Thatcher had been in power for two years; there were riots in Brixton and Toxteth as the black community protested against unemployment, living conditions and police harassment. Political correctness was a long way away. The woke brigade weren't even born. British Rail, British Steel and British Leyland were locked in disputes. Even with Mrs T in power, women only played marginal parts in government with just 20 women MPs. The jobless total would soon hit three million.

Punk was in vogue, there were constant IRA threats, the Cold War was always in the background and a nuclear holocaust seemed a possibility with the government advising us to shelter under the table with a couple of pillows to withstand the shock. Cruise missiles were the topic of conversation. But on the plus side, the postman still came twice a day.

Spurs won the FA Cup after a replay against Manchester City. At Headingley, England won one of the great Test victories against the Australians. It was the third match of the Ashes series with Australia needing just 130 runs to win in the final innings. Ian Botham had given England a hint of a chance with an unbeaten 149. Bob Willis then took eight wickets as Australia were bowled out for just 111. A never to be forgotten match, said the press in unison.

Burnley was still in the grip of poor housing, unemployment, coal mines one by one closing, ill health, low wages and poor social conditions. Crowds at Turf Moor were low, the club so poor that it couldn't even afford a new wheelbarrow for the groundsman who repaired his broken spades and forks regularly. The new wheelbarrow came from the newly formed supporters' club.

But groundsman Roy Oldfield witnessed and noted in his own diary that the new broom was benefitting him. No longer did he go to secretary Albert Maddox with purchase requests that were immediately turned down. New director Colin Sanderson allowed him to spend up to £50 without the need for a request. And the new chairman was never happier than when, in winter, helping clear the pitch of snow with the borrowed dumper that he drove around. If Bob Lord had ever helped, it was only to take pot shots at the pigeons that descended on the turf at seeding time.

At this point in time there was boardroom harmony at Burnley, but Brian Clough's analysis of directors was brutal. He saw three categories: duplicitous, devious backstabbers, who'd have given Julius Caesar a good going over; feckless sycophants who hid in dark corners when the flak flew; and the egotists, running a football club to get their photograph on the back pages of newspapers when nothing else would. Clough subscribed to the view of Len Shackleton, who, in his autobiography, famously headed one chapter 'The Average Director's Knowledge of Football' and then left the page blank.

It has to be said that at Turf Moor, in 1981, this was not the case. Both Gill and Jackson had followed football and Burnley since boyhood and most certainly knew and understood the game. They had seen the great team of 1959/60 and then the Adamson side of 1973/74. Their football education was impressive.

There were reports that Brian Miller had tried to sign Stuart Pearson and John Aldridge, but Newport County wanted £100,000 for the striker. At this point at the beginning of the season Gill had yet to begin coining in the deals that he would eventually set up, so there was no way that Aldridge could join. He went on to become one of the game's most prolific scorers. Old-timers like defender Jim Thomson were shipped out and the season began badly with a 3-1 defeat at faraway Gillingham. 'Improve or else,' said a grim-faced Miller.

It was the game when several of Burnley fans, including local reporter Peter Higgs, charity-walked to Gillingham. All that way to see them lose. They were swiftly booted out of the League Cup and the future looked anything but Claret. It wasn't long, after four consecutive defeats, that Burnley were 22nd. Manager Miller was hospitalised with appendicitis; it never rains but it pours.

Derek Gill records very little of that triumphant season in his diaries save for something he wrote about the end of the season, 'Our minds were over the proverbial moon as we won the championship of the Third Division and many wild statements came in its wake. The worst of them goes down to me when I asserted in the press that Burnley had played their last ever match in the Third Division. There were those who later never let me forget it when the rot set in with a vengeance such a short time later.'

But that was yet to come and, in the meantime, it developed into a season to remember.

Gill, company secretary as well as finance director, added, 'All problems of organisation and finance were quickly swept aside as we suddenly began to win games and the shareholders' meeting was immediately followed by six consecutive victories which inevitably gave us a lift up the Third Division league table. The eventual winning of the championship was looked on as nothing more than the first step towards the restoration of our birthright.'

It was to everyone's credit that promotion was achieved on a shoestring; it was not until nearer the end of the season and the beginning of the next that the money began to roll in. The Trustee Savings Bank gave the club very generous banking terms and the Burnley Building Society sponsored a stand to the tune of £100,000, a huge sum in those days. It then added another £25,000 to have its name on the back of the tracksuits. By the end of the following season a bid of £300,000 had been accepted for Trevor Steven. Prior to all this, of course, had been the windfall from Lord's Lowerhouse land deal. The money coming in was therefore considerable so that by the end of the promotion season the financial garden was rosy and bright.

Gill noted all of this in his diaries:

'Once we'd gone up, we were quite favoured. Multipart came in. TSB came in and took over our bank accounts. TSB were known in banking circles as "those silly buggers". I soon found out why. The bloke came to see me about taking over our accounts and offered us banking terms that were unbelievable. They were so daft we couldn't possibly turn them down. They were throwing money at us. I had my own business account at Barclays and when I told them about this they looked heavenwards and said to me, "Well you've got to take it haven't you."

'And then the Burnley Building Society came on board. They were being absorbed by another building society, the National and Provincial I think, and they were taking a lot of criticism. So, they came to me and they wanted to sponsor a stand; I'd never heard anything so stupid in my life and I kick myself to this day about it. I thought to myself, "I'll quote them some silly figure because negotiation obviously wasn't their strong point."

'I asked for £100,000 and they just said, "Yeah, right then." I immediately regretted not asking them for more because it was clear they would have paid it. But it was a fortune for us back then; our turnover was only half a million. And just for pasting their name along the top of the Cricket Field Stand, they thought it was a stroke of genius. They just wanted to deflect a lot of the local criticism about the merger and didn't seem to care about the money. So, I went away racking my brains about what else I could do and a couple of weeks later I invited the bloke back and I said to him, "We could put Burnley Building Society on the back of the tracksuits." And he gave us another £25,000.

'So we had fantastic banking facilities, all bank charges had been waived, and it meant we could pay our way. We settled quite a few of our debts, we'd been given a £300,000 overdraft by the TSB and the season ticket money was coming in. So, all of a sudden, we have a lot of money, and we are up a league.'

But prior to all that money flooding in there was a promotion to win. Luckily, just before Brian Miller was taken to hospital with appendicitis, he and Frank Casper had planned how to arrest the slide and the poor results. Martin Dobson would be moved back to play as a sweeper enabling the full-backs to bomb forward on the attack. Both Laws and Wharton were naturals. November 1981 and Burnley were at Bristol City; the newly formed Social Democratic Party won their first seat, at Crosby and England had qualified for the World Cup finals in Spain where Burnley's Billy Hamilton would star for Northern Ireland.

It was a key game at Bristol, a club in total disarray, and they were winning 2-1 at half-time. Casper, in temporary charge along with Jackson and Gill, could have been forgiven for thinking the new plan was going nowhere. But playing for Burnley was an 18-year-old Trevor Steven, with a 'face not out of place in a church choir' according to one report, putting on an absolute master show, and a new star had arrived. It was a sublime performance and Burnley equalised. At last Bristol capitulated to constant pressure and conceded a penalty that was slammed home to win the game. Burnley were still in relegation trouble, but there was a sense that this was a turning point.

December was as good as wiped out by atrocious winter weather. Snow hit Burnley with a vengeance and outlying villages were cut off for several days. Roads were littered with abandoned vehicles. Raging snowstorms were accompanied by gale-force winds. Roads into Burnley were closed and children gleefully found their schools closed. Forty drivers and passengers snuggled up for the night at the Waggoners Inn on Manchester Road, barely out of Burnley. Conditions were horrendous, high winds causing huge drifts between Burnley and Bacup ten feet deep. Roy Oldfield found the stadium buried in snow. It needed a tractor and plough to shift it off the pitch. Two dumpers were hired, all hands to the pumps as it were, the chairman speeding around on one of the dumpers.

The whole of Britain shivered and it was colder than Iceland in some areas. Motorists crawled along roads until they became gridlocked. Hundreds of people were stranded. There was a national outcry that the nation's roads were so badly affected but snowploughs and gritting teams were simply no match for the weather. Airports were closed, scores of football matches cancelled; sales of sledges and toboggans rocketed.

Newspaper editorials asked, could 1982 be any worse than 1981, when there was the worst economic recession and unemployment since the war. By and large the public were fed up with both Tories and Labour so that they were turning to the Social Democrat Party. Lawlessness, crimes of violence, rioting and sectarian killings in Ulster had all increased. It had not been the best of years.

In fact, 1982 was the year of the Falklands War when Argentina had invaded the island and Margaret Thatcher decided this was unacceptable. In April, the Royal Navy armada set sail and headed south in a massive operation and a long, long voyage. Britain and Argentina were at war and it seemed quite surreal with it all being played out so far away. It was a television war inasmuch as all of it was brought to the screens in gory detail and we watched open-mouthed. Sunken ships, submarines, ships under attack, planes screaming overhead, Exocet missiles, the yomp across the island to liberate Port Stanley, the deaths and injuries, we saw it all from our armchairs as if we were watching a film.

Oldfield related in his book, *Mud, Sweat and Shears*, how they were still so hard-up, even with, by now, a winning team. Did Gill and Jackson ever hear about the cheap yellow footballs they used in the snow? There were only two, and slowly through the first half the yellow turned near-white. The second ball was brought out for the second half and survived the pummelling. George Courtney was the same referee there for another game, when the goalpost corners where the post met the crossbar had been taped up, because they were in such poor condition. This time Courtney was aware of the problem and simply crossed his fingers that the crossbar wouldn't go flying six feet up in the air if there was a thunderbolt shot.

As the side rose up the table, another newspaper feature about the chairman appeared, this time by Don Evans. Fourteen weeks after he had taken over at the club, people were beginning to sit up and take notice, wrote Evans. 'A revolution was taking place around the magnificent stadium and stubby streets of Burnley Football Club … Jackson discreetly avoids talking about his professional career, a Northern Circuit advocate, but pleads with a passion Burnley's betterment in the public eye … Many people have asked me how difficult it was to follow Mr Lord in the chair at Burnley FC. It is in fact a nice easy job … Mine is a public relations job.' How he would later come to rue those few simple words. It undoubtedly was a nice easy job at that point as the accolades descended.

The final two games of the season saw promotion clinched at Southend United and then the title won at home to Chesterfield. Oldfield recalled the final games in *Mud, Sweat and Shears*. There had been a totally unexpected 5-3 defeat at home to Southend but after that there were no more defeats. In the final seven matches there were five wins and two draws with promotion secured with a resounding 4-1 scoreline in Essex. That left one game, against Chesterfield, on a pitch that was a morass after heavy rain. The monsoon rain was so bad that earlier in the season it was a game that would have been postponed.

Roy's book explained, '"TURF MOOR NIGHT TO REMEMBER" headlined the *Evening Star*. This was the night Margaret Thatcher had her finger poised over the war button as Admiral Sandy Westwood waited for the order to head south and re-take the Falklands. Thatcher's patience had run out and hopes of a peace settlement were bleak and a huge task force was poised close to the islands in readiness.

'But thoughts of that were a long way away from Turf Moor on a night of celebration, although the game was only drawn. It gave Burnley 80 points and the title was theirs as long as Carlisle didn't beat Chester by seven clear goals. Even the worst of pessimists gave that no thought at all. A giant crowd of 18,655 watched a tense encounter given added nervousness when Chesterfield took the lead. But a Kevin Young equaliser meant that the champagne corks could be popped even though the team had already had a civic reception at the Town Hall that afternoon.

'The date was Tuesday, 28 May 1982. It was exactly 100 years to the day since the club had been formed. No one was more delighted than the office staff who each pocketed £1,200 as a result of the group bet that they had made on promotion back in October.

'Roy looked on both thrilled and horrified as his precious pitch was submerged beneath thousands of feet who ran on, churning up the soaked surface.

'Roy was delighted when Frank Casper came along to our next meeting. He talked about the game at Southend when Burnley had clinched promotion. The image that he retains is chairman John Jackson, who sometimes used to come to the club straight from court in his barrister's silks, strolling down the touchline past the dugout with the score at 3-0. The gist of his remarks to Brian Miller and Casper were to say, "What about this then and I've only been chairman six months." And already there was a promotion. Casper saw the writing on the wall more or less there and then and remarked to Miller that promotion or not, they would both be replaced before long. Within a year both of them were gone.'

'CHAMPION CLARETS WE'RE UP' announced the now-defunct *Evening Star* souvenir edition, in which the late Keith McNee summed up the season:

'Burnley's superb surge into the Second Division must be rated as the greatest comeback in the club's 100-year history. Who could possibly have thought on 3 October, that the Clarets were on their way to a promotion? On that Saturday they went down 2-0 at home to Swindon Town. It was their fourth consecutive league defeat. The sad result left Brian Miller's team third from the bottom of the table with relegation to the Fourth Division for the first time looking on the cards.

'The turning point came seven days later when Burnley made the long trek to Fratton Park to play Portsmouth. Manager Miller and coach Casper decided something had to be done to tighten up the defence that had made far too many careless mistakes in the opening eight fixtures of the season. Their answer was to switch Martin Dobson to a sweeper role behind the two central defenders and the move proved a tremendous success. Portsmouth were beaten 2-1 thanks to goals by Kevin Young and Andy Wharton.

'On Friday, 14 May the Clarets hammered Southend 4-1 at Roots Hall to become the 11th club to take the leadership of the Third Division and the first to clinch a promotion spot. This magnificent victory at Southend took the Turf Moor club's successful sequence to 37 matches with only two defeats. Perhaps the freak 5-3 defeat at home to Southend in April was in retrospect not such a severe disaster as it seemed at the time. It gave Dobson and his team-mates an extra edge and determination, and they went on to gain four more wins.

'Thirty-four-year-old Dobson, honoured by his fellow professionals when they named him in the PFA select team for the Third Division, has of course been a major influence over the Burnley side this season. With the former Everton and England player always steady and often inspired in his sweeper role, the defence has been very tight since the early days of the campaign.

'Dobson and another long-serving Claret, goalkeeper Alan Stevenson, have provided the necessary experience in defence while 31-year-old Tommy Cassidy has added much to the team with his midfield know-how and passing skills. Cassidy, again dogged by injury, as was the case last season, fittingly created the first of the four goals in the clinching game at Southend with a classic long pass to scorer Wharton.

'But if the Clarets are to make a strong impact in the Second Division next season, as could well happen in my view, they will clearly have to rely heavily on youngsters. They are well-equipped in this respect. Full-backs Brian Laws and Wharton have fitted in perfectly with the sweeper system, pushing forward effectively from defence at every opportunity to both make and take some important goals. Wharton's splendidly struck efforts at Southend, Doncaster and Portsmouth were good examples of this while Laws will do well to better the spectacular goal he got at Chesterfield.

'Vince Overson, who reached his 20th birthday the day after the win at Southend, has been a powerhouse at the centre of the defence alongside several different partners. Michael Phelan would probably have had a long run in this position but for a broken bone in his foot and then a cheekbone fracture at Wimbledon. Paul Dixon has had a number of matches alongside Overson but mostly the job has gone to the experienced David Holt who has proved he is more than a useful asset as a centre-half than in his more customary left-back position.

'At 18, Trevor Steven looks to be Burnley's finest prospect since the teenage days of Welshman Leighton James. Up to the start of the season, Berwick-born Trevor had made only one senior appearance as substitute, but he has been a vital part of this side with his clever play on the ball, strong running and excellent distribution. He looks certain to go a long way but as he told me after the Southend match, he will always look back with great satisfaction on being part of the team that put Burnley back into the Second Division at the second attempt.

'Young, another midfield player, has been inconsistent at times but I rate him very highly and he deserves a lot of credit for his contribution to the promotion drive. In attack, Burnley have been magnificently served by centre-forward Billy Hamilton, Steve Taylor and Paul McGee. Hamilton was generally regarded by managers as the best centre-forward in the Third Division this season and one would have to go a long way to find a more wholehearted player than the big Irishman from Belfast who joined the Clarets from Queens Park Rangers after starting his career with Irish club Linfield. Taylor, like local-born Phelan, has been desperately unlucky with injuries after ankle ligament strains sustained way back in February. With Taylor injured, Burnley beat the transfer deadline in March to sign Ireland international Paul McGee from Preston North End for £25,000. Sligo-born McGee had made a big impression during his loan period earlier in the season but took some time to settle back into the side. He came good after scoring the winner against Carlisle, then scoring against Walsall and two more at Southend.

'But as Brian Miller has been so eager to emphasise, Burnley's triumph in escaping from the Third Division, after looking doomed to a campaign of mediocrity, at best has been due to the strength of the squad rather than just 11 players. Derek Scott is one who has been in and out of the team, a dedicated player for the club who has filled in at a number of positions and contributed much to the Turf Moor cause.

'I rate the win over Southend as Burnley's most impressive performance in a long and eventful season. Other outstanding displays came in victories over Reading, Chesterfield, Carlisle and Preston and surely Burnley's goal of the season was Hamilton's effort against Preston when he took the ball 60 yards before firing into the net.

'No review of the season would be complete without reference to the boardroom changes that took place in October, with barrister John Jackson taking over as chairman and long-serving Doc Iven becoming vice-chairman. The mood of the club is right for further success and there are many who believe that Burnley will be a considerable force in Division Two during 1982/83.'

Of course, the spotlight fell on chairman John Jackson and why shouldn't it? He was the man at the top who had reformed the club, instigated change, brought new ideas and a freshness to the place after the years of Lord inertia in the late 1970s. He was still young, only 43, enthusiastic, and had shown that he could roll up his sleeves and 'muck in'. McNee paid tribute to him:

'John Jackson, Burnley's 43-year-old barrister chairman, is convinced that the club's sparkling return to the Second Division is only the start of something good for the Turf Moor club and their supporters. Mr Jackson who took over as chairman from Bob Lord in October, the month in which the long unbeaten sequence began, was first into the dressing room with congratulations for Brian Miller and the team after the stunning win at Southend. It was a scene of great happiness for all concerned.

'Said Mr Jackson, "Getting out of the Third Division is one ambition achieved. And obviously we are all delighted. We have come along a hard road since the dark early season of poor results and low gates. What I would like to say to supporters is this. We thank them for their terrific backing which has helped the players on the field more than people might imagine. Now we need their continued support in order to help us keep this team of ours together. The best way they can help is in the matter of buying season tickets. Every penny spent will help the club keep on the right lines for the future."

'Over the last few months there have been several changes in the Turf Moor boardroom set-up. Mr Jackson now heads a board that also includes Dr David Iven, Mr Jack Eglin, Mr Derek Gill and the newest director Mr Alan Hutchinson. The chairman commented, "I see myself as the head of the boardroom team working in unison with Brian Miller who heads the team which goes out every week on to the pitch and plays. I don't think we have done too badly since the new board was formed. But we certainly need every supporter we can get and I am sure people will continue to rally round us. We want fans to feel part of this club and to share in anything we can achieve."

'"It is not going to be easy but we are confident we will make our mark in the Second Division with the players we have. If you go through the team, the quality is easy to spot. An international-class goalkeeper, a superb international as club captain, playing behind a defence of highly promising youngsters, plus a man such as David Holt who has played a heroic part in the promotion push. Then there are others such as Trevor Steven and Billy Hamilton. Yes, I believe we are well equipped for the stiff challenge ahead and I am quietly confident about the future."'

Martin Dobson had his say; how it brought back great memories of the 1972/73 promotion. There was no question that he was the mentor and inspiration for the younger players in the side. Been there, done it and got the t-shirt. The 1972/73 side was the best he had played in, he said, but this new one had the makings of another fine side.

'It will be very interesting to see how we fare in the Second Division. My contract with Burnley will expire in the summer of 1983 and I wouldn't have fancied what could be my last season, in the Third Division. It is possible I will finish my playing career after the 1982/83 campaign and I will be giving the matter much thought over the next 12 months.'

As it happened, he would soldier on through the 1982/83 season and on into the next. But in that one, he would encounter a new manager, John Bond. It would be a far from happy experience.

In a town bedevilled by economic hardship, the withdrawal of government aid, jobs few and far between, the decline of manufacturing and increasing youth unemployment, the success of the club was a huge boost. Footballing success lifts gloom, increases morale and gives a focal point. The air of dejection was briefly lifted.

Roy Oldfield worked like a trojan to get the pitch back in shape during the summer, and then wondered if the chairman and directors ever spared a thought for all the work that went into it. Did they think that every season would be like this?

'They would soon find out in the coming months,' he wrote. 'All good things come to an end, and sometimes sooner than you think.'

4

What could possibly go wrong?

FOR THE first game of the season at home to Bolton Wanderers, Brian Miller was proud but cautious in his programme notes. He wrote about the magnificent achievement of the battle to win promotion but was disappointed about the mediocre pre-season results. He saw no reason why they should not do well in the new division; they could be successful and entertaining. And, he added, he hoped to bring in new players to strengthen the squad.

Glenn Cockerill was one target, as was John Aldridge. Then there were Danny Wilson and Peter Reid. All of them would go on to become stellar players, but, alas, not at Burnley. When I met Miller some years ago, he said it was chairman John Jackson who said no to his requests.

The guest programme writer was Martin Tyler, freshly returned from the 1982 World Cup where he noted that he had struggled with two names. There was Spanish forward Roberto López Ufarte and from Kuwait there was Fathi Kameel. He looked forward to the easier English names in the new season.

Ray Lott of the blossoming supporters' club warned anyone thinking of attending a game looking for a bit of 'bovver' – don't. Anyone involved would be banned from the supporters' club.

The featured player was goalkeeper Alan Stevenson, who had totalled over 400 league games and was hoping to continue. If

Dino Zoff could play in the World Cup at the age of 40, then why could he not continue to the same age? 'I think we'll do well,' he said about the coming season. But he didn't like the new four-step rule that had been introduced to make goalkeepers speed up their game.

That most lyrical of writers and Burnley fan Tim Quelch set the scene for what was to be a memorable new season – for all the wrong reasons. He was filled with optimism after the enjoyment of the previous campaign. It was a good time to be a Burnley supporter.

'Saturday, 28 August was a magnificent day. Arriving early, I parked the car at Crown Point and cooled for a while in the swishing air, reading the Friday *Evening Star*. The view was superb. Across the valley stood Pendle Hill, tanned by the warm sunlight and there, below me, was Turf Moor, its totemic floodlights dominating the terraced housing. Just a few scrambled clouds populated the sky, enough to disperse the distant sunshine, enough to impress a patchwork pattern upon the valley. It was a blithely reassuring moment. All seemed well. The prospects appeared as fair as the weather. Dexys' "Come on Eileen" was number one but Sting's "Spread a Little Happiness" was on my mind. It seemed fitting until I realised later that it was from the musical version of that dark drama, *Brimstone and Treacle*.

'There was the regulation pre-season team photo. This one had club chairman John Jackson laughing uproariously. Behind him, Lee Dixon (yes, that one) was smiling very uncertainly. Everyone had been told to look bright and breezy. Only Andy Wharton seemed to have forgotten what he was told.

'Keith McNee headlined his preview with "Now for the big challenge". With the Second Division campaign about to start, Keith was much more cautious in his assessment of Burnley's chances, contrasting markedly with his euphoric end-of-season review. His concern couldn't have been eased by the pre-season games. He quoted chief coach Frank Casper as saying, "It was disappointing to be involved in a second successive 0-0 draw against Bury. We should have won easily but the goal touch was missing." Injuries to Vince Overson, Paul McGee and Tommy Cassidy hadn't helped. However, Billy Hamilton's brilliant showing in the World Cup finals had been a massive boost.

'Despite almost £100,000 being gained in advance season ticket sales, £65 for the Bob Lord Stand and £50 for the Cricket Field Stand, there were no incoming moves.

'It is unclear whether Brian had tried and failed to sign new players[5]. Defender David Holt predicted a further upward push, though. He said, "We won't give a lot of goals away and if we can find our scoring touch then we'll be up there with the leaders."'

The first home game with Bolton on 28 August was a goalless anti-climax. But after the rather tame opener, Burnley found their wings. Bury were beaten 5-3 at Gigg Lane in the Milk Cup and then on the following Saturday Middlesbrough were beaten 4-1 at Ayresome Park. Billy Hamilton scored three in a 4-1 win against Carlisle at Turf Moor. Hopes of a good season were high.

Derek Gill had said little in his diaries of the promotion season but season 1982/83 saw him writing in earnest as he gave an overview of the season:

'Negative thoughts had no place at the club. In our innocence, which must also have affected the manager, we had hardly given a moment's notice to strengthening the team. We had been buoyed by the sale of season tickets and the sale of the Lowerhouse land, and there was a very significant increase in the sale of season tickets for the coming season. The only addition to the playing staff came after a couple of months when Willie Donachie joined us on a

5 This was not for the want of trying by Brian Miller. Years later, when I met Miller to speak about another book, he told me he had wanted to sign new players in the summer, one being Danny Wilson. His efforts were not supported by chairman John Jackson, he said. He had to wait well into the season to sign Brian Flynn and Willie Donachie, the latter for free.

genuine free move from the American league, and I have to say what delight he was in every respect. A multi-capped Scottish international who was so wonderfully calm in all that he did and a quietly spoken but really genuine man who was respected wherever he went.

'I do not care what anyone says about the lack of football knowledge among directors, but I was not slow to make my opinions felt. That is running ahead of myself slightly but the manager then was John Bond whose best friend would be hard-pressed to defend his judgement on the Burnley full-backs. To say it was flawed would be an act of generosity which I am not prepared to grant. It is still painful to remember the disposable trio who between them brought in less than £35,000 (forget what you read in the press) in transfer fees. The trio were Brian Laws, transferred totally against his wishes to Huddersfield Town, Lee Dixon who went on a free transfer to Chester City, and Willie Donachie. No less a manager than Joe Royle of Oldham Athletic has told me on more than one occasion that he could not believe his ears when he heard that Willie was available on a free.

'All that was for the future and as was our divine right, we set off like a house on fire on the field of play and our self-delusion was such (or was it just me) that after our first game at home to Bolton Wanderers, I was thoroughly disappointed to learn that it had ended in a goalless draw. I say "learn of it" because I had been "drawn" out of the boardroom hat to accompany the reserve team to a fixture at Wigan. No problem for me though, as the first two away fixtures saw us score five times against Bury and settle for four at Middlesbrough. If we add to those the four that we scored in our final away game at Southend in the previous season, that came to no less than 13 goals in just three games. Tuesday night following the weekend win at Middlesbrough saw us sweep aside Carlisle by the same 4-1 scoreline and the set of clever buggers in the boardroom were supremely confident that the Second Division title was within our grasp. The incomparable Brian Clough and his "directors know bugger all about football" could only be strengthened in that view, had he been a fly on the wall.

'The Carlisle game had been number 41 in the run of games of which only two had been lost. However, somebody had not read the script and we were dumbfounded to lose the next four games in the league and even more so as two of them were at home against clubs expected to number among the weaker opponents. The warts began to surface and although we did not realise it at the time we were heading for deep trouble and with frustrations surfacing, the rapid decline must have been inevitable.

'The cash position remained reasonably secure from the Bob Lord Lowerhouse land deal, plus season ticket revenue, and then on to the scene were coming the TSB, currently very keen to get into commercial banking with privatisation just round the corner, and us, a sudden new-found outlet for their massive funds. We were offered banking terms that no company in their right senses could refuse and in addition TSB agreed to sponsor the team shirts for a fee that at the time was quite handsome. We were slightly concerned at the time as we feared that the shirt sponsorship might conflict with the even better deal that we concluded with the Burnley Building Society, whose management seemed more than a little anxious to deflect considerable unfavourable local publicity, which was affecting their merger with the much bigger National and Provincial. The introduction had been provided by Colin Sanderson and his ever-present bonhomie was instrumental in enabling this astonishingly beneficial deal to go through.

'As the chairman and majority shareholder of an engineering and die-casting business, I simply cannot resist making a comparison between bankers and leaders in the financial sector of commerce, with those engaged in the sharp end of manufacturing and production. They were child's play to deal with and their lack of appreciation of the value of money would be funny if it were not so bloody sad and ultimately dangerous.

'The upshot of it all was *Alice in Wonderland* stuff for the new regime as we danced a 180-degree turnaround, moving from having no money and winning matches, to working with some ease with our overdraft facility, but losing games one after the other.

'Brian Miller was still the team manager having been named Manager of the Year for the previous season, an honour that follows the winners of the divisional championships with predictable regularity. Quite naturally he was called into the boardroom to explain to us what was a completely unexpected turn in our fortunes. Just as all managers want to do, he wanted to strengthen the squad and the question of who to bring in was discussed[6].

'As is the norm at Burnley, the credentials of possible signings were invariably weighted in favour of players who had been with the club in the past and we had heard that Swansea City had an urgent need to reduce their wage bill and that Leighton James might even be available on a free. Me, the standard Clough director, allegedly not knowing much about football, strongly fancied Leighton back at Burnley, but Brian did not, and that was the end of that. Knowledgeable or not, I still believe that if Leighton had been brought back, the relegation that came at the end of the season would never have happened.

'We opted to sign another great servant to the club and bring back Brian Flynn from Leeds United for a very modest fee made possible by the then impecunious state of Leeds United. Brian performed heroically for us and what a pleasure it was to have him round the place. With the benefit of hindsight, we should have taken them both and the golden rule in any boardroom/manager

---

6 He had already wanted to make signings, you may remember, but his requests had fallen on deaf ears.

relationship is "back him or sack him" but Leighton remained at Swansea. There is no satisfactory halfway house.

'The transfer of Brian Flynn was the first one I was called upon to handle personally although I had to get approval before it was implemented. The parameters had been agreed before I met him at the club and therefore the approval amounted to no more than rubber stamping. But: I particularly want to mention this transfer to acknowledge the super integrity of the player who took a reduction in wages to come to Burnley and was simply "full of it" and bursting to go as soon as the transaction was completed. It was all done in one meeting and there was no question of agents or percentage merchants and associated hangers-on; just simple straight dealing with him. When, at later times, I had the dubious pleasure of confronting one or two who were not fit to clean Brian's boots, I was even more grateful to him. You can go to war with men like Brian Flynn, and I am glad to have known him.

'Brian's comeback match for us was at Sheffield Wednesday where we achieved a very creditable draw when he had to fill in at left-back after an early injury to Willie Donachie making just his second appearance for us. The following game was at Turf Moor when we met Derby County and drew a match we should have won by the proverbial panful. And then the midweek saw us defeat First Division Birmingham City, taking us into the dizzying heights of the quarter-finals of the League Cup. The next draw was awaited with a fair degree of excitement, more than vindicated when we were given a visit to Tottenham Hotspur which we could hardly expect to win, but would surely enhance the kitty very nicely, thank you. We also thought that the league table was coming round a bit after our poor away form had plummeted us down among the stragglers.

'But: shocks were in store. The whole of December became a nightmare when five games were played and all five were lost. The results were crazy and it is not being blindly prejudiced to claim that at least two and probably three of them could have been won. The Leicester City game was fantasy football in which we took an early lead which was shortly followed by the dismissal of a Leicester player and all then appeared to be plain sailing. The referee that day had better remain anonymous[7] to anyone not in possession of the match programme, but the fact that he took centre stage usually says enough.

'We were landed with the same genius for a quarter-final FA Cup tie later that season when he gave another virtuoso performance. Referring to this game as "there for the taking" the story went haywire in a manner I have no wish to witness again. Alan Stevenson had dived at the feet of an oncoming forward and to my claret and blue eyes had taken the ball quite cleanly. Our referee decided otherwise and awarded a penalty kick and dismissed Alan from the field. The game went barmy and no doubt feeling that he needed to balance matters on penalties, in addition to the dismissal, proceeded to give, in every sense of the word, two penalties to Burnley. Both were missed and for the pottiest quiz question one might ask which team had three goalkeepers in one match and two of them missed penalty kicks. Culprits were my good friend Brian Laws and Paul McGee. It was a defeat that hurt us badly.

'Back to December and we lost by a last-minute winner at Grimsby and then horror of horrors went down to the old enemies from Ewood Park in a dismal game that we actually did deserve to lose. I can't actually bring myself to admit that Blackburn did deserve to win. Next up in December, after a really good performance at Molineux and having a perfectly good goal disallowed, we lost by two late goals to Wolverhampton. Rock bottom was close and we were in a bad hole and the possibility of an immediate relegation was taking on the realms of a real possibility.

---

7 The referee was George Tyson.

'It was the defeat at Chelsea that had the major impact although the match meant little against the unhappy incident involving the chairman who had travelled independently to London with a friend and, after what we assume was a pleasurable lunch, arrived quite late at the ground and looked for additional complimentary tickets[8].

'His request was turned down and he was obliged to issue a personal cheque on which he wrote words to the effect "I hope it chokes you". Chelsea chairman Ken Bates, who many years earlier might have had a beneficial relationship with Burnley, was not the sort to accept that lying down and the edition of the *Daily Mirror* on the following Monday had some sport at our expense. I was asked to comment and simply stated that it was the first time I had ever known us to be asked to pay for tickets to the "box". The atmosphere in the Chelsea boardroom was a bad one and I was in there alone for a time on behalf of Burnley.

'The next four games were lost. I tell you that directors have rarely if ever won a match, but the number of times they have lost games must be legion. The road to nowhere now loomed large woven into the tapestries of fantasies too far-fetched for any plausible novel. Sadly, for Burnley, they were all too real.

'I do not know if Brian Miller's outburst on the coach home from Chelsea was ever relayed to John Jackson[9]. But I do know from that day he was on an ever-shortening fuse. I have already told that all five games in December were lost including a defeat at home on Boxing Day to arch rivals Blackburn Rovers. The fixture list was kind to us that year with home games scheduled for both days on which attendances and therefore bumper cash

---

8 John Jackson as chairman of BFC was rightly aggrieved to be asked for payment. It was appalling by Chelsea FC, but one does wonder if it was long-delayed retribution by Ken Bates who had been rebuffed in no uncertain terms by the old warhorse Bob Lord, when he had attempted to join the board of Burnley FC.

9 Following an incident involving the chairman and the catering on board the coach, manager Brian Miller declared loudly that the chairman was a 'big spoilt kid'.

receipts could be anticipated with confidence. The fixture on New Year's Day saw us at home to Sheffield Wednesday and it was decided that the team should spend New Year's Eve tucked up in a motel off the M6 motorway. No prizes for guessing which director drew the short straw to accompany the party. The players, as ever, behaved in an exemplary way and I spent the evening in a card game with Brian, Frank Casper and team physio Jimmy Holland.

'Early to bed and up early to arrive at Turf Moor an hour before the start but any deprivations were quickly forgotten when we ran out winners by four goals to one. A few days later we were home again, this time to Middlesbrough but we were disappointed to have to settle for a drawn match. An interlude for a third round FA Cup tie with Carlisle United saw us making progress after a replay.

'We were then required to visit another Lancashire neighbour at Burnden Park, the home of friendly Bolton Wanderers. I had some pre-match banter with Wanderers' George Warburton and I well remember thinking how grand it would be if we had a director or two like George. He had given me a quiet chuckle when asked in the Burnley boardroom one pre-season how much did he miss Bob Lord? "Like a sore arse," was his reply.

'It was an atrocious day and the game was played in heavy rain with a very strong wind blowing straight down the pitch and the two elements conspired with goalkeeper Jim McDonough, the Wanderers goalkeeper, to join a select band who have scored a goal when he released the ball with a tremendous punt upfield. It bounced just once, but that was enough to pass it over the head of our goalkeeper, who on that occasion was the unfortunate Billy O'Rourke. We lost the game by three clear goals and my other memory is of McDonough trying to repeat the feat and damned nearly succeeding. Nobody on our board could see the funny side and John Jackson was not the only one to be a picture of abject misery, and had barely a word to say in the post-match proceedings in the Bolton boardroom.

'There was no gathering of the board that weekend but the directors' telephones were red hot with the chairman seeking the opinions of his colleagues on a one-to-one basis. It was blindingly obvious that he wanted to dismiss Miller and he may have been crafty in the way he passed the question to each of us, certainly if my experience was typical. I was told that all the others had been sounded and that it was the unanimous view among them all that Brian should be dismissed. The timing worried me with the ritual slaughter due at White Hart Lane just three days away. My own view was that a change was indeed necessary and the sooner we got it over with the better it would be all round. But the succession needed addressing.

'Brian Miller had served the club long and faithfully to the very best of his ability. Beginning as a player who gained England honours and subsequently in every imaginable post culminating in the uneasy crown reserved for the manager. There is a cynical theory that by staying in one place long enough, one will eventually be promoted to his eventual level of inefficiency. But in Brian's case, he had much to offer and his integrity was as unquestionable as his real love for Burnley. I have stated here that I agreed with his removal from the managership, but it was to the eternal shame of the club that the news should come to him as it did, after more than a quarter of a century of devoted service. I understand that he was told by the chairman that he was not required to travel with the team on the journey to Tottenham and that "things would be sorted out afterwards". He was not told face to face and the news that he must have known to be obvious was emblazoned across the press during the following days.

'It was not that there was any disagreement with the removal of Brian Miller from the position of manager, it was just such a pathetic way to carry it out.

'My opinion of Brian was that he was such a nice and friendly guy that he would go to great lengths to avoid internal confrontations, causing him to be too loyal to his staff when ruthlessness was needed. His anger could then be pent-up until it exploded. I remember a very odd interlude when after a match at Queens Park Rangers, the board were offered a player on loan. Incredible as it may seem now, the manager, Brian, was not party to the discussions instigated by Jim Gregory, a chairman of renown, and who had past negotiations with Mr Bob Lord and there was a history of transfers between the two clubs. We were told he would be very good for us and it was only their own strength in forward players which allowed them to loan him out for a month with the option of signing him permanently.

'Brian clearly did not care for what in effect was insulting; being given a player without his personal input. He made his point as clearly as could be by playing his new loan signing for just one full match and then employing him as a substitute on just one other occasion when he scored an opportunistic goal at Leeds. Unsurprisingly Brian did not wish to keep the player and off he trooped back to the smoke before eventually reappearing for Tranmere Rovers when he, Ian Muir, broke all sorts of scoring records. A sign of things to come for the next season and a big-hitting circus hit town with a bang that reverberates to this day.

'By this time, we had lost poor Jack Eglin, called to the Elysian Fields far too soon, and the board was reduced to five. The despair in the club and my growing dissatisfaction with the chairman was getting to me, both at home and at work. Frank Casper was told that he would be in charge of the team for the trip to Tottenham and his immediate reaction was one of extreme sympathy for Brian Miller allied to an immediate request for the upgrading of Gordon Clayton from chief scout to assistant manager. Obviously, this had to be granted there and then and the pair of them took the team down to our London hotel where once again I was the director in charge to be joined by the others prior to the match itself. It was an interesting pre-match evening with Frank and Gordon and I had the impression that they had a clear view of what was likely to lie ahead for them and how to handle things.

'Every Burnley fan knows what happened that night at White Hart Lane as Ardiles, Hoddle et al were pulverised by four goals to one and suddenly a good time was had by all. Perhaps too much so by some in our official party, unable to restrain themselves in these wholly unexpected circumstances. My abiding recollection is of being approached by some worthy, clearly unaware of my allegiances, to be told, "Hell fire, this lot only had three shots and scored four times. I can't believe it."

'Not very original I know, but I gave the time-honoured response, "Look in tomorrow's papers and you'll find it is certainly true." It is possible, indeed quite easy, to lose gracefully, and to win in the same manner, but it was disappointing that both codes suffered in the post-match gatherings. Boardroom etiquette-cum-behaviour is an odd sort of charade when there is excessive pre-match politeness (usually), while hoping for a good game, but hoping secretly that your team stuffs the other one by six goals or more. After the jousting is over one of the good things inherited from Bob Lord was an instruction not to get into discussions about the game during the first quarter of an hour after returning to the boardroom.

'That element of detachment is good and it brings to mind two separate delightful boardroom pantomimes both involving matches against Walsall. The first was at Turf Moor when the niceties had been played out to perfection and John Jackson and I were in anodyne conversation with an elderly visitor and just a few minutes before the witching hour of three o'clock we noticed our visitor had fallen hard and fast asleep. I suppose there remains something of the schoolboy humour in each of us and we exchanged amused glances and thought, "Should we?" But common sense prevailed for once and our soporific friend was in his seat in time.

'The other occasion was after a game at Walsall and the usual after-match procedure for directors and guests is to gather around the TV to tune in to the results service. In we went and the Burnley contingent were very eager to get the results of the other matches involving the relegation struggle which had considerable effects on us. The normal ritual involves emotions swinging wildly with each result and there is usually one anorak who can immediately tell you the effect on the league positions after every result. But not at the friendly Walsall club. Here they had different priorities which you might say took the Bob Lord principle of say nowt for 15 minutes to new extremes. Instead, these Walsall worthies sat laughing their sides out at a *Tom and Jerry*-type cartoon and the football results were kept in abeyance for the next 15 minutes. With all the turmoil we were beginning to endure, who is to say that the Walsall directors did not have the right idea?

'To get back to the matters in hand, we had won at Tottenham, but we did not have a manager and Frank Casper was left in no doubt that the post was up for grabs at the end of the season. What this could possibly do for his confidence seemed all too clear to me at the time and I have always believed that the "caretaker manager" syndrome was unsatisfactory. I firmly believe that it should not have been allowed to continue one minute longer than was avoidable. Furthermore, it was avoidable if the board had exercised some thought before taking the drastic step to dismiss Brian Miller.

'This gives me the opportunity to sound off on a particular hobby horse of mine which I had thought about from the early days of my involvement in football and from the outside, even before that. Nothing causes me to change my opinion, even now, and although it is clearly a minority view, I would be more than ready to argue it with anyone.

'If I may borrow from and paraphrase the amusing Len Shackleton book of yesteryear when his memories included a chapter under the heading of "The Average Director's Knowledge of Football", which was followed by the most celebrated blank page in football journalism, then I think there would not be much to write about the average football manager's knowledge of business. Exceptions there are of course, but there is certainly no correlation between success as a player and the ability to manage, and most certainly not in the aspects of finance that now rule the game. If it were not so serious, it would be funny to see individuals who exchange their football studs for silk suits become financial wizards overnight, or so they think.

'It seems to me that the very word "manager" is a misnomer and the title should be "team coach" and the job description marked accordingly. One hears of figures of millions of pounds being talked about in a most glib way, and without any appreciation of the financial consequences of raising and financing that sort of money. The job of the "team coach" should be to get the best possible team on to the field of play and to determine the tactics to which they conform, and if and when changes in personnel are called for, he can be told the financial limits within which he must work. But the negotiations and detail must be left to the chairman of the club.

'Certainly, the team coach should have the final say in whom he wishes to sign or sell but he should be made fully aware of the proportion of the club finances that are being discussed. I contend that the game would be far healthier in such a scenario and most chairmen are sound-headed executives who collectively could soon rid the game of the parasites and percentage merchants who degrade the very name of the sport. I recently read that Graham Kelly [Football League secretary 1978–1989; Football Association chief executive 1989–1998] had said that he would not cross the street to talk to representatives of the agents and he is 100 per cent right. Elsewhere I can recall having to meet one such gentleman and one of his endearing terms was that I should sign a secret agreement by which "his" player was to be granted a free transfer seven months after joining us for which he requested a nominal signing-on fee of £45,000. Needless to say, I refused but was amazed to find the same player had signed for another major club within days of our negotiations falling down. Seven months later, he was transferred and I would take a healthy bet that it was on a free transfer. Let the coaches coach, and let finance men deal with the money, and let the agents go to hell.

'Frank Casper is the perfect example of the coach rather than manager. It was of course Frank who was thrown in the deep end following the sacking of Brian Miller. Frank had seen his playing career cut down in vicious circumstances just as he was reaching his peak. International honours should have been his. Disastrously for the club the injury was in the week preceding our appearance in the semi-final of the FA Cup against Newcastle. Whilst I can sympathise and to an extent understand it, I cannot describe him as other than bitter, as one shocking foul act had taken away his playing career, decimated his wage packet and seen the culprit (Norman Hunter) escape scot free and go on to achieve England recognition.

'To me, at least, Frank was a coach par excellence, and I do think that others, if not most, of the board shared this view. Unfortunately, it appeared that John Jackson simply did not like Frank Casper at all, which prompts the obvious question, why did he allow him to be appointed as acting manager? Somebody might know the answer, but I certainly do not. What I do know is that lawyers as a breed rarely, if ever, make good man managers. In my opinion their very legal upbringing invariably brings them into contact with the "underclasses", when the peasants are in a spot of bother or need advice on matters with which the lawyers are unfamiliar. Or, the overbearing atmosphere of the court room takes over, and horses' hair for head gear is regarded with some weird sort of mystique.

'The only explanation for Casper's appointment which stands up clearly lies in the undue and unconsidered haste with which Brian Miller was removed. The Bolton Wanderers howler of a goal might well have been the final straw such is the fickleness of the wacky world of football. No matter what, it is not good news to sack the manager unless you have the succession in place or virtually so. John Jackson made it clear that the job would be advertised at the end of the season, and would serve as an exercise in motivation of the key employee of the club. It would have made good copy for one of the John Cleese *How Not to Do It* management videos.

'I tried all I knew to encourage Casper in every way I could imagine, but I could not even get his pay increased, even nominally from the derisory level at which it was fixed, significantly below that of the better-paid players. He did not help his cause by refusing to use the manager's room. "I'll use it when I get the job properly," was his cry. In the boardroom one would expect the acid test to be the results on the field and in Casper's case the first two months included five league games of which four were won and one was drawn. Concurrently we also progressed through two further rounds of the FA Cup to reach the quarter-final stage. And the sensational victory at Tottenham was followed by two League Cup semi-final games against Liverpool, then riding high on the crest of ten successive victories and their normal excess of penalty kicks. Excuse me but I just had to get that one in.

'Although we were beaten by three clear goals at Anfield, one a penalty of course, we had performed with credit and to general rejoicing we actually won the second leg at Turf Moor. At this point John Jackson and I seemed to be in agreement about the coach as opposed to the manager role, and I would have had no hesitation in appointing Casper and Gordon Clayton there and then. But: the chairman would not move from his assertion that the best interests of the club would be best served by advertising the job at the end of the season when Casper could apply if he wanted to.

'Of course, he wanted the job; it was obvious to anyone with eyes to see, but when no confirmation of his appointment was forthcoming after the cup runs and dramatic improvement in league form, the writing was on the wall in letters that could not be misunderstood.

'It can never be proved but I feel that if I had had my way and Casper had been appointed, the relegation that followed would not have happened. Brian Laws and Lee Dixon would have continued their education at Burnley for some time to come and Willie Donachie would not have been given away to Oldham Athletic. When I think like that, I could scream with frustration.

'The FA Cup quarter-final was against Sheffield Wednesday and they had been soundly beaten just a few weeks earlier, 4-1. We blamed a missed penalty for our failure to win the home game and were then faced with a replay at Hillsborough, where we were well beaten, 5-0. But, at this juncture the spectre of dreaded relegation, unthinkable at the start of the season, had been greatly eased by the improvement in our league form. Alas, following Frank's elevation to the hot seat, it was proving to be far too hot without the full support of the chairman. Once again, little did we know and there followed a sudden collapse in form and let nobody who knows the first thing about the game tell me that it had nothing to do with the poor relationship between Frank Casper and John Jackson.

'We suddenly found ourselves in an uphill battle for the final few games and the showdown came with the final fixture at Crystal Palace, another victim of our cup run. The vagaries of the fixture list meant that victory for us would send Palace down, but any other result would consign us to an immediate return to the Third Division. We lost of course but there was the inexplicable penultimate game when we visited Leicester City who had assured themselves of promotion to the First Division a few days previously and were in near party mood. Prior to that match Burnley needed three points to maintain our league status and it would have mattered not one jot if we had lost one of the last two games by a dozen goals as long as we won the other. Put simply, a draw was of no use to us.

'It is not for directors to comment on team tactics but for all their faults, directors are fans too. But at Leicester the team gave the impression of being content with the draw. On the face of it, there was no great urgency in the later stages of the game to go for broke, or that the plan might have been to catch the jubilant Leicester on the break and snatch the win that way. I am absolutely certain that after that, not even victory at Crystal Palace would have saved Frank's job and I felt that while still defending him and without doubt would have stood by him, he had made himself a hostage to fortune, and fortune for Frank Casper was in short supply from the chairman. It was a pity, as I was firmly of the opinion that Casper the coach had so much to offer.

'I had missed the final fixture at Crystal Palace as I was away on holiday in Tenerife, a holiday that had been postponed from February when I cancelled, as there was no way on earth that I was going to miss the Liverpool semi-final games. But during that Palace game I was pretty much permanently on the phone during that traumatic one and a half hours. My misery was unconfined when the dreaded result was known and I spent the rest of that night in our apartment morosely downing whisky to finish in a state no one ever saw me in at a football match.

'Defending Frank Casper against the chairman's preference would have been well-nigh impossible after the inexplicable (to us at least) tactics in the Leicester fiasco and I still had the best part of two weeks' holiday to enjoy while my mind was half on trying to formulate new ideas for the next season. The appointment of a new manager I had to recognise as being inevitable, as by now I was the only one on the board who would have carried on with Casper and Clayton, whose dismissal I will always contend was an avoidable error.

'I took some small comfort from the budget revenue to come from the Leicester and Palace gates which came in aggregate to well over 50,000. In those days there was still the gate-sharing arrangement that gave visitors a per-capita share of crowd receipts. I have always regarded it as a pity that the majority of league clubs were railroaded into the abandonment of this equitable system by the "big few" who have never looked at the general good health of the game, if it in any way conflicted with their private interests. In the end there can be no league worth having if there are insufficient clubs to participate. I do not think it is to the good of the game that it should be ever more structured to the supposed benefit of the few, who in any event have the big city populations to buttress them.

'But in our own little world we were relatively rich and we were bound soon to come into really big money for the transfer out of the marvellously gifted Trevor Steven as it was clearly impossible to keep him at our now Third Division (again) club. All of which reminds me of my ill-advised comment that Burnley had played their last game in the Third.

'Ever the optimist, I believed, as did the rest of the board, that we still retained a squad of players who could surely redeem this catastrophe at the first attempt and I repeat ad nauseam that if we had retained Casper as coach with Gordon Clayton to assist, I am as sure as one can be in writing the history that never happened, we would have returned to the Second Division the next year much wiser and better prepared for it. It is not for a director to select the team but I would be failing myself if I did not list here some of the players who were at the club and ready to do battle again.

'The very least Frank Casper deserves is for it to be recorded here that while he was in charge there were 26 games and of these 11 were won, six were drawn while nine were lost. This was comfortable mid-table form achieved in difficult circumstances. In essence now, it is clear beyond dispute that to all intents and purposes we were relegated before he took charge of the team. It is not simply hindsight to have a glimpse of the obvious, that Frank never had a chance and was not even given a whiff of one from an unsupportive board.

'Already contracted for the next season were eight or nine players whom I will contend to my dying day would have formed the nucleus of a team which would have returned us to the Second Division at the first attempt. I know I can be accused of having claret and blue spectacles and would plead guilty as charged, but this squad stood head and shoulders above the standards of the Third Division. And, we were shortly to be in the unique position of having substantial finance to add more quality to it.

'Ready and eager to do battle were Brian Laws, heart and soul in the club and devastated to be discarded by the new management before they even saw him in a competitive match; Lee Dixon was to get just one match before being moved on a free transfer, and Willie Donachie for me was a truly super professional in everything he did and who was good enough to play in the top flight some five years after he left and being told he was past his sell-by date. Try to find me another Third Division club with three full-backs of that quality and I assure you that it will be a long and fruitless search.

'When I think of some of their replacements for whom we paid fees, I know I was in the centre of a nut house.

'Also committed to the club were skipper Martin Dobson, Brian Flynn and Billy Hamilton, internationals all, and every one of them a genuine man, highly skilled and competitive and in love with the town and club. I know they would give their all and they had the skills to go with it. Also contracted was Derek

Scott; a more honest and devoted player never passed my door. I remember well, after the new management had been at the club for at least a couple of months, asking them why they never utilised the exceptional long throw that he possessed. None of them were aware of this element to his game.

'On the little subject regarding director's knowledge of the game, I might add a snippet of a conversation I had with Martin Dobson, when at Bury, when I told him that I had questioned John Bond about seeing off Brian Laws. Bond's reply to me was to say, "Do you think you know more about football than I do?" Martin said I should answer with just one word, "Yes."

'Quite new to the club was Terry Donovan, signed from Aston Villa for a modest fee and who had performed creditably during the last few desperate games that year. After the departure of Trevor Steven there was the new jewel in the crown, Michael Phelan, who any fool could see had real quality and with it a love for his hometown club. There were developing youngsters all in place and with the insertion of two or three experienced players that were easily affordable, there were grounds for optimism and the relegation nightmare could have been exorcised very quickly. All we had to do was to keep our heads and all pull in the same direction.

'The records show that this was all too much to ask and it is to the shame of us all that we made such an appalling hash of things. It can never be proved of course, but if the players we had did not form the basis of a side good enough to stride through the Third Division, then I have to plead guilty to knowing nothing about football at all. We knew that we needed a goalkeeper and a left-sided midfield player but we were custodians of wealth beyond the most extravagant dreams of only a year ago. We had performed the crazy double of putting the finances straight and getting relegated in the same season. But our playing staff were a resilient lot and I deplore the permanent pessimism that gets you nowhere and I had no doubts that we could get back to work during the summer break which is the busy time to bring in new players.

'A morning or two later I strolled down to the Tenerife front and bought a newspaper. The sports page heading stopped me in my tracks. The ball game was about to change with a vengeance.'

* * *

For the record, lest this chapter be seen to be rather one-sided, John Jackson did explain his reasoning behind the dismissal of Brian Miller. At Christmas, he had seen them lose to rivals Blackburn Rovers, a bitter pill to swallow, and in January Burnley were next to bottom of the division. The defeat at Bolton was described as 'gutless'. He felt it was time to act decisively and that was his prerogative:

'We are nine points adrift in the relegation battle. We have lost more league games than any other Football League club. Of our last 11 away league games, we have drawn one and lost ten. It is an appalling situation. A decision was therefore made to change the manager. The next question relates to the timing of the announcement. Bearing all things in mind, we took the view that nothing could happen at Tottenham that would make an appointment after the game more sensible.'

The chairman added in another interview that they had discussed the situation at Christmas and the run of results but had done their best to help him put it right. The Bolton result was singled out, 'The performance at Bolton was appalling, the worst ever. Clearly some action had to be taken.' It was also pointed out that an alternative role at the club had been offered but with no mention of what that role would be.

Had Burnley lost at Tottenham nobody would have given the decision or the timing a second thought. But the astonishing victory certainly complicated the dismissal. It was also Brian Miller's birthday the following day. Football doesn't get much crueller than that.

5

The trauma of relegation

TO SAY the chairman and the directors were left stunned at the relegation is an understatement. Two games to go and salvation was still possible but the ending was just tame and spineless. Tim Quelch describes the final agonies:

'[Saturday] 14 May was a day of warm hazy sunshine. Michael Jackson's *Thriller* was the number one album while at the top of the singles charts Spandau Ballet's "True" held sway. The Hitler diaries weren't true. Despite the premature claims of learned historian Lord Dacre, formerly Professor Hugh Trevor-Roper, the *Hitler Diaries* were just a scam, dreamed up by some journalists on the make.

'Getting into the game was like being churned in a huge scrum. Outside Filbert Street, thousands pressed hard to reach the entrances, filling up the narrow streets and gangways, milling, heaving, rolling, a helplessly shifting, sweaty tide. We seemed to be propelled through the turnstiles by the force of the throng. It remains one of my most alarming football experiences.

'Despite having the greater possession, Leicester looked ragged and edgy but Burnley did little to threaten. But they could justify the classiest moment of the half. It came from Martin Dobson at his most imperious. He went off on one of his surging runs, combining the power of a Scania with the grace of a Rolls-Royce.

Three Leicester players lunged in at him but with deft control and timed acceleration he left them for dead. His run deserved better, petering out in yet another blunt attack. We needed to win.

'Hamilton might have stolen the points. Flynn's weighted ball gave him the opportunity to run down the inside of the right channel of the Leicester goal. Alas this was not the Billy of White Hart Lane. The pressure of carrying a struggling side had worn away his sharpness. Instead of the crashing drive, which had flashed past Clemence's left hand, all Billy could muster was a wretched mis-kick. There was so little power in this effort that it barely crept over the byline.

'The draw suited Leicester. They were promoted. A 0-0 result was an excellent achievement but it meant that Burnley still had to win their final midweek game at Crystal Palace in order to secure safety. We expected a night of high passion and drama but it was nothing of the sort. The lights went out with barely a whimper. This was a desperate way to bid farewell to the Second Division after just one season.'

The esteemed writer Brian Glanville was at the Leicester game and paints an entirely different picture to that of Derek Gill, who wrote that he was baffled at the Burnley tactics of not going for a result. Glanville was full of praise for Burnley, citing several scoring chances and attacking moves. He was also baffled as to why they were down at the bottom of the division, stating that they had no real business being there. The last time he had seen them was when they thrashed Tottenham Hotspur.

The Palace game, on the other hand, wrote Mihir Bose, ended in boredom. Apart from the brave Hamilton there was hardly a decent Burnley attack. Maybe they could have had a penalty early in the second half when Gilbert appeared to foul Kevin Young in the box. But teams don't get penalties when they are fated to be relegated. Towards the end, the boredom factor was so great that one Palace fan entered the fray, dribbled the ball into the Burnley net and acclaimed himself a hero. It was the highlight of a game in which a lethargic and almost disinterested Burnley seemed to have totally forgotten, or never knew in the first place, that a win, however improbable, would have saved their season. It left people scratching their heads; how could a team that had such stirring cup runs perform so badly in the league? How could any side that beat Spurs 4-1 at their own ground end up being relegated?

Journalist Keith McNee concluded that it was difficult to put a finger on the reason for the weirdly contrasting fortunes but felt perhaps that the players were under much more pressure in the league games. In cup ties they could be far more relaxed and this allowed them to rise to each occasion brilliantly.

Local Clarets reporter Peter Higgs referred to the Tottenham game and the Miller dismissal in his piece, 'What A Week That Was', in the now long-gone *Evening Star.* He was most certainly supportive of the decision to replace Miller:

'The events of last week will receive a special chapter in my memoirs, if ever I get round to writing them. But that, I'm sure, is true of many people connected with Burnley Football Club. It was certainly the newsiest, most dramatic week since January 1976, when the Clarets lost at Blackpool to go out of the FA Cup, had a widely publicised dressing room row, and within three days manager Jimmy Adamson had parted company with the club.

'Eleven days ago, as I sat in my car outside Burnden Park having seen the most appalling Burnley performance I could remember, someone asked what, if I was a director, I would do? I replied that Brian Miller would have to go. But what? Before the Milk Cup quarter-final at Spurs? Yes, I replied, it would only complicate matters if the decision was delayed. So, while unlike some supporters, I agreed with the timing of Mr Miller's removal from office, it was still a shock when it came.

'The decision was made by the board on Monday evening and relayed to Mr Miller the following day, a few hours before the team left for Spurs and the day before his 46th birthday. It was bound to be a difficult decision because Brian, a true gentleman, is well liked throughout the club. But results are a hard master to satisfy.

'While I back the board's actions, the manner in which it was executed left something to be desired. Acting manager Frank Casper was told only 20 minutes before he left for White Hart Lane that he was in charge of the team, with no time to select the players he wanted, or begin the preparation his own way. The publicity was also badly handled with no official statement emerging from the club until Friday, three days after the news broke. Such complaints were inevitably overshadowed by the events of Wednesday night.

'I travelled down to London on the Burnley FC staff coach and found the mood surprisingly optimistic. Youth team coach Arthur Bellamy, for example, said, "I really believe we can do it. I just have a feeling about this match."

'Traffic conditions were so good that we arrived by 6pm. In plenty of time for the 7.45pm kick-off. Many fans, having left Burnley around 12 noon, were in the Tottenham area by 4pm. As I waited outside the ground, watched the crowds arrive, I was amazed by the number of people I recognised. At a guess I'd say there was a noticeable reduction in staff levels at offices and factories throughout Burnley on Wednesday afternoon. Probably Thursday morning too.

'White Hart Lane has always been a favourite ground of mine with a special atmosphere of its own. The multimillion-pound stand has done nothing to destroy the image and with 30,000 fans ready to roar their heads off, the stage was set for a great occasion. The match itself is now history. Even though I saw it with my own eyes, I still find it hard to believe.

'Spurs ranged from the sublime to the ridiculous, showing some neat, sharp touches for an hour, before folding up like a second-rate schoolboy team in the last 25 minutes. Burnley battled bravely, stuck to their task and were dictating things by the end. But such was the bizarre nature of the first three goals that I am tempted to say that they were simply fated to win.

'The press room at Spurs, in addition to providing some delicious sandwiches, also contained a video recorder which showed all the goals at normal speed and then in slow action replay, immediately after the match. Such a facility was not only a rare treat but ensured that reporters got their facts right.

'The four-hour journey home was, as you might expect, noisy and high-spirited. It featured plenty of noise and singing. I know three members of the party who had difficulty speaking the following day. Martin Dobson, having led his troops into battle, finished the trip in the role of chef, serving up the team's hot meal with the able assistance of Brian Flynn and Derek Scott. The coach arrived back at Turf Moor shortly before 4am to be followed by the choking sounds of straining engines as players struggled to start their frost-covered cars.

'Me? I left my uncooperative car and headed straight for the office. With so much to write it wasn't worth going home. So, in the small hours, the sound of a lonely typewriter could be heard over Bull Street. It was not until 4.30 on Thursday afternoon that the job was done, the paper was finished and I was ... tired. I went home and slept for 13 hours. By Friday morning Burnley had issued a statement about the managerial situation and plans were well underway for the defeat of Barnsley.

'Life goes on and the headlines change, but for a few days Burnley rocked the football world. How soon will they do so again?'

If Peter Higgs had possessed a crystal ball, he would have seen another result that would give Liverpool a real shock. But a little further down the line he would have been utterly shocked himself to read the headlines about who was to replace Frank Casper at the end of the season. It was to be an appointment that most certainly rocked the football world.

The chairman expressed his delight, of course. It was unbelievable, he said, adding that it was hard to believe that a team that had played so badly at Bolton just days earlier could win so deservedly against such illustrious opponents.

Casper said he wished to take no credit for the performance because it was down to the players. He pointed to Martin Dobson in particular. They had beaten three First Division clubs and now he looked forward to taking on Liverpool in the semi-finals. In the first leg at Anfield the history books say that Liverpool won 3-0, but don't mention how well Burnley played on the night. They were not disgraced, and more composed finishing in good situations might have seen a far closer result. The second leg at Turf Moor, however, was one of those special night games under the floodlights that live long in the memory and when the drama and spectacle is made more vivid by the lights. The word 'theatre' would not go amiss as Burnley won 1-0 and over 22,000 crammed in, filling the coffers and delighting Derek Gill. Higgs was there:

'Thousands of happy fans summed it up far better than any words of mine. "We're proud of you, we're proud of you," they sang as their heroes not only beat but humbled the mighty Liverpool, on a night of great emotion at Turf Moor. If the victory at Tottenham was the result of the century, this was the performance to overshadow it. From the moment a raucous, ear-splitting roar greeted their arrival and caused a Liverpool reporter accustomed to crowd atmosphere to turn to me and say, "Hey, this really is like the old days," to the time they dragged themselves away to a standing ovation, the Clarets provided undiluted pleasure.

'In the days of television, Jimmy Hill, bare terraces and bad publicity, football isn't often like this. People who shared it on Tuesday night were so lucky. Without any exaggeration, Burnley were magnificent. They were so good that they might easily have wiped out the 3-0 deficit from the first leg, and now be on their way to Wembley. A multitude of memories will remain with the cheering masses for years to come.

'To pick out individuals in what was essentially a team performance would be inviting controversy and I wouldn't argue with manager Frank Casper's claim that they were all incredible. But Brian Flynn had an outstanding performance to tackle like a terrier in the first half and end up running the game as Burnley went from strength to strength. And Derek Scott must be mentioned in despatches for an all-action display which deserved to boost his popularity immeasurably. He scored the match-winning goal, got knocked out, was booked, and would have run through a brick wall if it meant Burnley getting to the final.

'Burnley were unquestionably on top in the first half and they showed no sign of slacking the pressure in the second. Highlight of the first half was a 30-yard power drive from Brian Laws that was so desperately close to being goal of the season. I can't remember when I last saw a shot hit so hard. In the first minute of the second half he had a 20-yard drive pushed away at full stretch by Grobbelaar.

'Within nine minutes came the goal that lifted the roof off. A diagonal cross from Laws was headed down by Hamilton for SCOTT to hook a left-footed volley between Hansen and Souness and past Grobbelaar's despairing dive. A minute later there was a goal-line clearance by Lawrenson. Had Burnley scored that second goal in the space of 60 seconds, with 35 minutes still remaining, they might surely have staged one of the fightbacks of the century.

'The final whistle brought glorious triumph for Burnley even though their illustrious opponents took their expected place in the final on 26 March. The Clarets' victory was Liverpool's first setback in 15 matches and prevented them equalling Nottingham Forest's record run of 25 League Cup matches without defeat.

'If only Burnley had taken their chances at Anfield, if only a debatable penalty had not been awarded against them, if only they had not conceded a third goal.

'If only ... But it's no good crying over spilt Milk Cup hopes. Let's savour a marvellous run in the competition climaxed by a remarkable victory. What a treat it was.'

Let it be repeated that this was a club firmly entrenched in the relegation places and the prognosis was not good. Yet they had excelled in their cup ties.

The Gill diaries make no mention of the horrendous game at Ewood Park at Easter, when Burnley lost again to Blackburn Rovers and fans went berserk. It was a shameful episode in the club's history. Phil Whalley described it:

'By mid-March Burnley were out of both knockout competitions and their cup commitments left them facing a backlog of league fixtures from the daunting perspective of bottom place. Defeats against Cambridge and Wolves built up the pressure on players and fans alike as Burnley took on mid-table Blackburn Rovers at Ewood. Although the Clarets desperately needed to win, just the avoidance of defeat would have been an acceptable outcome, something upon which to build.

'The first half was depressing in its familiarity as Blackburn went two goals up in the face of another poor display from the Clarets. Fans aware of the importance of the game feared the worst. It was at half-time, with Blackburn cruising and in complete control, that the first unrest occurred. The police decided to make a stand against a small and frivolous act of foolery; a lone wellington boot was being tossed randomly around the away end. Granted there might have been one poor soul hopping about but since when have the police ever been concerned about the right to wear matching footwear.

'A few policemen waded in to try and grab some of those they had seen throwing the boot around, but this merely started off isolated scuffles. The police retreated empty-handed and this should have been the end of the matter. However, fans making their way to the snack bar reported a rapid build-up of police and dogs in the area between the Darwen End and the main stand. No one was prepared for what happened next. With no warning, the police let their canine friends loose on the Darwen End and followed with truncheons drawn. Fans returning to the terraces from the snack bar emerged into a scene of chaos, surrounded by snapping, snarling dogs and policemen cracking heads indiscriminately. I've no wish to romanticise a certain section of Burnley support; they were tough, hard lads who liked nothing better than a public brawl, but few of the many innocents caught in the middle of this crass act of police violence could find it in themselves to condemn those Burnley fans that fought back.

'This was how they utilised the roof: faced with an uncompromising constabulary, some of those hundreds of fans cornered in the Darwen End began to rip and kick pieces of plastic and asbestos from the rotten timber frame of the enclosure. At first these crude missiles were directed at their aggressors standing on the other side of no man's land that had now appeared on the terrace. By this time the second half was due to start but the players remained in the dressing room. This was a significant moment. Up to that point, the throwing of missiles had been a straightforward statement against the police and their arrogant aggression.

'But now, the actions of the fans had come to confront another factor, the resumption of play, and this deepened the symbolism of the disorder. It wasn't just about police tactics now; the disorder had encroached upon the wider issue of the team itself and its performance on the pitch. Frank Casper made his way to the police box from which the PA system was controlled and let forth a stream of hollow rhetoric along the lines of, "We don't want you; we never want to see you at Turf Moor again. Those arrested are a shame on the club."

'The response was immediate as yet more asbestos came down from the roof. This time it was thrown on the pitch in utter contempt of one of the men who had presided over the decline of their club that they spent a large chunk of their incomes following. Their message was clear: our club is dying and you are responsible. Don't you dare tell us we can't support our team.

'Significantly, no cheers of righteous indignation greeted the cries of the manager. The Burnley fans in the main stand, seated in the section closest to the away terrace, had seen everything and their mood, although tinged with irritation at the delay, was one of reserved sadness. They knew what they were witnessing, another away defeat, another nail in the coffin, and the visible decay of the very social fabric of the club. The hasty and misguided nature of Casper's words was illustrated in the following week as the police conceded that they could not bring charges against any of the 32 fans that had been arrested. Many of these 32 had been assaulted and grabbed as all they did was emerge from the tea hut.

'Vince Overson, a Longside hero and the last of the class of '82 to leave the club, came out on to the pitch and appealed for calm as did Norman Jones, one of the Darwen End instigators, who had somehow made his way round to the tunnel entrance. Eventually, the boiling anger subsided to a simmer and the players emerged for the second half. Without ever looking likely to salvage anything from the game, the Clarets responded to their predicament. Derek Scott made a timely arrival at the end of a hopeful Kevin Young cross and poked the ball past Gennoe. But Burnley simply did not have the nous or spirit to conjure an equaliser.

'This 2-1 reverse turned out to be the third of five consecutive defeats that left the Clarets with the unrealistic task of winning five of their last seven games to stay up. It was to their credit that they were relegated only after losing the very last game against Crystal Palace. But the desperately poor performance served up by the

Clarets in that do-or-die game at Selhurst Park only underlined how corroded the Turf Moor underbelly had become.

'The Easter Monday clash with Blackburn went down in official annals as a dark moment in the history of the club. I would like to proffer a different conclusion. Quite simply the Ewood riots represented the moment when Burnley fans lost any remaining sense of humorous cynicism at the plight of their club. With a board that allowed no input from the fans whatsoever, only two options were left. Voice or exit. The latter option was eventually taken by all but a couple of thousand diehard Clarets in the next few seasons. The former option was exercised regularly in newspapers and on the terraces, but to no avail. The club was deaf to the voice of its supporters.

'Martin Luther King once made a famous observation about public disorder. "Riots," said King, infuriated by ignorant condemnation of radical black activism, "riots are the language of the unheard."'

In the league there was precious little to enthuse about, although after the awful game at Bolton there was a brief flurry. It came to nothing. One of the matches was a 7-1 win against Charlton Athletic. Good grief, 7-1. Fans went home quite stunned at the goal feast, wondering if there was hope after all. John Ashley reported in the *Sunday Express*:

'Burnley's battle for Second Division survival finally took off yesterday. At last, they found the form that they have been producing in cup competitions. And no matter how long former European Footballer of the Year Allan Simonsen stays with Charlton, he will never forget this nightmare for the London club. Burnley really went to town in the last 13 minutes. Hamilton crashed in their third goal after good work by Kevin Young. Taylor further increased the lead after a long run from Hamilton and then came three more goals in the last six minutes from Trevor Steven and Hamilton again.'

The more thoughtful fans in the Burnley crowd would have remained cautious. For the last 20 minutes Charlton were down to nine men. But there were two more goals for Billy Hamilton, who today remains a Burnley icon, and his two goals in the cup game at Tottenham sealed his place in the Burnley Hall of Fame. Ray Simpson, in his epic book *The Complete Clarets Collection*, provides an account of Hamilton's career:

'Billy Hamilton was a centre-forward of the old-fashioned variety. Big, strong, good in the air and fully committed to the cause. At a time of vastly fluctuating fortunes at Turf Moor, he never let the Clarets down, and the fans loved him.

'His career began with Linfield in the Irish league and he was already an under-23 international with Northern Ireland when he came to England to join QPR for a fee of £25,000 in April 1978. He won his first full cap before he had played a game at Loftus Road and never really established himself as a regular there before Brian Miller made him his first signing for Burnley, paying a fee of £38,000 to bring him to Turf Moor in November 1979.

'He immediately replaced Paul Fletcher in the number nine shirt and went on to become the Clarets' top scorer in 1979/80, his first goal coming in a memorable 3-2 win against Newcastle. Such occasions were extremely rare that season and at the end of it, Burnley were relegated to the Third Division for the first time in the club's history.

'Two years later the Clarets were back up and Hamilton's partnerships up front with Steve Taylor and then Paul McGee were major factors in that success. Hamilton was the target man, never a prolific scorer but always making life easier for his strike partners and always a difficult customer for opposing defenders. His international career blossomed and, in the summer of 1982, he was a key member of the Northern Ireland side that reached the group stage at the World Cup finals in Spain. He was the creator of Gerry Armstrong's winning goal against the host nation and scored twice himself in a 2-2 draw against Austria.

'1982/83 was a peculiar season for the Clarets with good runs in both cup competitions but coinciding with relegation back to the Third Division. Hamilton's finest moments of the campaign came at White Hart Lane, scoring twice against England keeper Ray Clemence to reach the semi-final of the League Cup.

'Hamilton survived the changes that came with John Bond's arrival as manager in 1983. Bond's one season in charge was also Hamilton's most productive time in front of goal with 18 in the league alone. He formed a fine partnership with Bond's major signing, Kevin Reeves, and then following Reeves's career-ending injury, with Wayne Biggins.

'He left Turf Moor in 1984, rather surprisingly joining Oxford, just promoted to the Second Division, for £95,000 plus Neil Whatmore in part exchange. Oxford were on a roll under manager Jim Smith and they won a second successive promotion in 1985 with Hamilton playing his part until injury struck. That injury would as good as end his career in English football; he rarely appeared in Oxford's first-team in their first season in the top flight. He played his last game for the club in October 1986.

'There is little doubt that Billy Hamilton enjoyed the best years of his football career at Burnley and he is remembered with great fondness by all who saw him play for the club.'

Hamilton made 200 Football League appearances and scored 58 goals across his career. In total he made 248 appearances in all competitions and scored 76 goals, playing 41 times for Northern Ireland. He ended his playing career at Limerick in the League of Ireland and was that competition's top scorer in 1988/89. He moved to Distillery in the north, playing until 1992 and remaining as manager for another three years. After retiring from the game, he opened a sports shop in Bangor.

6

How John Bond came to Burnley

BURNLEY SUPPORTER Stephen Tinshill still remembers being sat in the Bob Lord Stand for an evening game when Bond had only just been appointed as manager, 'A guy, probably no longer with us as he looked to be in his mid-50s, stood up and looked at John Bond as he approached the dugout in a flash suit and beige overcoat, and shouted in a strong Burnley accent, "Bloody hell Bond, you look like a club turn." The area where we sat burst out in loud laughter.' Is it any wonder the Bond year was doomed to failure? Over 35 years later, people still remember stories like this.

* * *

Derek Gill wrote in his diary in February 2005, 'It is worth recording that for all the faults and fracture lines of the John Bond appointment and subsequent era, he himself suffered a fate in that he never again held a position in football similar to that which he had held at Manchester City, and previously held with considerable distinction at Norwich, a club that I know he held in high esteem and always regretted leaving after seven years in charge.

'The very name of John Bond is spat out in Burnley and district, and while his tenure was nothing short of a disaster for the club, he, too, also suffered loss from it. I have nothing but contempt for those who drooled over him in his presence, wasting his time and mine, solely to be seen in his company. There are plenty of them.

'Some years ago, I foolishly gave a short comment to a red top newspaper in which I said that Burnley should have ended his reign earlier. This angered him very much and his reply was inevitable. He wrote to me expressing his disappointment at my remarks. But he should have known that reporting out of context is par for the course. My view was that the marriage between Bond and the club was unsustainable and should have been terminated to the benefit of both parties.

'I have to say that I found his style of man-management strange in the extreme, and thought that his judgement of players, certainly in his time at Burnley, was flawed. But at the same time, he commanded the respect of men such as Tommy Hutchison and Kevin Reeves, two quite exceptional players and real men's men.

'It needs a cleverer man than me to unravel the personality of John Bond. This is what I wrote at the time:.

* * *

'"John Bond to manage Burnley" boomed the headline.

'I could not have been more surprised but first I needed to ring the chairman to see whether this was fact or simply speculative journalism. It would be later that evening before I spoke to John Jackson, who simply said, "Every word is true."

'I was indignant but also at that distance totally restrained, not as has been imagined because Bond had been appointed, but because nobody had bothered to let me know, nor had my opinion been sought. My holiday phone number had been available and just simple courtesy to the hardest working, although obviously not the most influential, director, should surely not have been too much to ask.

'Nothing in all this should be taken to imply that Bond would not have been appointed if I had been in town. I was told by John

Jackson that it was unanimous among all four available directors and here was the right man for the job. In fairness I have to record that the chairman gave me the chance to meet "the new manager" prior to the exchange of letters of appointment, but I did not take it up. I had met Mr Bond during the previous season when he brought the full Manchester City team to play in a testimonial match for Alan Stevenson, our long-serving goalkeeper, and the manner in which he seemed to be in control of his players and the dignified talk he gave to an assembled post-match gathering in the club's social centre had been impressive.

'I remained sorry for Casper and secretly hoped he would be kept on as coach for which I had some reason to anticipate, despite John Jackson's personal dislike of him, as the chairman had always been adamant that nobody would come to the club and bring an entourage along with him.

'This was the first and would certainly not prove to be the last occasion when some individuals were literally falling over themselves to be near the great man, and it fills me with contempt when I now hear the same people prattling on about what a stupid appointment it was.

'Here in the real world, Mr John Bond, the new manager of Burnley FC, rolled up, and it has to be said that it attracted an unprecedented gathering of the press and TV. John Jackson told me, and I quote from memory but I know it to be accurate to the last syllable, "Up to now we have been playing at it," and went on along the lines that we were about to witness a level of professionalism within the club that would revolutionise the place. It sure did, as we all know.

'But back to first principles: "Back him or sack him", the only sane course and from that day until the day that he actually was sacked, he received full support on football matters with certain issues thrashed out privately, and from the day I became managing director he understood the allowed limits of spending available to him and the fact of the matter is that I had no difficulty with him keeping to them. If he was given the chance to spend money, he would grab it with both hands and I would expect him now to confirm my description of any relationship with him. As a man to work with he was not a problem but I often wondered about his relationships with players, some of whom, notably Martin Dobson and Joe Gallagher, made no secret of their dislike for the regime and the man himself.

'In no time at all the really critical relationship between chairman and manager was so fraught that the entire club was caught up in a charade of gossip which would not have been out of place in an Agatha Christie novel. It became sheer hell to try to work in it and the labour of love upon which I had embarked two years earlier was now robbing me of sleep and peace of mind and degenerated into a cross between compulsory community work and an ego trip gone wrong.

'I will not attempt to define an "entourage" but the following Johns came aboard to supplement the Jackson and Bond variety; John Benson as assistant manager, John Doherty as youth development officer, and John Sainty as something else. We had unceremoniously dumped Frank Casper and Gordon Clayton and how ironic that the parting advice of Gordon was simply to tell us to hold on to Lee Dixon no matter what. He said Lee would become better than Brian Laws. Lee played just once and Brian never had a single competitive game. Oh dear.

'Poor Gordon was to pass away suddenly and tragically at the early age of 51 and I attended his Requiem Mass at St Annes, Manchester, where there was a marvellous turnout for him from his true love Manchester United. It was terrible that such a good and devoted man should pass away, having had no reward for all that he gave to the game. A posthumous testimonial dinner for him at least brought some belated financial consolation to his family. Gordon had played just one game for Manchester United and it is to their credit that they arranged so much for his family. Not everybody in football is bad and such memories live on.

'But here we were with our new-found professionalism ready to take the Third Division by storm, and a part of the pre-season training included a semi-competitive and enjoyable competition in the Isle of Man. As the director who regularly took the reserves to places such as Scunthorpe, Derby and Middlesbrough, and arrived back home in the early hours while my hardworking colleagues were in bed, a few days in the friendly island was no problem at all, in fact the very opposite. If then I give the impression that it was usually me that accompanied the team and the reserves on the unglamorous trips, it is only because in reality that is precisely what happened. On this visit I was joined by Colin Sanderson, recently appointed, and keen as mustard.

'We travelled by ferry and I was taken aback by a conversation with Martin Dobson, club captain, or so I thought, and a player of great distinction and experience and who to me personified all that was good in sport. I learned of heated arguments in training and Martin told me he was being targeted to be got out of the club. I found this hard to believe but there was no doubt in the mind of Martin[10]. He had been stripped of the captaincy and humiliatingly been referred to as "Colin" Dobson as if he were of such insignificance, that the management confused him with another professional of that name. Despite never having any contact with Colin, I would be very surprised if he compared himself to Martin. An intelligent and mature man, Martin took it all in his stride and let the water run over the proverbial duck's back. I know that the games on the island are basically for fairly gentle practice purposes but I could not believe my eyes when I saw Dobson being instructed to play up front and be the "runner" alongside Billy Hamilton.

---

10 This is confirmed in the interview conducted with Bond by Phil Whalley and reproduced later in full.

'What happened to Martin faded into insignificance when attention was turned to Brian Laws. A great favourite with the crowd at Burnley and with me personally. Brian was still a young lad and still learning and really keen to do so and better himself, and he was head over heels in love with Burnley Football Club. Apart from an obvious natural ability he had guts on the field and had the courage to be the penalty taker as a very young player, when some of the seniors looked the other way. Brian was quiet on his travels and I had many an hour with him on his chessboard. Some footballers do have brains. He received a computerised chessboard from home on his 21st birthday which was a great delight to him. To my eye, he was, and still is, exactly the sort of young man to have with you if you have any pretensions to future development of your football club. Of all the compliments paid to me at the club, none pleased or flattered me more than to be invited to his wedding celebrations, and I will never lose my affection for him. I always look for his name on the team sheets he graces wherever he is playing.

'After being transferred so much against his will, he took the time to write to me to thank me for all that I had done for him. And to say he hoped to wear the Claret shirt again one day[11]. Unfortunately, at this early stage of his career and development, he was sufficiently insecure to be destroyed by his experience on that friendly island, the Isle of Man, and was never to be seen in a competitive match for the club again.

'Bond wanted Laws to play in a totally different manner to the way he had learned previously and in the Manx games one could not fail to hear every word the manager bawled at him. Laws was made to look foolish, which he most certainly is not, and the more that the abuse was piled on him, the worse he became, as he desperately tried to conform to the manager's ideas, but without

11 Laws returned as manager one day, replacing Owen Coyle, but without success.

any success. It was as sure as night follows day that Laws was on his way out and this was the time that I questioned the manager's judgement of a player. I suppose I got the inevitable answer. "Do you think you know more about football than me?"

'I should have taken Martin Dobson's advice and in this case said just one word, "Yes." Is there anybody out there who would not now say that, on that matter, I was right?

'The sponsors' lounge was the ideal setting for a pre-season dinner at which the twin objectives were to introduce the new management team to the most influential supporters, and possible suppliers of finance through match sponsorship, or any associated enterprises. Here, they could be sounded out in a cordial atmosphere and they had the chance to question the two Johns. There was no doubt that the new management team possessed a level of presentation superior to that with which we had been accustomed. All wind and you know what, as it came to in next to no time thereafter. The fact that previous management never had the opportunity to perform in similar circumstances might have something to do with it, one might think.

'The wining, dining and speaking provided a humorous and without doubt pleasant evening and a good time was had by all, capped by one local worthy known by name to at least half the population of Burnley interested in the club, who distinguished himself by eating the table flowers, thereby leaving the two Johns in no doubt that they were in uncharted waters. Despite having a low opinion of the worthy gent, I will refrain from naming him as it might deter him from doing it again, when others could see what a prat he is. Lest anyone should think wrongly, it was not John Jackson.

'Quickly established in the manager's office, John Bond set to work at a pace that astonished me and no doubt everyone else, and there was activity in the transfer market the like of which I had never seen before and am never likely to see again. From the point of view of the manager, the rationale behind it all was devastatingly simple.

'"You." To the end of his time he used "you" when discussing the club, which suggested to me he never felt part of it. "You" have been relegated so by simple definition the players must not be good enough. Like all managers, he had a shopping list of players with whom he had worked and whose qualities he claimed to know. It was clear that he wanted rid of Martin Dobson and Brian Laws, by coincidence regarded by the chairman as culprits in our relegation of the previous season.

'The transfer or bombing out, as I prefer to remember it of Brian Laws, was done and dusted in no time. Off he went to Huddersfield Town so much against his wishes. I recall seeing him pay at the gate for a midweek game at Turf Moor a couple of months later. I had a very quick chat and it was abundantly clear where his heart still lay. When he saw the line-up, he must have felt truly gutted as it cried out for someone of his stature. Brian was sold for a fee much below his market worth and for the first of only two occasions I deliberately gave incorrect information to the press. With a shade of reluctance, I gave an incorrect statement to the press when we led them to believe that the fee exceeded the true figure which I felt was embarrassingly low for a player of his potential. His subsequent performances have proved me right on that one. I thought that the fans would be still more irritated if they were told the truth and when we compare that fee with some that we paid for replacements; we were barmy to allow it.

'This chapter took but a little time to write and even less time for the dramatic events of the first few weeks of the John Bond season to explode. And explode they certainly did. One of the points always made by John Bond is that he was booed the first time he crossed Turf Moor before the kick-off at our first home game in the league. He has asserted that this demonstrated a pre-conditioned dislike of him and that Burnley could never accept him as an outside manager. This was not the case at all. He was jeered and heckled for two reasons above all others. The first cause of dissatisfaction was the treatment of the two much-respected players, Dobson having been stripped of the captaincy in a humiliating way, and the departure of Brian Laws. In little Burnley that sort of news is round like wildfire and can be exaggerated, but in these two cases the crowd were spot on in their assessment.

'Without doubt, I, along with many others, was right on the Laws affair but I must confess to being equally wrong on my reaction to being told that the manager wanted to bring in Tommy Hutchison. This seemed more than just a radical departure from all that we associated with Burnley Football Club and its proud history, and seemed to border on the crazy. Hutchison was 37 years old and I reacted with despair and disbelief. I had never met or spoken to him and my knowledge of him was restricted to admiration of his great skills when seeing him from the terraces in years long gone. He had once given a torrid time to the great John Angus when playing for Blackpool at Turf Moor, and that is something I cannot recall being achieved by any other player. However, in he came and was quickly signed up and was immediately subjected to crowd abuse, where two and two had been put together and made into five. There were absurd rumours that he had received a massive signing-on fee and was being paid an exorbitant salary. This type of gossip was strong in the accelerating rumour factories of Burnley, where football is the main topic of conversation, followed closely by the price of fags and a pint.

'This for the record deserves to be put straight once and for all. Tommy Hutchison neither asked for, neither did he receive, one penny to come to Burnley and his contracted wages were in line with the maximum put in place before Mr Bond came to the club.

'Furthermore, when the next close season came round, Tommy requested permission to go to play in Hong Kong for seven weeks and I remember speaking to John Bond thinking that this man is now 38 and must need a break.

'"Not so," said Bond. "This man is unique." And I have to agree to exactly that. By then I was the half emasculated, don't ask which half, managing director and Tommy came to see me and thanked me for the consent of the club. He told me that it was beneficial to him and then did something I have never heard of from a professional footballer, and I doubt I shall hear the like again. He simply said he would be well paid in Hong Kong and he thought the club was struggling (it sure was), and proceeded to waive his wages entitlement for that seven-week period.

'He always amazed me by his fitness and leadership qualities and went on to become the oldest playing professional in the entire league and never lost his appetite for football. Eventually he won over the grumpy Burnley crowd but was unable to erase the Bond association which became a mark of derision for all who inherited it. For Hutchison the criticism was as unfair as it was uneducated, and I repeat that if I was right about Laws, then I was just as wrong on this outstanding man.

'It still surprises me that he has not yet managed a club and it would be a task for which he is admirably suited. He is the complete all-round sportsman, he played golf off one and two [handicaps], and never take him on at snooker. He is a genuine leader of men and Burnley should have utilised his talents better than they did.

'Hutchison was not the only new face to arrive in time for the new season, being joined by goalkeeper Roger Hansbury also from Hong Kong, Joe Gallagher from West Ham and within a few days Gerry Gow from Rotherham. The total fees paid for these three was covered by the 50 per cent deposit we received for Trevor Steven and the peanuts we received for Brian Laws.

'Much has been said and written by folk who neither know the facts nor I suspect would have much interest in having them revealed now about the "financial recklessness" of that era. The simple and demonstrable reality is that the club could afford to pay them in full, and on completion, which put us in a rare position back in those days. Additionally, we had not disturbed the wage structure apart from adding the salaries of John Bond and the entourage that nobody was going to bring. Remember? These were set by the chairman when he was agreeing terms at their Manchester luncheon meeting.

'That though was not the problem. Put simply it was no more than the statement of the obvious that the players brought in were not as good as those sold or even given away. Burnley is the ultimate football town and the crowd might not have much of an idea on the finances, but they most surely do know their football and they were on to it in no time and gate receipts began a downward spiral which was not to be reversed until the excruciating, dramatic, call it what you like, Orient game when consignment to the Vauxhall Conference looked to be odds on. This was the first time that automatic demotion from the Football League had operated, this fate reserved for the club finishing in bottom place of the bottom division.

'John Jackson and I were subjected to some very strong criticism from some quarters in due course, but the transfers I have mentioned above, Gallagher, Hutchison and Hansbury, had not strained the funds at that time. It is the understanding of the simple basic fact that the loss of income at the gate, and much worse the eventual loss of sponsorship of the bank, and their restriction suddenly imposed upon is, which accelerated, and I could argue was the underlying cause of, the appalling decline which was to follow.

'I repeat, it was not the sums spent on transfers and wages which brought on the financial crisis. It was the starvation of income through the turnstiles and ultimately the withdrawal of sponsorship monies that led to such distress and specifically put our backs to the wall when we were later negotiating the transfer of Billy Hamilton. The bank cost us very close to £100,000 from the sum we would have obtained from Oxford United if the bank had allowed us the time to go to arbitration on the fee. Now: I realise that the board should have been able to finance the interim running costs without the bank, but we were not that sort of board and you may read into that what you will[12].

'Predictably and with justification, John Bond was seen as the creation of John Jackson and it was the chairman who took the barrage of personal abuse that followed, when indifferent playing results began to surface. But prior to all that I had the job of completing the administrative transfer details for the newcomers. The agreement for the signing of Kevin Reeves was quite complex but we were able to complete it at a total cost of about half of the ultimate proceeds from the sale of Trevor Steven. And: when we were eventually to lose the services of Kevin a few months later, we were able to recoup the costs through our insurers.

'Speculation is a fine thing on a par with hindsight but there are many that will argue that promotion would have been achieved in that troubled season had Kevin remained fit to play. One can only surmise at what might have been and just how things would have developed if that had happened.

'The fees for Hansbury, Gallagher and Gerry Gow were straightforward with none of the hidden extras that gossip imagined. As a matter of record, I never agreed a signing-on fee for a single player which will be news to the supporters and general know-alls. Roger Hansbury was a fit and athletic lad, a very pleasant and amenable young man but one or two howlers found the back of our net and at one time the crowd cheered sarcastically if he caught a crossed ball. He did settle down in time

12 The board were not prepared to put their hands into their own pockets, which is how many impoverished football clubs survived. Fair enough. None of them were wealthy men.

but never established himself with the supporters or indeed with the management[13].

'As for Gallagher and Gow, words really do fail me and the description of walking wounded would not be amiss. These signings were accepted with a resigned sort of communal shrug from supporters, who always yearned for their lost sons, but Gow in particular was well recalled for his performance against us the previous season when he single-handedly terrorised our entire midfield. We all looked on him as the "dirty bastard" who should have been sent off every time we saw him play, but in time-honoured fashion his signing for us miraculously transformed him into the respected midfield "ball winner" indispensable to any team. There were very few, if any, voices raised to question this signing. However, when he began to play for us "Gow the Kicker" became "Gow the Elder Statesman" who would never lower himself to such things. The manager calmly announced that his legs had gone and he would be unable to last. Quite why the hell we signed him without first seeing him in action is a legitimate question to ask and we have no defence for it.

'Gow then was a great disappointment to the manager and was to make but a handful of appearances. He did provide me with one moment of amusement when I took the reserve team to Liverpool, the others being engaged as usual and in this particular game one up and coming Liverpudlian took it upon himself to lay one on him, as you might say. Some minutes went by and when the chance came, the old warrior in him returned, and with consummate ease bided his time and then did what I thought we had signed him for in the first place. For all I know, they might still be looking around Anfield for the missing part from this ill-advised young man.

---

13 Supporters with their usual gallows humour christened him 'Roger Nohansbury'.

'The Gallagher signing led to a fiasco at the club so bizarre that no self-respecting fiction writer would give it space. One needs some inkling of the background to appreciate the full story and firstly it should be remembered that our relegation the previous season had not been helped by having to play almost the entire season without our first-choice central defender. Vince Overson was and is a big and strong, solid defender certain to dominate any forward light on physical courage. His appearances were limited to just two or three at the end of the season and the medical team doubted that he would ever regain full fitness. The centre of our defence had been manned in most games by Martin Dobson and Michael Phelan, each of whom had played in a near Corinthian style with only two or three cautions between them, an unheard of statistic. I do remember a visiting official once commenting and commending the character and quality of them both, but suggesting that they were almost too gentlemanly as a pair and we needed a big fellow to put it about, in his words. We knew that a big, strong, central defender was a priority signing for us and Frank Casper, before his sacking, had made this a priority along with an attacker to help Billy Hamilton.

'Most people in the football village knew that Joe Gallagher had had a bad injury, but were also aware that he had been making some appearances with West Ham, including a sixth-round cup tie. Mr Bond claimed that he had the reference of a well-known manager to the effect that Joe would struggle in the First Division but would walk through the Third. Regardless of that, players of the ability of Gallagher do not normally get transferred without a good reason for a fee of just £25,000 and we divined that the reason was probably because West Ham would be keen to reduce their wages thus providing a situation that lower division clubs could use to their advantage.

'Contrary to latter-day opinion, we were not complete fools, on that matter at least, and took the precaution of obtaining our own expert medical advice, from a Manchester specialist, supported by the opinion of our own experienced vice-chairman, Dr David Iven, whose CV bears a string of letters a foot long. I am not in the least qualified to question that level of understanding and although we were advised of some retraction on the knee, Joe was considered fit to play professional football for the next three years.

'It did not form part of his medical report but it could be added that he is also a very good negotiator. Sensing our eagerness to conclude the deal, he held out for the four-year contract that he wanted and declined our offer of a three-year deal. David Iven said that he believed Gallagher would be fit for three years but could not recommend any longer. My own strictly non-medical opinion was to think that it did not add up to say a man was fit for three years but not four years. I also knew that if unfitness were to overtake Gallagher, then the agreed contractual regulations made it a simple matter to serve a six-month notice of termination on him, which in effect meant six months' pay in lieu, if push came to shove.

'The upshot of it was that Gallagher got his four-year deal, and additionally became the first and only player to breach the wages limit in our budget by getting an inflation clause added after each anniversary. This was to operate in line with the Cost of Living Index and it was reasoned by Mr Jackson and I, and doubtless all the other directors, that annual inflationary increases would be expected and reasonable for all existing staff. Thus, we excused ourselves for the breach of our previously jealously guarded pay limits. It does not say much for our ability to manage.

'Joe was the very essence of discretion and in any case for a year at least he was earning the same as all the other senior professionals. He kicked the ball around for us in the Isle of Man and never even needed to break sweat. The trouble was to start when Joe Gallagher played in our first league fixture.'

* * *

In truth, the signing of Joe Gallagher was seen as quite a coup. He was an above-average, uncompromising central defender and had starred for Birmingham City. From there it was to Wolves and then West Ham. It was certainly reasonable for the Burnley board to think that West Ham were keen to reduce their wage bill where Joe had been on £500 a week. But that was only for one year so the contract for £300 a week for four years was not one to be turned down. At the age of just 28 he was at the peak of his career, was 6ft 2in and his signing was seen as being in the same class as Kevin Reeves. Medicals run by the club had deemed him fit, and the course was set for a long and successful spell at the club. Make no mistake, a fully fit Gallagher would have been an outstanding acquisition. Sadly, it was not to be and in no way can Gallagher himself ever be blamed for the situation he found himself in.

If only Vince Overson had not been injured and been out of the side for so long, how differently things might have turned out, you could imagine Derek Gill thinking. It can never be proved, but the side might not have been relegated in 1982/83 and there would never have been the need to purchase Malcolm Waldron. John Jackson might still have wanted to dispose of the management, and appoint John Bond. Who knows? A whole football book could be written under the title *IF*. In one of the programmes from that fateful season, Overson was the subject of one of the regular player profiles and, in it, his predicament was laid bare:

'While Burnley have had their ups and downs on the field of play, the season has been one of sheer frustration for 20-year-old Vince Overson. With half the campaign completed he still hasn't played a competitive match and he's had to sit on the sidelines watching his team-mates battling to make their mark in the Second Division, unable to help in any way. A troublesome groin strain has caused his inactivity and the road to full fitness has proved long and, at times, painful.

'The trouble began last January when he first began to suffer from the injury. But he played on, often in spite of the discomfort, and missed only a handful of games up to the end of the season. Does he regret not resting during that period?

'"No, not really," said Vince, "I was under no pressure from the manager to turn out and I felt I could carry the injury. I've been told I'll make a full recovery, so a few months out, taken over a whole career, need not matter."

'At the end of last season, Vince was ordered to rest with the hope of being fully recovered for the 1982/83 campaign. But when the injury failed to respond as expected during the summer, he contacted the manager and specialists were called in. One of them, from Manchester, had experience of treating a similar injury suffered by England midfield man Ray Wilkins. Since then, Vince has undergone numerous types of treatment to heal the injury. It has included courses of injections, manipulative operations, physiotherapy and exercises. But there have been setbacks along the way.

'"Five weeks before Christmas I set myself a target of being fit for the Blackburn Rovers match on Boxing Day," he said. "But then I slipped doing light training and strained a tendon, which set off a reaction in the groin injury. So, I had to rule out the Blackburn match. Now I'm setting no targets, but I hope to be playing again before the end of this season."

'Inevitably the long injury has brought Vince spells of depression. He explains, "I've been used to training every day for the past four years and when you spend all that time in the treatment room it's a big change in your life. I've had spells when I've been really ratty and I've had rows with Jimmy Holland, the physiotherapist, just because we've seen so much of each other that it's got on our nerves. I've also heard the rumours that I'm finished and that I'm joining the police force and all sorts of things. It's upsetting, but I'm determined to prove those rumours are wrong.

I've had long talks with the manager, with Jimmy Holland and the specialist, and now I realise it's up to me."

'Overson, the big centre-half who looked such an outstanding prospect when he broke through into the first-team at only 17, received encouraging news when a fortnight ago he could perform an exercise which previously had proved too painful.

'"I will have to take it a step at a time," he says. "But the great thing at my age is that there's so many years ahead of me to make up for lost time."'

And lo it came to pass that Overson did indeed recover. But by then, Burnley, as Derek Gill relates, had spent thousands on replacement Mal Waldron. Overson came back into the team. Waldron was superfluous and sold at a £20,000 loss. Such is football. Or such was football during the crazy John Bond season at Burnley Football Club.

7

Phil Whalley and Martin Dobson speak

PHIL WHALLEY gives his overview of the John Bond season:

'With the bitter taste of relegation not yet rinsed from the palate, the rumours began to crystallise. Just days later, the appointment was confirmed, John Bond, one of the game's most flamboyant figures had made Turf Moor his latest managerial home. Instantly, the profile of the club was raised. Burnley became the subject of a pre-season feature on ITV's *Saint and Greavsie* show, where the consensus was that Bond would do well, if he could find the place. That quip from Greaves seemed to indicate a wider perception of Burnley as a provincial club, a perception that Bond was to find unerringly true and summed up the incredulity with which the football world looked upon Bond's appointment at Turf Moor.

'Bond's attitude to the players certainly inflamed passions on the training ground. Initially Bond brought the players together and told them they faced big challenges if they were to meet his expectations. They would all have the chance to show him what they could do, but some would definitely be discarded. Had they not been relegated? Did this not prove that many of them were not good enough. The policy was clear; the family club approach was out and for Bond this was no bad thing.

'[Bond said,] "The people who had remained at Burnley were feeling that they were having their noses put out of joint but that wasn't something I did casually; that was something I wanted to do, because I felt that at that time there was too much about Burnley and the Burnley players, and that maybe a lot of them were getting soft rides at the football club. The club wasn't doing too well, and that needed to change."

'Whatever the merits of this opinion, it is true that a number of the squad flourished under Bond. Derek Scott recalls that the training sessions were thoughtful and innovative and developed him as a player. Vince Overson rates Bond as the best coach he has ever worked under. Billy Hamilton, Michael Phelan and Brian Flynn have had no complaints about Bond's methods.

'Against this however, one must consider the wider impact on the club of moving away from the hereditary principles of appointments from within. This Burnley tradition, set in place when Alan Brown succeeded Cliff Britton, is not without implications for the relationship between the management and the players.

'Establishing the proper space that ought to exist between manager and player can be a problem when a new manager finds himself in charge of players that he has previously coached or played with. There is anecdotal evidence that senior professionals at Burnley have sometimes had more influence over team affairs than one might normally expect.

'This might provide some insight into the dreadful relationship between John Bond and Martin Dobson. As club captain and senior professional, Dobson might well have had a significant role under the Frank Casper management. They were, after all, old team-mates. It is also the case that Dobson valued the family ethos of the club, and enjoyed the responsibilities that his status inferred, being particularly good with the youngsters. He also had managerial ambitions of his own.

'One can see, then, that the spectacular entrance of John Bond and his entourage might have set Dobson's hackles[14] rising. There is no evidence that Dobson applied for the job, although Bond has wondered aloud whether Dobson had been expecting the call. Either way, the arrival of John Bond had real implications for Martin Dobson and what happened next. Bond stripped Dobson of the captaincy and handed it to one of his signings, Tommy Hutchison. This ill-judged action, a crude attempt by Bond to impose his authority, merely gave the impression that the squad was dividing into two factions, with the manager and his men a minority clique, albeit one with all the power.

'From the perspective of the players, this divide was very real indeed. The established professionals at Burnley opposed Hutchison's captaincy; Bond's decision merely served to highlight the inequalities between them and the newcomers. Bond's signings enjoyed much higher wages[15] and kept their own counsel on the training field. Although Bond could be an inspiring coach, the benefits of his coaching were often offset by his goading and bullying manner, which seemed specifically aimed at certain players. Vince Overson says that Bond "crucified" him. Kevin Young and Brian Laws were other targets. But most of all it was Martin Dobson, the player that represented everything about the old Burnley that Bond wanted to change, who received the most flak.

'For the apprentices, life under Bond was very different. Youth team coach Arthur Bellamy was used to treating the young lads like they were his own, but his instructions under Bond were very different. The youngsters were to be trained hard and strictly regimented. Bellamy was soon instructed to cull his nursery and one of those released was local youngster Andy Payton[16]. Not long

---

14 This is Phil's word. I think I might have preferred 'misgivings'.

15 All Bond's signings went straight to the maximum wage of £300 a week.

16 Payton went on to have a very successful career and today uses that release as part of his motivational work.

after, Bellamy himself would be removed entirely from the coaching staff. His replacement, John Sainty, was another acquaintance of Bond. Though respected for his coaching skills, Sainty appeared to be cut from the same cloth as Bond in his man-management and motivation. Ashley Hoskin, the only apprentice from this era to progress to a regular first-team place, remembers this about the Bond regime:

'"The change was unbelievable, from being a family club and everyone getting on. Arthur Bellamy just became a different person. You know, Bond had his own ways. You'd call him 'Boss'.

'"That was one of the first things he said. 'I'm the boss around here. Anyone who fails to call me boss, anyone not fastening their bootlaces, will be fined.'

'"And it became so it wasn't a family. I know the apprentices I was with were frightened of doing something wrong. And before: it was like Arthur was the father and we were his pupils. Everyone respected him and I think to a certain extent he respected all of us. The things that we did were good and we enjoyed doing them. Everyone wanted to play for him. We went training with Arthur and we'd stop in the afternoon and he'd help us to sweep up, and it was brilliant. That went, kit just disappeared. Bond called a fellow in called John Sainty. We had no respect for him, it just changed. We were frightened of him, he would be effing and blinding, he'd never give you any encouragement. If you did well, he never said anything. We were top of the league when he took over and I don't think we won another game."

'Another apprentice, Chris Grimshaw, has similar memories about the impact of John Bond's arrival:

'"With Casper and Miller, you always felt as though you had a chance; you saw the likes of Trevor Steven go straight into the first-team and you knew that if you were good enough that you'd get all the support you needed. Up until then, I'd been really well thought of at Burnley and I was part of it. But John Sainty never spoke to me at all, never looked at me. From Arthur Bellamy to him. Arthur was brilliant. George Bray was really good as well. With them it was like a close family, you had a laugh and everything. But all that went out the window. You had no confidence at all with the new lot. They were very arrogant people. You went from working with people who were very down to earth, to someone who wouldn't give you the time of day. It just changed completely, overnight. It was the worst thing that could have happened."

'It was partly this treatment of the youngsters that brought matters to a head between Bond and Dobson. Chris Grimshaw remembers the treatment meted out to Dobson in training:

'"It was horrible to see people like Dobbo being treated the way he was treated. They used to talk down to him in training in front of every other player. I mean he was a class player, wasn't he? I remember that. It sticks in my mind."

'Bond, too, admits that he had some preconceived impressions of Dobson, thinking him "on his way out", envisaging the ex-England man in a filling-in role as and when needed. Dobson was faced with the task of convincing a sceptical manager that he was worth a starting place. But Bond thought his attitude was lacking:

'"The best thing I could say about Martin Dobson was that he was a wonderful player, as long as things were going well for him. As long as things were working out for Martin Dobson, he was a good lad. But all of a sudden, he's got to battle and fight for his place, and he didn't like it one bit. He didn't like the fact that I didn't see him as an automatic choice."

'After the shambolic opening-day 4-1 defeat away at Hull, where Dobson was reduced to the role of an unused sub, the following Monday's training saw Bond push things too far with the former captain and a heated confrontation ensued. Dobson accused Bond of destroying the fabric of the club and the row became personal. Dobson's immediate fear was that he would be dismissed. But Bond appeared to relent, calling a truce via his assistant, John Benson, and reinstating Dobson into his midfield role. As Vince Overson found, Bond's respect was more likely to be earned standing up to the barrage of criticism:

'"When John Bond came to the club, I couldn't stand the bloke. I'll go on record saying, I couldn't stand the bloke. I was struggling badly with an injury and I wasn't physically strong enough to do the pre-season. I'd been out that long. And he crucified me, he absolutely slaughtered me. You know, he'd have treated his dog better than he'd treated me. And I was maybe a bit naive and I felt sorry for myself, but in the end, I thought, 'He just wants a reaction from me.' And that's all he wanted, a reaction. I think some people, rather than face him, they backed down, and I think that's the worst thing they could have done with Bond. You just don't let yourself get hammered into the ground every day, which is what he would try and do. If some of them had stood up to Bond face to face, they would have got more out of him. If you stood up to him, he'd respect you. In the end I got on very well with him."

'It is instructive to note that Bond's verbal assaults could be relentless, an attritional tactic designed to test character. Teams do thrive if they have strong characters, that's for sure. But Bond's method was not only too blunt, a one-size-fits-all approach to man-management, but was also completely at odds with the prevailing culture of the club. As such, there was bound to be an enormous clash and numerous casualties, particularly among the younger, less-experienced players, not all of whom, in retrospect, Bond could dismiss as simply not good enough or strong enough. It was understandable that Bond wanted to be his own man and run things his way, but the manner with which he disregarded his newness to the place, his refusal to consider the impact of his management style on the social fabric of the club, the disregard for the opinions of others, could only be interpreted as arrogance.

'Vince Overson, always close to the fans and grounded enough to understand the relationship between club and townsfolk, offered this shrewd assessment:

'"We might have been just a couple of players away from having a good side. But when John Bond came in, he wanted to do everything his way and he wanted his players. And not just him; I think most managers in general get their own men in. But I think he could have waited a bit longer just to try and get to know the players, the set-up, the feeling of the town, before he started doing it. He's a very knowledgeable man in football terms, but you've got to live in Burnley to have that insight into the real nature of the club. You've got to live in Burnley to know that.

'"It was a family club and it changed overnight. Everybody was terrified of John Bond, me included. He didn't have to say anything. People used to train and get out so they'd be out of his way. There was just something about the very presence of the man. It's hard to describe, he's an awesome character. Was it a character suited to Burnley? Possibly not, but they wanted a big name and they got a big name. And they got a big man to go with it as well."

'When tackled about the harshness of his approach, especially towards the youngsters, Bond claimed to have supported the family approach, and denied that John Sainty was the ogre he was painted to be:

'"If you really knew John Sainty, you'd know that he is one of the easiest-going people you'll meet and an outstanding coach so I brought him in because I thought he'd be a good coach with the kids. Bringing the kids along in a family-like atmosphere, encouraging them and so on is exactly the way to do it. But my first job when I got to Burnley was not the youth team. My priority was to get that first-team going as quickly as possible."

'Clearly, this does not remotely resemble the stories told by the former apprentices and Bond does admit that he paid little attention to what was going on with the trainees. So, if he wanted the kids to be tutored within a family environment, then why force through changes to the existing routines? Why demote Arthur Bellamy to cutting the grass? Brian Laws bluntly condemned the Bond approach:

'"He started a clear-out when he brought his own players. If your face didn't fit, then it was out. I was very disillusioned when Bond came to the club and I certainly haven't changed my mind since. He was the wrong person for the job. He had his big-time thoughts and he'd come from a big club and he tried to make Burnley into a big-time club in a very short space of time. It failed miserably and it cost the club dearly. Burnley Football Club wasn't run like that; it was a family club.

'"We were all young players; in fact, the average age was just 24, something like that. So, we had a very young side, even when Martin Dobson was playing. That gives you four or five years of building a new structure and bringing the youth through because you've already got a good side and a good youth policy in the club. There was a real chance to get back to where it used to be.

'"The quality was there. Each individual player, and as a team, was good enough. We did well in the cups and the financial gains the club made were enormous. That could have kept the club in business for many years to come. The players that did go down were definitely good enough to go back up. But John Bond comes in and disperses everybody. We only needed two faces in certain areas and we would have been a very hard team to beat. Maybe there was a lack of quality in reserve, but there was money in the club to go out and buy some.

'"I've no sympathy for John Bond. I don't hold any grudges but I've got no sympathy for him. What happened to, and at, Burnley firmly lay on his shoulders."

'Despite the turmoil going on behind the scenes, gradually improving form on the pitch started to heal the fractured spirit of the squad. The one undoubted success of Bond's team building was the attacking prowess offered by Kevin Reeves and Tommy Hutchison. With Brian Flynn also encouraged to attack whenever possible, Burnley were capable of piercing the most well-marshalled defences.

'Burnley's own defence, however, was more problematic. Lee Dixon, having impressed enough through pre-season to merit the number two shirt at Hull, was promptly dropped and, by February, had been sold to Chester. With Bond having also moved Brian Laws, there was little option other than for Derek Scott to revert to his original right-back role. Although Phelan and Overson resumed their effective partnership in the centre of defence, Bond never resolved the full-back problem. Scott, though as wholehearted as ever, lacked pace and Willie Donachie, too, failed to perform to expectations. In the defensive parts of midfield, neither Gerry Gow nor Mal Waldron provided the competitive bite that Bond was looking for.

'So long as their attacking instincts allowed them to pin the opposition back, Bond's Burnley looked solid, confident and even creative. However, teams that succeeded in disrupting the supply line to Hutchison and Reeves found the Clarets an easier proposition, as did teams able to hit on the counter, as Crewe proved in the League Cup, when the Clarets embarrassingly shipped four first-half goals and lost the tie.

'At Turf Moor, where Burnley could give full vent to their attacking intentions, the team exhibited some excellent football, and while they retained the purpose to eke out draws, and the occasional away win from home, promotion remained a possibility. No objective analysis of Bond's season in charge can fail to mention the near-flawless first-half performance against Port Vale when the Clarets utterly destroyed their opponents with a sumptuous display of attacking football, 7-0.

'A Granada feature showcased the game interviewing Bond and showing all the goals. "My life has changed drastically," said

Bond. "I'm happy to be in a job. I've never been happier. In a couple or three years the club will be run how I want it to be run, the atmosphere, the way the team plays, the socialising, the dressing room, training. Football is a game of todays, not tomorrows, spectators want us to win today." After the game and the emphatic win, he said again, "I can say I've never been happier than when I was at Bournemouth with the likes of [Ted] McDougall and [Phil] Boyer and we were beating teams 5-0 and 6-0." After this game he could have been forgiven for being totally optimistic. But success was not to be.

'A handy Sheffield United side were beaten in a memorable end-to-end game 2-1, Hutchison in particular impressing with his ability to beat his man and send over quality crosses. A derby win, against Preston 2-1, was less eventful but notable for a superb display in goal from Roger Hansbury, of whom the Burnley crowd had been particularly sceptical. In addition to these, Bournemouth, Wigan, Southend and Scunthorpe were all sent home on the back of sound defeats.

'Were it not for the indifferent form away from home, Bond's Burnley would have been challenging at the very top of the table. As it was, they found away wins elusive. Draws at Oxford and Bolton were decent points gained but poor defeats at Lincoln and Bristol Rovers kept the Clarets from the very heart of the promotion battle. As Christmas approached, however, cautious optimism prevailed. The team were playing good football and looked to attack whenever possible. For all the worries about the stewardship of the club, John Bond was proving to be faithful at least to the traditions of passing and movement that the great sides of the 1960s had engendered.

'When Burnley travelled to Wimbledon the week before Christmas and came away with a 4-1 victory, everyone hoped that this would be the kick-start to a serious promotion challenge. Those at the game reported an excellent team performance and once again the Reeves and Hamilton partnership found the net, making it 22 goals in 19 league matches. Coming as it did on John Bond's 51st birthday, the Burnley manager must have savoured the win. To the press, he expressed his satisfaction with the way things were going. Though the team were to throw away the Boxing Day encounter with Bradford City, conceding two late goals in defeat, they compensated with a 5-0 hammering of Scunthorpe and another victory in the capital at Orient, Hamilton scoring the winner.'

* * *

At this point, a break from the Phil Whalley overview allows us to recall what now seems a quite astonishing turn of events in the story. 'A NEW BOND!' was the *Burnley Express* header in December, and what followed was hugely surprising, bearing in mind that twice already, the directors had contemplated dismissing Bond. Admittedly, results since then had been picking up.

The newspaper reported, 'John Bond is poised to make one of his most important signings. Himself. The manager, his assistant John Benson and youth officer John Doherty have agreed to sign contracts that will keep them at Turf Moor until the end of season 1985/86. They mark the latest stage in the growing unity between Burnley Football Club and Mr Bond.

'Describing his decision to sign a new contract Mr Bond said, "I'm really happy here, I love it. Burnley has now become the football club I always thought it was. In my early days there were too many people here who thought that the club was their property and I don't just mean directors and players. There were other people involved who felt it was wrong for someone to come in from the outside and do something different. I have tried to get people on my side by getting a good team on the pitch and that's the way that 'them' and 'us' have knitted together. It would take a complete disaster to come between us now."

'The news of the contracts was due to be announced at the annual shareholders' meeting. Before it took place managing director Derek Gill said, "All the members of the board are delighted that Mr Bond, Mr Benson and Mr Doherty are committing their futures to Burnley Football Club. We have been most impressed by their achievements so far and are highly confident that these latest moves will be of benefit to the club."'

* * *

Alas, the disaster that Bond referred to was not far away and any delight felt by the board of directors would dissipate along with it. Phil Whalley continues:

'For any of those in doubt that football fortunes really do rest on the bounce of a ball, events from hereon in were to prove the old adage. Having dispatched Hyde United and Chesterfield in the cup, Burnley were drawn at home to Oxford United in the third round. Their opponents were on the rise, funded by the largesse of chairman Robert Maxwell, and the game was, as expected, competitive and extremely tight. With chances at a premium, it was Brian Flynn who was presented with the match-winning opportunity when a beautifully executed one-two sent him through on goal. Flynn did everything right, slipping his shot under the advancing keeper, but the ball hit the inside of the post and rebounded to a grateful Oxford defender.

'On such tiny fractions do seasons rest. The replay at Oxford was to be a fateful night for Burnley and John Bond. Crowd disorder marred the evening and despite yet another Hamilton goal, the Clarets went out 2-1. But worst of all was the hip injury incurred by Kevin Reeves, for what was thought to be just a painful knock burgeoned into the discovery that the Burnley striker had an arthritic hip joint that necessitated his retirement from the game.

'The loss of Reeves was pivotal. Bond shored up his attacking options with the signing of Dennis Tueart, another old boy from his Maine Road days. Then, more astutely with the signing of Wayne Biggins from Matlock Town. Though Biggins would soon prove himself a worthy buy, neither he nor Tueart could forge a fruitful partnership with Billy Hamilton. For poor old Bill, the season was effectively over. In just over half a season he and Reeves had plundered 32 league and cup goals between them. Without Reeves, the man with the touch and vision to exploit Hamilton's strengths in the box, Billy managed just four more Burnley goals before an admiring Robert Maxwell took him to Oxford.

'In March the club bade farewell to another talisman: Martin Dobson left to begin a managerial career at Bury. The conflict between Bond and Dobson remained a source of tension behind the scenes. To Dobson's satisfaction, Bond had come to rely on his proven midfield skills but the relationship between the two was never healed.

'Despite the loss of these two mainstays, Burnley continued to hang on to the fringes of the promotion race but the feelings enveloping the club's supporters was that Bond's Burnley, now with so many unfamiliar faces, didn't have the togetherness or the collective spirit to go up. As it transpired, the shocking manner in which the season ended indicated a disintegration that even the most pessimistic Claret would not have suspected. A draw and a win punctuated the misery of eight defeats, including a 4-0 humiliation at Scunthorpe. Team morale, high over Christmas and the new year period, turned out also to be brittle and by the end of April it had crumbled completely.

'Derek Scott recalls that Bond, too, called a premature end to the season, rarely taking the training at Gawthorpe, spending most of his time setting up deals for new players. If gates were any yardstick, there would be precious little income to spend. The Turf Moor faithful gave their verdict in the predictable way; as the season drew to a close, gates dwindled to less than 4,000 and the club posted a loss of £227,015 on the season.

'Bond remained in charge through the summer and recruited another set of players, but their calibre reflected the more severe financial restrictions now in place. Once more, only a few would bed in successfully but Bond would not be here to see Neil Grewcock, Kevin Hird or Peter Hampton kick off the new season. He had been quoted in the *Daily Mail* as saying that his job was being made well-nigh impossible by boardroom politics, and mused out loud that the board had better sort out their disagreements. The implied threat to walk out on the club was obvious.

'With a board meeting due on Monday, 20 August, Bond made a now infamous statement to the local press in which he clarified his position, "All I want to do is manage the club in my own way. I am as prepared as ever to make Burnley a First Division club again but I am afraid that is impossible for any manager when there is friction between him and the chairman. It has to be sorted out one way or another."

'Even if Bond was hoping for backing from those board members who he thought might still have supported him, and this seems unlikely, his statement was received as just another in a series of tactless gestures. Bond was duly summoned to attend the board meeting and even this descended into farce. As if in a final act of revenge, Bond found himself locked out.

'Sidekick John Benson scurried away to locate a key, leaving the manager loitering outside in the company of a group of journalists. For Bond, this must have been an inexcusable humiliation. Two hours later, it was all over. Bond had been sacked with his assistant John Benson placed in charge. Bond dashed out of the door, passing the hacks with a brusque, "I have absolutely nothing to say." Jumping into his executive car, he sped off to his Cheshire home, never to return to Turf Moor or Burnley again.

'If one was to encapsulate the short, eventful reign of John Bond in a couple of descriptors, "mismanagement" and "misfortune" would capture the essence of what happened at Turf Moor between

May 1983 and August 1984. Bond always appeared an unlikely figure, never outwardly comfortable in the plain environs of a northern working-class town, but neither was he ignorant of the ways and traditions of the small-town football club. To this extent, the way in which he managed people he inherited at the club is regrettable, and, to his credit, Bond has recognised this. Certainly, by the time of his sacking, the tinge of glamour that he brought to proceedings looked grotesque among the wreckage of a football club on the very breadline of existence. Even if the image was just that, a public persona that bore no relation to the real person, it remains inconceivable that he could have stayed on.

'As for misfortune, Bond undeniably had his share; the loss of Reeves in particular is seen by most observers to have been a massive setback that stopped in its tracks a team developing a winning rhythm. Whether or not the team with Reeves and Dobson could have sustained a promotion challenge will remain one of those tantalising "what ifs" for Burnley fans to debate. John Bond himself in his managerial bones felt that the squad was insufficient in depth and character to go up. Derek Scott, on the other hand, asserts that the squad, at the turn of the year, fancied its chances.

'Perhaps the best way to consider the reign of John Bond is to place it into the longer-term picture of decline at the club. The club had been losing serious amounts of money for years. The scouting system, once Burnley's financial guarantor, had been gradually pruned until it was merely a husk of the operation that brought so much talent to the club. Relegation to the Third Division duly followed. But somehow the desiccated roots of the old scouting system had produced one last harvest and these youngsters flowered dramatically as Burnley stormed back to the Third Division title in 1982.

'Looking back, it seems that this should have been a crucial moment in Burnley's history, where the collision of a few arbitrary and unpredictable factors pointed the way to a more secure future. A group of talented youngsters maturing together, a simple tactical ploy, a sweeper system that cleverly maximised the classy guile of Martin Dobson; a team that found goalscorers in every department, including full-backs, and a midfield prodigy in Trevor Steven. All these combined to such an effect that few observers predicted the relegation battle that would ultimately be lost the following season. It was Burnley's failure to consolidate at this juncture that was essential to what followed, and we can point to errors of management here that weigh equally with those made by John Bond.

'This isn't to forgive what followed under John Bond, but merely to try and put his year in charge into some kind of perspective. He arrived at a demoralised club that had just thrown away a rare opportunity for which any number of similar clubs would have thanked the football gods. Bond did indeed significantly worsen Burnley's plight. In his hubris, he dismantled a team that required just a few operational changes.

'Martin Dobson is essential to the story of Bond at Burnley. Bond missed the chance to make better use of him, to make use of his experience at the club and his standing with the other players. He was management material as he would prove at Bury, but Bond tried to discard him far too quickly and with indecent haste.'

* * *

Years later, Dobson expressed his thoughts in a *Lancashire Telegraph* article, reproduced here:

'While sipping a cold beer and enjoying the sights along Spain's Costa coastline, I met up with a number of Liverpool players who were relaxing after another successful season. They were winning everything and totally dominating at home and abroad. The year was 1983. They informed me that Burnley had appointed a new manager, John Bond. Many names had been put forward in the media for the coveted position but not the former high-profile Man City boss[17].

'To say that their comments were uncomplimentary would be an understatement. I listened. You do, when you hear opinions that you respect from the league and League Cup winners of the previous season. I was about to start the final year of my contract at Turf Moor. At 35, I had been lucky to play for two magnificent clubs and was fortunate to still hold down a regular position. I always felt that I would know when I had become a liability, and then the pre-season wasn't something to look forward to with the same relish. Running up and down sand dunes with the thighs wobbling, or along the streets of Padiham with an oxygen cylinder strapped to the hip, is no joke.

'I was naturally a bit apprehensive as to how it would pan out. I was soon to find out. The first day of pre-season training made an immediate impression, not on the training ground but in the car park. An E Type Jag looked a bit out of place among the Novas and Escorts.

'Within a few days I knew my days were numbered[18]. Indeed, not just for myself but for other players. Every mistake was highlighted and Bond seemed determined to belittle individuals. He would stop the play, point the finger and raise doubts as to our ability to perform at this level. I have played under a lot of different managers and coaches, and the only thing you ask for is to be given a fair crack of the whip.

'New managers will quickly decide which players will figure in their plans. For the others, notification of their availability to

---

17 What emerged was that he had been offered the job and told to keep quiet. The ensuing interviews with Jimmy Frizzell, Ian Duncan, Ian Branfoot and Stewart Houston were just a pretence.

18 Interviewed for this book, Dobson says he has no idea why Bond ever had such preconceived notions about him or wanted him out, but could only assume that Bond and John Jackson had hatched the plan together; out with the old and in with the new.

other clubs is usually the next step. If the manager goes down the other route of trying to destroy confidence and embarrass players in front of their team-mates, then respect has gone.

'Young players talked to me about their positions. They were low because of the criticisms and they didn't have the experience to be able to cope with it. As a senior pro, I could only advise them to keep their heads up, let a lot of what was said on the training ground go right over their heads, and just keep on battling. An enormous gulf in the camp had taken place. Senior players and backroom staff had arrived from Manchester and there seemed a definite ploy to blow away all the traditions and beliefs of the club in one fell swoop.

'The club was built on talented young players brought through the youth system teams who were desperate to play in the famous claret jersey. The next generation were already in place. Trevor Steven, Brian Laws, Michael Phelan, Vince Overson, Derek Scott, Lee Dixon and Billy Hamilton, players who would have been the backbone of the side for the next ten seasons. Sadly, it didn't happen. Dixon was freed; Laws went to Huddersfield and Steven to Everton all within three months. The heart was cut out.

'You might remember the first game of the season, Hull City away. I was sub. We lost 4-1 and I didn't get on. In the dressing room afterwards, Bond had a go and it was to continue all the following week. Monday afternoon arrived and on a glorious sunny day after the training session, the manager got us together to discuss Saturday's performance. He asked me what I thought. I started but he cut in and had another dig.

'It was one of those defining moments that everybody has in life. Six weeks of frustration had built up. I had taken the criticism like everybody else but there was no way I was going to allow this to pass over. I stepped forward. Everybody else stepped back two paces. And then it all came out. No swearing, no histrionics, just how I felt he was destroying the core foundation of a once great football club. It did become personal but I felt it had to be done. My playing career didn't matter, but the club did.

'Some of the younger players and some of the staff made it clear they supported me but as you can imagine, I wasn't the most popular player with the manager that afternoon. Let's say I wasn't the first name on his Christmas card list. I left the ground and told the family what had happened. I even suggested that hitching up the caravan would be advisable. I went in the following day convinced that Bond would tell me my services were no longer required; but it was his assistant John Benson that had a word with me.

'Bond said nothing. I must admit though, the tackles were flying in for the next few training days and there was a definite edge round the place. By Easter I was away but I have often reflected on that period and where the club would be now and where it would have moved on to; if those excellent young players had been allowed to blossom together. I suspect and maybe the majority of supporters would agree, the problems of the next few seasons would not have surfaced so dramatically.'

Indeed, the problems were dramatic. Derek Gill would continue with the diaries on and into the season after John Bond when, under John Benson, another relegation ensued. Financial problems increased so that two years after the Bond season ended, the club was four days away from liquidation. It survived, but then, three years later, what followed was what is forever called the 'Orient Season', and only on the very last day of the season was the club saved from exiting the Football League, with a 2-1 win and hundreds of chewed fingernails.

The club paid a heavy price for the folly of appointing Bond and to this day conjecture and speculation continues along the 'what if' debate among supporters. Would the club have ever had to endure seven seasons in the bottom division is the question that will never go away.

8

Growing tensions

TUESDAY, 16 August 1983, Burnley versus Blackburn Rovers in the Lancashire FA Manx Cup, and John Bond wrote his first programme notes. Of course, he was proud to be at Burnley and the notes are optimistic and hopeful. But in hindsight they were quite the portent of things to come. They were also brash, blunt, abrasive, bombastic, critical, challenging, scornful even, with several eyebrow-raising statements. Before the season had even started you could look at them and think, this can only end in tears:

'When I took over as manager, I walked into the job with my eyes wide open and believe me I knew exactly what I was letting myself in for. There are very few clubs outside the First Division I would want to be in charge of, but Burnley, with this unique set-up, is definitely one of them. We are not a big club, but we are very sound financially; the basis of a formidable Third Division team has already been assembled and we have magnificent facilities.

'I have had a lovely reception from Burnley supporters. Many of them have greeted me with Lancastrian warmth and many of them have sent me marvellous letters. I intend to justify the confidence that they and the board of directors have shown in me. Other people appear to believe that John Bond, having parted company with Manchester City, took the Burnley job with the aim of getting back into the big time. They reckon I'm going to stay here until about Christmas, bankrupt the club with fancy signings and then disappear. How little they know me.

'I am absolutely convinced, that along with my assistant John Benson, we will make this club successful. I am going to be around for more than just a few months so I suggest you all get used to that idea and that remark is not just addressed to the minority of doubting supporters but to directors and players as well. As far as the board is concerned, they know exactly how I feel about the situation. I want cooperation but what I don't want is interference. I have had far too much of that in the past.

'The players? It has been spelled out to them very clearly that for me 99 per cent is not enough. I require total dedication and discipline will be strict. The players need that to be the case. The rules and regulations that I have brought in cover a wide range, including fines for dissent or retaliation and there will also be action taken for late attendance. The departure of Trevor Steven to Everton was a magnificent piece of business by the club. It has given us the money to construct a successful and formidable team without any delay. The process to that end continues constantly.

'I predict that Kevin Reeves will be a magic player for Burnley. I sold him from Norwich to Manchester City just over three years ago for £1m and bought him for Burnley for just one-tenth of that amount. His partnership with Billy Hamilton up front can set the Third Division alight. I have made Tommy Hutchison the new club captain and had no hesitation on deciding that. Tommy is not as young as he was, but he has a young head on old shoulders. There is no question about it; he will be great for this club whether it's on the wing, in the dressing room, or anywhere else. Joe Gallagher is the big man I want in the middle at the back. He'll do a fine job for us and so will Roger Hansbury, an experienced goalkeeper who in my book is as honest as the day is long.'

Bond went on to write about learning that seven or eight players would be suitable, others would need to do more and others would have to convince him that they were good enough. Some might just come up to his standards. As an exercise in putting players down, it was textbook. The remark to directors that he did not want interference was simply arrogant. Joe Gallagher, meanwhile, was a totally wasted signing and the glowing reference to him would come back to haunt Bond within days. Of course, he added he would need new players. His claim that they would be of the highest-possible quality was, to put it mildly, regrettable. The material for Derek Gill's diaries was already growing.

Gill continued, 'It is easy to be wise after the events of that time, but in retrospect I suppose that I was guilty as the next man in allowing my infatuation with the inside of football to overcome my better judgement. Within days of the Hull City game, I knew we had dropped an almighty clanger by appointing John Bond. Mr Bond had not had a happy time at Manchester City despite his team reaching an FA Cup Final, but it could not be denied that he had been successful at Norwich and for his sake alone that is where he should have stayed.

'It was radically different at Burnley and every participant became frustrated and this marriage from hell should have been ended before consummation. Grounds for annulment for those that don't know such things. Had that been the case I have little doubt that the chasm which existed between John Jackson and I would never have reached the width that it did, widely differing personalities notwithstanding, and which played a major part in my eventual departure from the scene and possibly his too.

'Relegated to the Third Division, we visited Hull City for the first fixture and as it was also the first game for them in a higher division, there was more than just the usual interest for an early season joust. Believe it or not, a director of Hull asked me before the start of the game if I knew why John Bond was there. Looking at it now, it was me that should have been asking that question.

'Times without number I have tried to tell myself, and others, that tactics on the field of play are best left alone by directors. Once again, Len Shackleton doubtless had a point with his famous blank page, but allowing for all that, we as a breed, contrary to popular opinion in Burnley, most of us have mums and dads and we know who they are. And: we do have eyes in our heads and any fool could see that Joe Gallagher was having problems with his mobility and it was so obvious, so early in the game, that I wondered if he had hurt himself in the pre-match warm-up session. The game was a nightmare for us and we lost it by four goals to one. The only bright spot was Kevin Reeves scoring on his first appearance for us and looking the class act that we expected him to be.

'Looking back, it must have been an indication of my mood that I was outside waiting for the coach before most of the players, simply wanting to get away and back home, when Joe came up to me and gave me my first culture shock of the new-born era. He said that he had been promised an "ex gratia" payment at the end of his contract and was clearly looking for some sort of confirmation. Now by its very definition, an "ex gratia" payment is one for which there is no entitlement. All this, I ask, within an hour of making his very first competitive appearance for us.

'I was taken aback and simply told him that he had no legal rights outside his contract and he then confirmed that this was in line with advice he had received from his solicitor. Even the dimmest of lawyers know that much. Anyone getting post-contractual payment, it would be on the basis of reward for services rendered and for which there was no legal requirement to pay. I also had to tell Joe that his chances of getting one were not on the agenda after one bloody bad game, and four years to go.

'As a matter of interest, when those four years were close to their expiry, although I had long since gone, I was contacted by the then chairman, Frank Teasdale, who claimed to know nothing of it. I gave him the facts here related and I have no idea if, or how, it was eventually resolved. What I do know is that when there was any question of deferred payments or any other matter with financial implications, they were religiously tabulated in the contract of the player. I was offended when a later director with a mouth more active than his brain, and as usual ignorant of the facts, accused me of agreeing to that sort of arrangement. A significant part of my time at Burnley Football Club had been spent putting to rights what for now I will be content to refer to as unusual aspects of the past[19].

'Some may argue that I was the worst ever director of Burnley Football Club, but I can shout "straight dealing" from the rooftops with no fear of being unmasked. And I will now go on record that when I was a director of Burnley Football Club, I continued to buy season tickets for my sons in the mistaken belief that it would stand me in good stead if the fat hit the fire. I was the mug of the decade and I regret it bitterly.

'The Gallagher contract was very soon to reach a truly crazy impasse and provides another tragicomic story which only a board with a preponderance of dimwits could allow to pass.

'Of the four managers with whom I had first-hand experience, there is not a shadow of doubt that John Bond stood head and shoulders above the others in his ability to handle the boardroom machinations which were beginning to bedevil us. He could, and would, set out exactly what he wanted to do and I think was aware, but definitely not concerned by, the financial implications of his objectives. Lurking inside him is a politician, a man with a quick tongue, an imposing personality and an innate instinct to divide and rule. With utterly disarming frankness he came to a board meeting and announced, and here I quote, "Gentlemen, I have dropped a ricket. Joe Gallagher is not fit."

---

19 It is reasonable to suggest here that Gill is referring to the less accurate aspects of Bob Lord's expense claims, and payment promises made to another player by Lord.

'My command of English does not run to understanding the precise definition of a ricket, but I and the rest of us got the drift all right. And on the board, there was a notable exception who doubtless did understand the plural of a ricket but would not take on board the meaning of the singular[20].

'The manager took full responsibility upon himself for Gallagher's lack of playing fitness and never tried to hide behind the medical reports which had been so crucial to his signing. The board then retreated into one of its Walter Mitty trances and a whisky or three later, the majority opinion boiled down to terminating his contract which required no more than a six-month notice of intent, supported by appropriate medical opinion.

'But then came the rub, as our very own medical expert, the vastly qualified Dr David Iven, insisted that Joe was fit for purpose, as one might say of any manufactured factory product. Chairman John and the board were in an impossible position, believing, as we did, that we had made a mistake but were restrained from correcting it by our very own medical expert, himself reinforced by the independent report in our possession. It was pure fantasy with all the non-medics lined up against the medical expert on a medical matter, a pure Mexican stand-off, and everybody standing with a loaded gun, but nobody daring to shoot.

'Then: to compound it all, who should suddenly return to centre stage but the forgotten Vince Overson who immediately set to work to restore our normal high rating in the caution stakes, and all thoughts on the Gallagher contract went on the back burner for a while.

'In the meantime, we had followed the disaster at Hull with a midweek loss to Crewe Alexandra by a single goal in the first leg of the League Cup competition, prior to the first meaningful game at Turf Moor under the management of John Bond. A hostile reception

---

20 Doc Iven, we might deduce.

from the Longside greeted him as he made his pre-match entrance and many times since he has quoted this undeniable fact as a result of him "coming from the outside". He claimed that there was a parochial attitude in Burnley and an unwillingness to accept him as an "outsider". But the simple truth was there were numerous supporters who had welcomed his appointment but were totally bemused and angered by the transfer of Laws, the humiliation of Martin Dobson sat absurdly on the bench at Hull, and saw the defeats at Hull and Crewe as all the vindication needed to confirm their views.

'That this particular home match was won by five goals to one, immediately followed by a two-goal victory and then a creditable draw at Oxford, changed few if any minds. Minds had been made up and there was no way that facts were going to be allowed to influence opinion.

'Then came the second leg of the Crewe cup tie and on that night died any possibility of John Bond being accepted by a very large section of Burnley supporters.

'There was something of a pre-match injury crisis and the combative Vince Overson, only recently introduced, was among the injured players and the manager had no choice but to bring back Joe Gallagher to the side. At half-time we were behind by 4-1 and in all my 50 years of watching Burnley, I have never witnessed or experienced booing and abuse remotely like that hurled at our own team. It was devastating to see Gallagher in particular struggling so hard against his handicap and although we scored two goals to reduce the final score to 4-3, we were dismissed from the competition in which we had performed with such distinction just those few months previously.

'We were distraught and the directors sat bewildered until the early hours of the next morning wondering just what we had let ourselves in for.

'The treatment of the Gallagher impasse took on a sort of ignore it and hope it will go away delusion, and it was later that I learned that Joe had been effectively thrown out of the training area by the manager and reduced to keeping himself in some sort of condition by solitary running, while not being allowed access to other members of the playing staff. It certainly says something about Joe that he evidently went about his limited training with no trouble to other staff but I have no means of knowing the effect on the other players. Hardly, I have to say, my idea of good management nor indeed to that of the expressed views of Bond himself. Not that he informed the board, at least at my level, and I cannot believe that the chairman would have known and said nothing to the rest of us. Gallagher turned up at my house one day, and that is how I first knew of this most unusual nonsense[21].

'More supposition, but I have suspected that Bond felt he had been taken in by Gallagher whom he believed must have been aware of his lack of mobility all along and had perhaps been able to conceal it from the medical experts. The medical report actually referred to testing Joe after strenuous running up and down the stairways. This poses an obvious question to a football simpleton like me. When did any football match ever take place on a stairway?

'As we all know, Gallagher went on to complete his four years and was part of the team in the legendary Orient match and I have to admit that had he been at full fitness he would, without doubt, been the best centre-half since Colin Waldron, who have, for my money, has not been replaced by anyone remotely close to his equal to this day.

'"TURF MOOR IN TURMOIL", a perceptive headline in the local press, gave the view of an outsider on the shenanigans and bitterness enveloping the club following the Crewe Alexandra debacle. Pent-up resentments and dissatisfactions exploded to the

---

21 Ironic that Joe Gallagher went on to become one of the Burnley heroes of the Orient game in 1987. By and large it was one of the worst sides that season ever assembled, but by escaping oblivion on the very last day it went on to be remembered forever.

surface and in retrospect it is unarguable that few if any participants behind the scenes came out with any credit. We were far down the wrong road by the time of the nightmare cup exit, but with hindsight it was not irretrievable if only we could have had the sense to put our internal divisions aside. None of us were blameless and I take my share of responsibility for the internal wreckage. All this time later it continues to make reading too silly for words, but it set the curse for many years of strife for the club.

'"Never mind the football; let's get on with the game." That just about sums up the Burnley FC boardroom for a short period after the Crewe debacle, but first we need to return to the Vince Overson story.

'Vince had reported himself unfit for that terrible Crewe tie and had missed all the previous season apart from the final match or two. There then followed a revealing affair between Bond and Overson whose unfitness was put down to a groin strain. As far as I understand this had been particularly difficult to diagnose and could possibly and partly have been as much in the mind of the player. It is accepted that some will play through "bits of niggles" while others will dwell on them until they convince themselves that they are unfit[22].

'John Bond thought that Vince, who feared nobody on the field, might just come into the latter category, summoned him to the office and effectively railroaded him into forgetting his aches and pains and to get out there and show what he could do. I know for sure that it had crossed his mind more than once that he had no future in football, and it is not going too far to suggest that John Bond saved Overson's career by literally kicking him out to play. I also think that Vince himself recognised this when he left Burnley at the end of his contract. Where did he elect to play? Right first time – it was Birmingham, managed by John Bond.

---

22 This is not to denigrate or be critical of Vince Overson in any way whatsoever.

'In the boardroom there were deep scars resulting from the Crewe debacle which had been in evidence before the kick-off and erupted uncontrollably afterwards. For the record, the directors arrived at their homes the next morning having left the club at ten past five, yes 5.10am, that morning. It was only the previous week that the chairman and manager had flown across the Atlantic and back to interview and agree terms with Steve Daley, not long since a member of the exclusive million pounds player clan. That was before they became two a penny as it were. There had been differences in the boardroom about that little matter.

'Sufficient to relate that it brought to the fore differences of opinion between John Jackson and myself and was leaving the board split with John Jackson and Doc Iven in one corner, with Alan Hutchinson, Colin Sanderson and me in the other. Crewe Alexandra and the League Cup result provided the catalyst and the local press had a succession of field days, correctly reporting Turf Moor in turmoil.

'That night Colin Sanderson put it to the chairman that he did not have the confidence of the majority of the board and that his position was untenable and he should quietly stand down and make way for a new appointee. John Jackson and Doc Iven were outraged at this suggestion and the good doctor regarded it as totally out of order to discuss such a drastic measure outside of a formal board meeting.

'I accused the chairman of high-handed unilateral actions of the type that must have been commonplace under his predecessor and I regarded Doc Iven's contributions as neither use nor ornament. John refused to stand down but I simply looked upon this as no more than delaying the inevitable.

'The impasse did give me time to take stock and talk to Alan Hutchinson whom I thought, and nothing has ever caused me to change my mind, was the obvious choice to take the chair as he was by far the coolest head among us and would provide a balance between the chairman and myself, when things were getting heated and emotions were in danger of boiling over.

'And yet, throughout all this difficult period and for much of the time beyond, I continued to enjoy a reasonable relationship with John Jackson and I give him full marks for separating issues from personalities. I hope that to some degree I can lay claim to the same.

'Regrettably there were people with big mouths and small brains unable to make this distinction and their tiny closed minds had a field day and the press boys thought it made good copy. John and I had one thing in common and that was a fanatical and myopic support for Burnley Football Club which no one could deny, and it was not diminished, despite us having a very differing view on how to act in the best interests of the club.

'However, Alan did not want to take the chair and thought it was my responsibility, especially as I was acknowledged by the entire board as the ever-present workhorse. With the mayhem at the ground, it was essential that there was a director in attendance with maximum authority for the foreseeable future. By no means was I afraid of the position, but I was very wary of a simple reversal of roles with John Jackson which might leave us no better off. But, after a long talk with Alan I really believed that I was headed for the hot seat.

'Shortly thereafter, John came round, obviously as aware as the rest of us that we had got ourselves into a predicament that somehow had to be resolved. His opening comment was revealing when he said, "You know, we have allowed Bond to split us apart." Whether or not Bond had full responsibility was a moot point, as for my part, I had thought that a split on the manner of the running of the club had been coming when Bond was not even on the horizon. In the sense that I had failed to confront him, or better still tried to have a quiet one-to-one dispassionate discussion with him, John may have had reason to think that I had let him down.

'Burnley Football Club was now manna from heaven for the press, whose back pages were sure of a good story every day, and the manager actually thought it was in our interests to keep it going. I well remember a rare day when nothing had gone adrift among the directors and he casually told the press that he fancied signing Joe Jordan, a signing so far beyond our capabilities that even a schoolboy would not have taken it in. Our intrepid reporters, despite being out of school, had a comment to work on, and of course the story had its prominence the next day.

'John and I were far from happy with all the media attention, and the chairman was subjected to fierce criticism which far exceeded my idea of decent reporting. By this time, I had learned better how to treat the journalists in the absence of the chairman and I had established a good rapport with them largely based on my premise that I would never feed them a bad line and it worked well right until the end of my tenure. Just once more after the Laws transfer fee, I was a bit shifty and added 2,000 to the attendance figure for the Plymouth Argyle game for the first match of the next season.

'Because of our high profile, anything and everything was getting into print and some of it was too close for comfort. In a wide-ranging discussion with John Jackson, the question of confidentiality and the image of the club gave us real cause for concern. Correctly, I am sure, we reasoned that the continuation of adverse publicity was putting into jeopardy the vital sponsorship income and this had to be corrected before the damage became irreparable. I knew the leaks were not from me, and John was equally sure that he was not to blame. It was unthinkable to look upon Alan Hutchinson or Doc Iven as culprits so that suspicion fell upon the director who was not present to defend himself.

'Nothing was ever proven or directly alleged regarding Colin Sanderson but the board was in such a state of turmoil that something just had to give. It was the next day when John came up with a proposal that we should reconstruct the board without a change in chairmanship. This would involve Doc Iven going "upstairs" to become club and company president. Colin Sanderson would be "asked" to resign and I would become managing director.

'Colin was to be the sacrificial lamb and on the face of it we had cured our divisions with the chairman effectively brought into line with the wishes of Alan and I[23].

'For me, Alan was the ideal partner and we were regularly in harmony both on club matters and we had keen mutual interests in the theatre and old-time music hall stories upon which we regaled each other on away trips. There was to be no loss of face for the chairman and the entire exercise could be carried through and presented as a natural progression for the good of the club.

'There is no doubt that John was capable of fronting the club in a most acceptable manner and where the "clever ones" questioned our motives, it was easy to point out that as a barrister tied up by the strict opening hours of the courts, it was often impossible for him to guarantee his attendance at the drop of a hat. Thus, he could claim he was prevented from devoting as much time as he would have wished, to the day-to-day affairs.

'Selfishly for me, it seemed the perfect solution as I could get back to the job in hand, with the added comfort of knowing that my role as linesman was now promoted to centre-forward. At my suggestion, John and I began to make a show of being seen together at neighbouring clubs when Burnley had a free night, and I have to say that there were some highly enjoyable trips. As a point of interest, it is amazing how much more one sees on the field of play, when your own team is not engaged.

'At this juncture, nothing but common decency compels me to put on record my profound apologies to Colin Sanderson. First

---

23 In fact, the leaks continued and to this day no one knows who the culprit was. Colin Sanderson was blameless.

and foremost, the leaks of which he had been wrongly suspected continued after his departure. As I had known him for many years, without ever being able to claim being a close friend, I really should have known better. After all, he had been solicitor to the club for many years and there must have been times without number when I had been in his company, when juicy morsels were there for the telling if he had chosen to talk. But never once had he broken a confidence to me.

'These were the days long before I had dreams of a seat on the board and I could hardly forget that it was Colin who had put my name forward to John Jackson and had been so instrumental in obtaining the critical sponsorship of the Burnley Building Society. I did him a great injustice in siding with those who opposed him and it is miraculous, and no credit to me, that we are today on decent terms, which is more than I deserve. Very little happens in Burnley that Colin does not get to hear about, and we lost valuable contacts with his departure.

'With the directors busy kicking each other, other injuries were sure to be inflicted and there were just four days for recovery after the Crewe game before we were due to entertain Sheffield United in the league. By one of those fateful chances when imagination and chaos combine, the manager reported a strange illness affecting his playing staff. From this, it seemed that knocks on knees, shins and the like had resulted in an outbreak of influenza among the players and we were unable to string together 11 bodies to fulfil our weekend fixture, and medical evidence was produced to prove it. Permission to postpone was granted and luckily the mystery ailment cleared up as fast as it had appeared and we were up and kicking in no time flat.

'Our nearest and dearest neighbours Blackburn Rovers came to our rescue on our blank Saturday by giving John Jackson and I and our wives a good day out at Maine Road when they contrived to lose to Manchester City by 6-0, which gave the East Lancashire press something to write about which did not concern us. Bill Cox, the chairman of Blackburn and later to become president of the Football League, took this thrashing of his beloved Rovers as best he could, and thought the presence of John and I the last straw. I have been known to say, only half in jest, that if only he had been born on the right side of Accrington, who knows what might have been.

'Anyway: the inevitable could only be postponed and a return to kicking footballs was awaited with some trepidation.'

* * *

In October 1983 and in the match programme for the game against Southend United, Derek Gill explained the rationale for the decision to make him managing director:

'The job of a managing director is to decide. To take advice, listen to all opinions, weigh pros and cons and then decide. I have never met the man who made every decision correctly, although all of us can bring to mind a few who think that they do. It may well be asked why Burnley should wish to appoint a managing director when the vast majority of clubs have not found it necessary. In reply to that I would say that similar appointments will become much more common in the future as time progresses and the ever-increasing burden on club chairmen make a division of responsibilities essential to the smooth running of the business.

'Yes, I did state "business" and for years now, a football club has been a complex and substantial business. In the case of Burnley, we think in terms of exceeding a million pounds when we consider our assets, our annual income and annual expenditure. That level of business can only run with any hope of success when it is managed, and managed on a day-to-day basis.

'At Burnley we shall have a small working board of three directors, comprising chairman John Jackson, vice-chairman Alan

Hutchinson and myself, with Dr Iven always available for advice in a future role of president and ex-officio director[24].

'After a very considerable discussion and heart-searching we decided that three acting directors were enough, not because others did not have functions to fulfil but because three can decide quicker and surer than a committee.

'Think, consider, listen, think again, decide, then act. That is the function of those privileged to be directors, and the role of the managing director is to implement those decisions and to encourage and assist those around him. Decisions, decisions, it is all about decisions. Decisions on sponsorship, ground improvements, admission charges, facilities, wages, and how to encourage those working around you, how to do their best.

'Oh, and then there is the football. Football is what it is all about, is it not? But then we have a manager, and those decisions are his.'

Alas, the programme notes were premature. Doc Iven decided not to become club president and that he would remain on the board. The board of three was a pipe dream and we might reasonably assume that Derek Gill had to grit his teeth and grimace at the news. It remained Jackson and Iven on one side of the table, with Gill and Hutchinson on the other. Impasse.

---

24 In fact this did not happen and Iven remained as a director on the board.

9

A warning of what is to come

DEREK GILL noted in February 2005, 'By the time I wrote this next chapter, all thoughts of publishing it had been forgotten and the draft notes had lain unread and of no concern to anybody. The Tenerife holidays had been abandoned for different climes with more interesting matters in hand. The thoughts I had harboured of a return to Burnley Football Club were long abandoned and any visits to the ground were few and far between and only then when there were grandchildren requiring an adult presence.

'I had been to another club of similar standing to Burnley at the invitation of a former Burnley hero, and I had met the chairman and there was a suggestion of me having a role with them. This was just 45 minutes from my home. It was a friendly club with a splendid ground and facilities; but after three visits I found myself quite unable to identify with the team and it all came to nothing[25].

'The simple fact of the matter is, my heart never left Turf Moor and with that door irrevocably closed, there were, and are, other things in life which gave me fulfilment.'

* * *

25 This was Oldham Athletic, managed by club legend Jimmy McIlroy and under the chairmanship of Ken Bates.

Continuing with his original diaries, Gill wrote, 'After the miraculous release from the mystery illness that resulted in the cancellation of the Sheffield United game, the realisation that football clubs do exist to fulfil fixtures came to the fore and we were due two difficult away fixtures at Brentford and Bolton. Vince Overson was playing regularly despite his niggles but there remained a doubt in the mind of the manager that he would stay the course of a long season.

'Because of the weekend cancellation we now had 11 days to purge the system of the more serious illness from the Crewe hangover and by now I was in the position of being the managing director (ho ho ho). These 11 days were dominated by the question of the centre of the defence and the manager was reluctant to place all his reliance on Vince Overson. Gallagher was beyond the pale, and he did not want to play either Dobson or Phelan in the middle of defence. Interestingly by now he had been forced to come round to recognising that Dobson was an outstanding player in his own right, and that Phelan was too valuable to be "wasted" in the middle of a defence when his creative abilities could be better used elsewhere.

'Utterly predictably he came to the standard conclusion that all managers come to, that he needed another signing to complete the squad and crucially allow him to offload Overson. Lawyers call it "caveat emptor" and in football it is the responsibility of the buying club to ensure the fitness of a player. That is not to say that clubs deliberately offload their crocks. We just seemed to be in the habit of buying them.

'I had personally told John Bond about the boardroom changes and without hesitation he immediately gave me his opinion that I would not be allowed to do the job and neither would it work. Bill Fox at Blackburn told me exactly the same, the next time we met.

'Of all the managers that I met, John Bond was much the most political and he was unconvinced by my assurances. It was put to the test there and then when he asked my consent to the signing of Malcolm Waldron, a central defender from Southampton[26].

'At the time the finances were hardly buoyant but the kitty was comfortably adequate and the manager was left in no doubt that this must be the last big signing, even though I knew there was a substantial sum still to come from the Trevor Steven fee. Add to that the understanding that there would be a decent fee for Vince Overson, I had no qualms on the financial implications.

'What the manager did not know was that the directors, with the new president-elect (except he had decided not to be president) David Iven, had met in the Belvedere Restaurant and had been very close to dismissing Bond. We hesitated by reasoning that the bed had been made and had of necessity to be laid on. And: at the same time there was a sort of honour among thieves that clubs would not be poaching each other's managers during mid-season. Two issues dominated my thinking.

'Firstly, I had made the manager aware of the finances and he had to sit with me through interminably boring lunches with bank officials who in my judgement wanted nothing more than to be seen out with him, and who in due course were to wash their hands of us so sanctimoniously after letting us down in a quite shocking manner, which eventually cost the club a great deal of money. Back him or sack him; first principles to the fore again and I felt that I had to back him.

'Secondly, the next reason does me less credit because I used it as a trial of strength with John Jackson and rang him to tell him that we had agreed to sign Waldron. He was dismayed, but accepted it as a fait accompli and never in my presence did he ever display any disagreement on the issue. As I have stated, the terms were not onerous, the total fee being £80,000 spread over

26 Gill does not record that Bond also wanted to sign Shaun Elliott from Sunderland for £120,000, Bond saying he would give a year of his life to get him. But even Bond realised that at that price there was no chance.

12 months, with a deferral of the full initial payment until he had made a certain number of appearances for us. And: with the Overson sale in the offing there should not have been anything to concern us, so long as the player performed. He made his first appearance in the away fixture at Bolton and as we came away with a goalless draw, the first omens were good, or so it seemed to me.

'Nobody was left in the slightest doubt that the spending spree was over and I was thinking that to all intents and purposes I was running the show. But then came a potential sting in the tail. David Iven collared me and proposed that he should not resign after all but remain on the board with a guarantee that he would support me in anything I chose to do for the club. As the only likely issue would be on future spending and spending was on the back burner, I took a deep breath and got on with things.

'This was a far cry from our "agreement" which had been announced in the press and in the matchday magazine of the club. But I could not force the issue and had to accept it. David Iven did indeed support me but it was clear that if ever the chips were down then a casting vote would still lie with the chairman. I think that John Bond had judged the situation pretty accurately and I had been outmanoeuvred again, now having outright responsibility with insufficient control.

'The frenetic reconstruction phase had ended with the only issue not completed being the finalisation of the Steve Daley transfer. Everybody was aware there was no more money for expensive signings and we had better pull together to make best use of the playing resources we had and get out of this wretched Third Division.

'But hold on, what about the transfer out of Vince Overson? Yet another strange and unpredictable twist was in store and ironically it was the big success of John Bond in getting Overson back into action that precipitated it. Not only did big Vince Overson bounce back into action but suddenly he was performing like a man inspired and the defence improved out of all recognition. We were conceding fewer than a goal a game which effectively meant we had signed Waldron unnecessarily and blown our last big spending opportunity. Thereafter, Waldron was unable to command a certain place in the side and hardly ever in the role for which he had been bought. Much of his short career was wasted with him isolated out wide on the right side of midfield. Meanwhile, Vince was totally revitalised and was happily kicking all and sundry in that endearing way of his – provided he was on your side of course.

'Looking back, I still find it difficult to believe that the club could get itself into such a hole as that which now began to manifest itself as a result of the signing of Steve Daley. I found him to be a pleasant and modest young man who on arrival at the club was simply bursting to get on to the field and perform. His wife was shortly expecting her third child and there was some urgency to get him housed. Promises had been made to him by the chairman and manager that were totally impractical and my immediate task was to somehow accommodate them. The three of them had met in an American airport lounge where a verbal agreement had been reached. In retrospect we should have reneged on it and paid Daley some reasonable compensation and got on with normal business. That is what I should have advocated and had I done so, history might have been very different.

'As I read of the money that slips off balance sheets today, and the murky world of agents prevails, I can only marvel at our innocence in those days.

'Without any doubt it was the signing of Steve Daley which proved to be the pivotal moment and the final straw and its consequences were to haunt me for a very long time. But what really hurts is the knowledge that it was all so unnecessary and could and should have been avoided.

'Results on the field of play had taken a slight turn for the better, they could hardly have gone worse, when we were to learn that Steve Daley, him of the celebrated million-pound transfer from Wolverhampton Wanderers to Manchester City, would be available as a "free" as a result of his club in the American National Football League going broke[27]. The manager believed this was an opportunity too good to miss. It now seems to me that this is quite a common medical condition among football managers and the usual early symptoms appear shortly after two or more bad results on the field.

'There is an equally engaging variation on this theme which oddly displays itself after a good run of results when "building on success" provides the motivation. Either way, John Bond can be a persuasive talker and the inevitable question of the terms likely to be demanded by Daley dominated discussions between Jackson, Bond and myself. Both the chairman and I were adamant that the club's wage structure should not be breached and we were justifiably jealous of the fact that this principle had been maintained. With hindsight I now wish that we had made this public knowledge as the town was alive with incorrect rumours about enormous pay cheques. In a small town like Burnley, where football is the main, and to many the one and only, topic of conversation, wild talk soon reached the ears of loyal players such as Derek Scott, Brian Flynn, Billy Hamilton, Michael Phelan and Martin Dobson. Martin had lost the captaincy of the club in circumstances so absurd that it is still difficult to believe it really happened. The whole scenario was beginning to take on a tragicomic pantomime routine and the only surprising days were when nothing surprising happened.

'Despite it all, the finances at that time were in reasonably good shape and we were in the near unique position of being able to finance transfers "up front". We had even been able to negotiate a meaningful discount from Leeds United by advancing the final payment of the Brian Flynn transfer which had been

---

27 As it turned out there was nothing free about it at all, not to mention the cost of flights to the USA and back, for the manager and chairman.

arranged the previous season on standard terms. This contrasted somewhat with our transfer of Malcolm Waldron to Portsmouth the following year at a time when they were pushing for promotion to the First Division and we were engaged in a desperate and ultimately unsuccessful fight against relegation to the unthinkable Fourth Division. The 50 per cent deposit cheque from Portsmouth bounced and after an angry exchange I was able to get it replaced and add a "keep it quiet" interest charge.

'These were pleasures deferred at the Daley time and although the blush of virginal innocence had faded, there were issues looking large which would radically alter the necessary financing of the transfer. The costs of something like £60,000 had been agreed between the chairman, manager and me, and other directors were informed rather than asked their opinions, as they readily accepted my belief that we could afford and indeed pay in full a transfer fee of that amount.

'The club was operating on a relatively modest overdraft and there were substantial sums still due and undoubted from Everton for the balance of the Trevor Steven fee. It is worth noting that the dealings with Everton were conducted in a most professional manner; instalments were paid exactly in time as agreed, and there was a further clause that if Trevor ever appeared in an England shirt while an Everton player Burnley would receive an additional £25,000. When he duly made his debut in Belfast, this was paid within days without any reminder from us. You remember that kind of business with satisfaction and with it was born a soft spot for Everton which I still retain.

'Unfortunately, Daley was not playing for Everton and we were aware that his registration would probably revert to the NFL, the American governing body, on the winding-up of Seattle Sounders[28], the club to which he was contracted. This was never going to be a

28 Here he was known as the Six Million Dollar Man.

case of agreeing a fee, and the player's terms, with a handshake, and then left to the secretary to complete the papers. At that time, as I was the director with more knowledge of the club's finances than the rest of the board put together, it seemed obvious to me that I should be the one to accompany the manager of the transatlantic trip to interview the player. There was some disagreement in the boardroom as to who should go but the chairman insisted that he was the person who should accompany the manager, as he was the only director with the authority to conclude negotiations.

'Undoubtedly that was true at the time but as it coincided with my own engineering business having matters to conduct in America, I offered to travel at my own expense, but was told it was unnecessary. There was a bizarre twist to the tale as at the time of this argument John did not possess an American visa and I remember his wife being asked to hurry round to get the required documentation. The discussions between the three of them were conducted at the airport, and the two Johns wasted no time, set off with a blare of trumpets and were back in little over 24 hours when I met them at Oxford where we were playing the next match.

'Arrangements were made for the player to fly over and I was left to try to tie up the loose pieces of a deal which had somehow grown to around £70,000 in various payments. Daley was to get the vast majority of this sum which I had already advised the board was affordable as a transfer fee. But it was a very different matter to get that sort of money into the hands of a private individual without a blatant bending of taxation and company law, which neither I, nor John Jackson, nor any other board member was willing to contemplate. The midnight oil was burned trying to concoct a legal way to meet the undertakings given to the player at the airport meeting. It was no joke running a capital-intensive engineering business in the early 1980s, but I am blessed with a reasonably calm disposition and I coped with these ups and downs without too much stress. But: the situation at Burnley Football

Club was deteriorating by the day and the proposed Daley contract was keeping me awake at nights for many an hour. I was worried to such an extent that friends I had made on the board of Blackburn Rovers thought it was having a bad effect on my health.

'Most players are discreet about their contractual arrangements but the Daley contract even in its embryo form soon became common knowledge among other players and inevitably there was dissatisfaction and unrest among them. When I relate that no less a player than Martin Dobson had been asked to take a pay cut and had agreed to it, I can only marvel at how restrained many of them were. I remember once talking to Brian Flynn and trying to assure him that no player was being paid more than the known maximum wage in force, and while I believe that Brian and I had a first-class relationship, and for the life of me I cannot imagine any player that caused less trouble, to this day I am not sure I convinced him.

'Somehow or other, the Daley contract had to be resolved and at that stage of my learning curve it had not dawned on me that the simplest way was to renege on it, alleging misunderstandings and unforeseen problems. The income from the club from attendances was beginning to fall away quite seriously, and the promotion that we naively believed before the season began was there for the taking was beginning to look a much more dubious prospect. The eagerly awaited debut of Daley had to be postponed for some weeks while his registration was sorted out and the manager, a man who never had a glass half empty, assured us that this was no bad thing as it enabled him to get up to the level of fitness needed in England.

'But: for me the most important thing by far was to come with the finalisation of his contract in line with the promises made to him. It was a nightmare to which the only legal solution which conformed to the stringent requirements of the Football League would be at a prohibitive cost to the club. It was necessary to play for time and soundings were made on the possibility of transferring

Daley on again, without him ever kicking a ball for us. With the top rate of tax standing at 60 per cent the cost to the club of making good its commitment to Daley was now in excess of £150,000 and we simply could not pay it. And: the bank that had so actively encouraged us to spend on players was now getting worried.

'Then there was the matter of the house that we had led Daley to believe we would buy for him at a cost of around £50,000. There is no doubt that this could have been done leaving Daley as a sitting tenant and leaving the resale problem for the tomorrow that never comes. I came up with a holding solution that is so daft I cannot believe I proposed it and carried it through. My four sons were all mad Burnley supporters and David, the eldest, had been back from university for a few years and was living alone in a pleasant three-bedroom semi that eventually became the first matrimonial home. I persuaded him to come back home to mum and dad for a time, which turned out to be three months, so that the Daley family could be housed while I tried to resolve the Daley issue that had given us such a combination of problems with finance, damaging team morale, and virtually wrecking the fragile relationship between the manager and the board; and bringing to a head differences of opinion between John Jackson and I, which could not possibly do other than harm the club[29].

'Football clubs defy all rational behaviour and thinking, and as if the above was not enough, Daley made his long-awaited debut and in no time the manager was telling us that he was overweight and could not play. After months of trying, we were able to arrange

---

29 While a house was being refurbished for Daley, David Gill moved out of his own home and went back to his parents. He remembers that Daley moved in with his three children, and his mother-in-law was also there for a while over the Christmas period. They were there for about three months and when they moved out, the house was spotless. David found Steve and his family very charming, and they often went for a drink at the local pub, The Craven Heifer in Briercliffe.

a transfer of the player back to the USA and even though no fee was involved, the transfer was so conducted that there was a saving for the club of over £100,000 on the possible full contract. This included a perfectly legal termination fee to Daley to be made over two years without interest and the entire matter was completed at a fraction of the total anticipated cost to the club. This brought to a conclusion the worst of the transfers with which I was involved. A very unhappy chapter indeed.

'With Bond now held on a tight financial rein, playing results improved so that by Christmas we were well placed for a strong challenge on promotion. On the pre-Christmas Saturday we visited Wimbledon and stuffed the boot boys by our favourite score of 4-1, despite missing a late penalty when Derek Scott was given the chance to register his first ever hat-trick. Spirits were high that night and the fact that the outstanding Kevin Reeves had needed on-field treatment on two occasions was hardly noticed. Little were we to know that it was to signal the beginning of the end of his career and with it went the best chance of the promotion we all wanted so badly and indeed which the club and its supporters demanded, as some sort of belated recompense for the loss of many of their favourite sons.

'During this relatively relaxed interval we had progressed nicely to the third round of the FA Cup. En route I had been able to persuade Hyde United that their best interests would be served by playing their home tie with us at Turf Moor and we then defeated Chesterfield in a replay that then gave us a home tie against Oxford United. Our high-profile manager was naturally eclipsed by the then unrumbled Robert Maxwell, although not to the readers of *Private Eye*. He was then chairman of Oxford United who along with ourselves were favourites for promotion. The game was drawn and we knew shortly thereafter that the winners were to have another home tie against Blackpool with a very strong chance of still further progress and a healthy boost to the bank balance.

'Unfortunately, a strange sort of paralysis was by now setting in, more than just a mere contrast to the frantic antics that had so characterised the first few weeks of the Bond era. Board meetings began to fall by the wayside and began to be conducted by word of mouth, usually between John Jackson and I. The board as an entity was sleepwalking into a period of drift and inactivity, with me effectively in a position to do whatever amused me at the time. An attitude of "ignore it and hope it will go away" was in danger of taking over, if indeed it had not already done so. No one else was interested in taking on the away trips with the reserve team and as I had come to look on these trips as the best part of the job, no fuss was made.

'It is fair to say that of my three colleagues on the board, only Alan Hutchinson seemed alive to the financial implications of a falling revenue, combined with fixed costs, which could not be reduced without transfers of players. The bankers had gone into their shells or ivory towers, as you might prefer, and I was beginning to worry that we were about to fall well short of our anticipated income. I prepared amended budgets to reflect this concern, laying down figures in parameters that could not be misunderstood. I did not walk out of Turf Moor with a bag full of confidential papers, but I did take the precaution of copying or retaining computer discs of some relevant papers prepared at critical times.

'Therefore, I can state with absolute certainty that on 4 March 1984, I presented the directors and the manager with an updated and very clear picture of the finances as they stood at that moment, and a projection of the expenditure to be met in the following season. Amongst the information that I presented was a figure of 13,600 which was the average attendance needed to break even, assuming our exit from both cup competitions at the first hurdle.

'Let nobody now turn to me and say they did not know or were not warned of the road we were treading. I do not possess copies of the garbage that passed for financial statements which were in place when I first went into the club, but they would not be out of place in a Sunday School raffle. My dilemma was made worse with Alan clearly not well and I despaired for the other two. Possibly they were thinking that I had got myself into a jam and should be left to get myself out of it. On my own I could have done so and I am certain that with some ease I could have arranged the appropriate finance.

'Consequently, far from activating the other directors, my reporting seemed to induce a still greater lack of interest in the real problems and we lurched from absolute zero to total panic as a board, which left the manager in a state of near bewilderment, to the extent that he made excuses to miss every one of our final eight league games. This must be some sort of record; giving as his excuse the need to watch as many other players as possible to prepare for another reconstruction for the next season. This from the guy who had brought in every man and his dog those few months earlier, had not even seen some of them play, and had been allowed to give long contracts and all at the club's maximum wage. In reality I do think he was finding it difficult to be in the same company of some, if not all of us. And he was glad therefore to have an excuse to absent himself from the madhouse. After all, he knew and had accepted that he was getting no more money for incoming transfers as on that matter, the board were quite unanimous. Necessity makes strange bedfellows of us all even in the barmy world of professional football.

'At this juncture I could and should have thrown the gauntlet to the board and come out cleanly and demanded that I become chairman with the responsibility and authority the position demanded. There were influential supporters urging me to effect an internal "coup" and to my everlasting regret I bottled it and allowed the circus to continue.'

* * *

Way back in 2004, one of the players interviewed for the John Bond chapter in *No Nay Never* was Derek Scott. He was a regular in the team of 1983/84 and spoke to me at some length about the season, discussing several positives about Bond. As a player he was committed, brave, box to box, and one of those players with endless stamina. The great Keith Newton was his mentor, he said. From being signed as an apprentice in 1974, Scott went on to make 356 appearances and scored 31 goals. He had no preconceived ideas about John Bond when the news came that he was the new manager.

He said, 'I knew he'd bring his own entourage with him but it didn't bother me either way. I was 25 at the time and ready to move if necessary. I was interested to see him work as a coach and what he had to offer. Training sessions were excellent and I did learn a lot. He was innovative and had been part of the famous West Ham Academy. Under him I was fortunate enough to be a regular in the team.'

I asked Scott if there was an 'us and them situation' which is the reason I include this little piece here about him. He replied, 'Well, he brought in his own people and players. I, and others, were never part of that group and they all came on bigger wages, some earning three times as much as us, with signing-on fees and relocation fees. This caused much discussion between players already at the club.'

Gill was right then; the players did learn that the 'new' players were on higher wages and maybe even thought, wrongly, that the old maximum wage of £300 a week was now a thing of the past and the new guys were exceeding that. Gill is adamant that it was never exceeded but interesting that he remained unsure whether or not that a player such as Brian Flynn was ever convinced, when they spoke about it.

Dissatisfaction or not at the higher wages the Bond players were on, Scott insists that up until Christmas they were playing well and team spirit and unity was good. It was the Reeves injury that changed everything, and then things went downhill during the last games of the season when they saw less and less of John Bond.

10

Goodbye Mr Bond

DEREK GILL'S notes of February 2005 record, 'At the time of writing this chapter I had been thinking that greater detail on a few issues and events should be welcome to anyone disposed to read my recollections of the period. The season had gone from initial horror to a flickering of hope still mixed with a simmering discontent and anger at the early season transfers both in and out. But: a realisation that Reeves was something special and even at 37 Hutchison was an extraordinary player.

'By the new year it was still possible to dream of promotion but this was soon to be dashed with a season ending in utter desolation with an absentee manager and performances on the field so bad that they were described to me by a highly respected visitor from the top flight as, "You have now scraped the bottom of the barrel." Twenty years on I have no difficulty in recalling the disappointment, frustration and utter misery of trying all I knew for the club and with Alan Hutchison very ill and soon to pass away.'

* * *

In his original diaries, Gill continued the story, 'There was a replayed cup tie at Oxford, an occasion in which my education was furthered in more ways than one. On the field there was a close and hard-fought match, level at one goal each into the second period, when our goalkeeper was felled by a missile thrown from behind the goal that he was defending. Other players were being pelted by coins and Tom Hutchison told me there was a reluctance to take up their defensive positions particularly from corner kicks. The game had been held up for several minutes while Roger Hansbury, our goalkeeper, received treatment. Almost immediately we surrendered a goal that ended the scoring and lost us the game.

'A major European cup tie had been set aside as a result of a missile hitting an Italian player whose side were being beaten by seven (yes, seven) goals to one. There was never a clearer case for a result to be set aside, a view supported by the precedents just stated and by subsequent similar acts of crowd misbehaviour. The difference was quite simply that, on the other occasions, the offending clubs did not possess such an influential boss.

'I submitted a very detailed telex to the Football Association the very next morning, having decided on this course of action in post-match discussion with the chairman. Within hours on the same day, I had a conciliatory sounding [Robert] Maxwell on the phone telling me in no uncertain terms that it would do us no good and it would only put a lot of people to a lot of trouble. Smart as you damn well like, almost before the ink was dry on my telex, came the exact same message from the proper authorities, that is to say the Football Association, which to me reflected appallingly on them. In fact, it was as good as made out that I was the offender and that they had better things with which to concern themselves.

'That second Oxford goal was also unique in another way as it remains the only one that I ever saw scored to be celebrated by the entire home box, congratulating their chairman in a display of unadulterated sycophancy they must now wish to forget. Probably for the first and hopefully only time during my directorship, I forgot my manners and asked one or two of them if they kissed Maxwell's arse every time they scored. As a reader of *Private Eye,*

I had, let us say, certain doubts on the man beautifully described in that magazine as the "Bouncing Czech".

'It was a bad blow to lose the potential income from the desired home tie with our neighbours Blackpool for which potential sponsorship was ready, along with our share of the gate money. But: we were soon to learn there was much worse news just around the corner. Kevin Reeves had limped out of the match and been substituted and minds went back to the injury at Wimbledon a week or two previously. At that point the worst was not suspected and no indication had been made to the board by our doctor, or training staff, that there might be a more serious cause than just a relatively simple knock or strain. We were stunned beyond words when the manager told us that Kevin would not recover and his loss effectively brought to a premature close all hopes of any playing success for that traumatic season.

'Hands up those that noticed that it was the manager who gave the news to the board, whose numbers included a multi-lettered medic and who had passed fit Gallagher and Gow to mention but two. Only an idiot would want to run an outfit in that state, and oh how I wished for the power to correct it.

'A point worth recording again is that in the John Bond era, the new players without exception began on the club's maximum wage, replacing players who had been paid significantly less. Directors, including me, must take responsibility for this absurdity. And: repeating it so that the most dim-witted director might understand it, it was not money spent on transfers that undermined the club, rather it was the simple fact that we sold and bought the wrong players and that the result of our excursions into the transfer market was to weaken the team. Concurrently, the departure of so many crowd favourites led to a discontent among supporters who began to vote with their feet in ever-increasing numbers. So, the income base necessary to sustain the business was fatally eroded and we got ourselves into a downward spiral which could

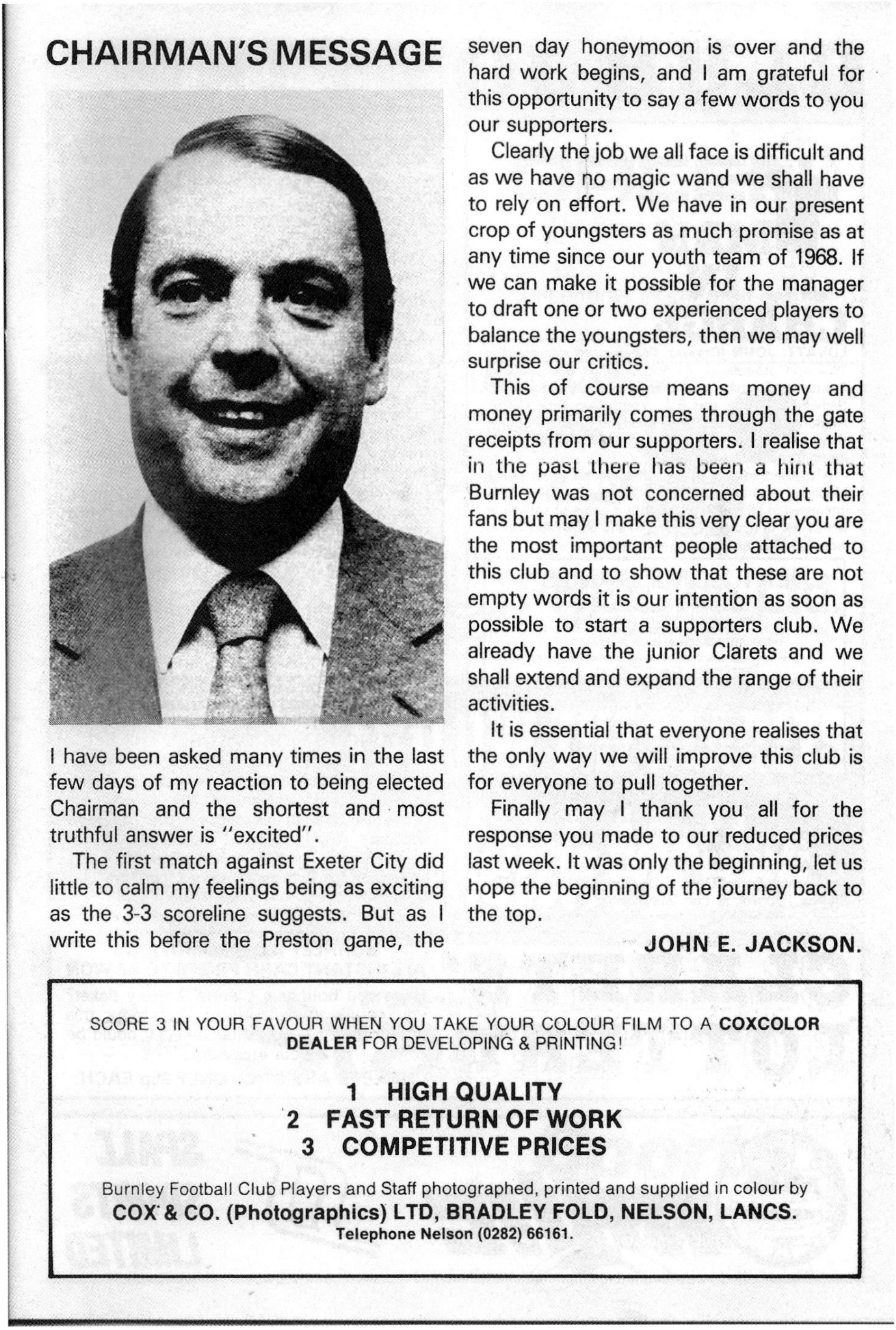

CHAIRMAN'S MESSAGE

I have been asked many times in the last few days of my reaction to being elected Chairman and the shortest and most truthful answer is "excited".

The first match against Exeter City did little to calm my feelings being as exciting as the 3-3 scoreline suggests. But as I write this before the Preston game, the seven day honeymoon is over and the hard work begins, and I am grateful for this opportunity to say a few words to you our supporters.

Clearly the job we all face is difficult and as we have no magic wand we shall have to rely on effort. We have in our present crop of youngsters as much promise as at any time since our youth team of 1968. If we can make it possible for the manager to draft one or two experienced players to balance the youngsters, then we may well surprise our critics.

This of course means money and money primarily comes through the gate receipts from our supporters. I realise that in the past there has been a hint that Burnley was not concerned about their fans but may I make this very clear you are the most important people attached to this club and to show that these are not empty words it is our intention as soon as possible to start a supporters club. We already have the junior Clarets and we shall extend and expand the range of their activities.

It is essential that everyone realises that the only way we will improve this club is for everyone to pull together.

Finally may I thank you all for the response you made to our reduced prices last week. It was only the beginning, let us hope the beginning of the journey back to the top.

JOHN E. JACKSON.

December 1981 and John Jackson replaces Bob Lord as chairman of Burnley Football Club

Happy Days, the last for many years. The winning of the 1981/82 Third Division title. Picture courtesy Burnley Express

The full squad. Picture by Howard Talbut

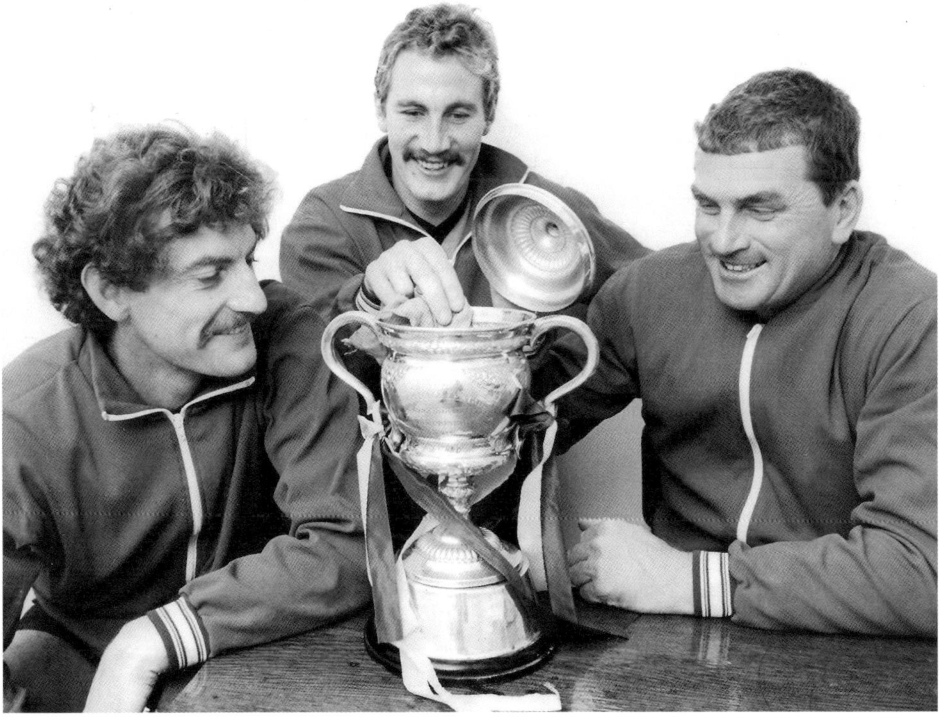

Brian Miller, Billy Hamilton, Martin Dobson and Division Three trophy

Two years later after the relegation, Derek Scott scores at Wimbledon on John Bond's birthday. Pictures courtesy Scott Family

Turf Moor with groundsman Roy Oldfield. Picture from the Oldfield family collection

The 1982/83 squad that was relegated. Picture by Howard Talbut

Hamilton scores v Spurs in the Milk Cup

Dobson celebrates. Both pictures by Burnley Civic Trust

Bond arrives at Burnley. Picture by Clive Lawrence

Burnley squad. Picture by Howard Talbut

From the strange season when there was a relegation but superb cup runs. Burnley won the home tie against the great Liverpool 1-0. Front cover. Hamilton scores. Courtesy. Burnley Football Club.

Chairman John Jackson. Picture by Howard Talbut

not be arrested without an introduction of new funds or a drastic retrenchment, in their absence.

'Now faced with the realisation that the season would end in failure, all the boardroom discontent returned with a vengeance. Board meetings which had been known to go on until the early hours, the record set at ten past five after the Crewe game, went by the board so to speak. There were plenty of weeks when I only saw my colleagues on matchdays. My own car was to be seen outside Turf Moor hour by hour; day by day.

'In addition to my duties as director, I had acted as company secretary following the retirement of Albert Maddox and it was always me who was called on to represent the club at the Football League or elsewhere. In what must have been my spare time I continued to be by far the most regular travelling director with the Central League team. Indeed, I well recall Gordon Taylor, the powerful secretary of the players' union, having assumed that I was a full-time employee of the club, being paid appropriately, and expressing his astonishment when I told him to the contrary.

'In any club the key relationship is that between chairman and manager, but in the spring of 1984 there was not a single person in the club unaware that the Jackson-Bond relationship was in tatters and there can be little doubt that the better informed had arrived at the correct conclusion. Both of them were men of intelligence and there were intermittent and extramural interludes between them when one or the other would have a go at peacemaking and there were odd days when things would quieten down. By one of those delightful coincidences which relate to professional sport these better interludes seemed to happen after we had won the occasional match.

'Possibly I was more affected at this juncture because I had been thinking that we had got over the worst. I had assumed the enhanced role of managing director thinking that my teeth were long enough to handle the David Iven change of mind. Whilst we had all recognised that the bed that we had elected to lie on was far from perfect, the only sensible course was to just get on with the job in hand.

'The best and most productive time of John Bond's time at Burnley took place during the two or three months prior to the injury to Kevin Reeves. The boardroom was more than quiet being as good as deserted and this was the time following the boardroom shake-up and my appointment as managing director. In common with others that I could think of, I certainly would not have minded being the absolute dictator implied in that scenario, and had I been so, I would have no doubt been at Burnley Football Club for the next ten years. One thing is sure, however, in that idyllic dream there would now be in place a board of directors capable of ensuring that the good of the club transcended the personal ambitions of any one individual.

'One of those in the history of the club is more than enough and a recurring theme of mine has always been to put a large share of the responsibility on to the one who dictated and then bequeathed the shambles[30].

'Only one who lived through it all really knows what went on behind the scenes in the early 1980s, and I was behind the scenes more than most. Possibly, it will come as a surprise to many, but for the first three months I found it quite easy to work with John Bond who had settled in as well as he ever would do in what he always considered to be something of an alien environment. Nirvana for John would have been to manage West Ham and I could easily understand that. Settling for Burnley would always be something of a second prize for him, and he owed a great deal to his assistant, John Benson, one of the very best men I met in football. He was

---

30 Bob Lord, of course, but a newspaper article in 1987 where Gill laid the blame for the woes of the club on Lord, after the Orient game, did not go down at all well. The survival of the club inspired euphoria and it was not the best time to blame the old curmudgeon.

extremely hardworking, level-headed, and supportive without ever being afraid to express his own opinions. I am sure John Bond recognised his debt to him and his preference for Benson as his number two, was a tacit acceptance of the benefit he gained from the association.

'Employed as chief scout was John Doherty, also a very intelligent man beyond football, himself a former player numbered among the famous Busby Babes and whose playing career had been cut short by injury. He too had a role to play and to him should go the credit for the discovery of Wayne Biggins who was signed for next to nothing and eventually left the club for a sizeable fee after giving splendid service.

'It may be feeding ammunition to the uninitiated and the knockers but I will go on record as saying that if, and it would be a big IF, John Bond had come to Burnley straight from Norwich, where his record speaks for itself, instead of his unhappy departure from Manchester City, and had I been chairman, the history of Burnley Football Club would have been very different and the thought of playing in the Fourth Division, let alone for an absurd seven years, would have been laughed out of court.

'I would have spent hours with him before making the appointment and he would have got the job only when he and the board were all fully aware of the parameters within which he would be expected to work. Clearing out some of the favourite sons, back to Brian Laws again, without seeing them in competitive action would have been unthinkable. Given optimum support from the board a productive relationship was possible; but with the board we had in place, I cannot think of any manager who would have succeeded.

'I have already indicated that I think the real job description is "team coach" and at the end of the previous season I would have confirmed Frank Casper in that role and it is not beyond the realms of possibility that we would have escaped relegation if that appointment had been made, the day he took over from Brian Miller. A sensible and popular move would have been to ensure the longer-term future of Martin Dobson and the club with those two and Gordon Clayton would have done for me. Please note that Dobson and Casper took Bury out of the Fourth Division and came close to another promotion to the Third, and that was on gates of about one-third of those at Burnley. I am not trying to be clever after the event as my views at the time were well recorded, but as everyone at Burnley knows, it was not to be and more is the pity.

'With no disruption from the board, thanks to their absence, there was a degree of peace in the camp between matchdays, and also now living with the discipline of knowing there was no more cash for transfers, attention had turned to the non-league scene and I had not forgotten a cup tie against Runcorn where we survived narrowly but significantly found our players pushed to the limit by part-time professionals whose numbers must surely include some capable of playing in the lower divisions of the league, if not at the very top. Thus, we invested petty cash to sign Wayne Biggins, who came to the club to play for an astonishingly low wage for the opportunity to prove himself. John Bond saw him play for the first time on a midweek reserve game and immediately threw him in at the deep end with the first-team to plug the gap left by Kevin Reeves. Wayne established himself as an automatic first choice literally from day one.

'Of course, John Bond made some horrific errors on the playing side, but a fair-minded person should not omit to mention the positive elements. Once having left the club I was not involved, nor do I know the eventual receipts on the Wayne Biggins transfer to Norwich City, but from reports it seemed to be rather lower than what I would have expected. But, at the very least, no one can deny that it was one Bond signing that made money for Burnley.

'I am not John Bond's keeper and I have met him just once since I left Burnley, this being in the boardroom at Oldham when he was manager at Birmingham City, and my intention is simply to put on record and give credit where credit is due, and to criticise constructively when I have something to say. So much at Burnley was childish and utterly pathetic and John Bond was subjected to abuse simply because he was particular and smart in his dress sense. Does anyone wonder why he failed to perform well, and what a shocking price he then had to pay for this sojourn at Burnley that damaged his reputation disastrously.

'Meanwhile: every now and then we had to get our minds off these things and play a football match.

'March had been an indifferent month on the field but promotion hopes were reawakened marginally when we won a hard game at Gillingham. Being a long way from home it followed that I was the only director there and I was very struck by their friendly boardroom, and by the obvious high regard in which John Bond was held. The much-respected commentator Brian Moore, himself a Gillingham director, was present and there was a telling observation that John Bond needed a major club to express himself. I felt that I understood precisely what he meant. John was not one for too much detail, a necessary ingredient for success in the lower divisions. He may well have had success at a club such as Manchester United where I believe he was once close to getting the job as manager.

'It was a very good win at Gillingham and we had two home games to follow against Oxford United and Bolton Wanderers, both fellow contenders for promotion, and victories in these fixtures would put us back in the frame. In the event, both games were drawn and this effectively meant that both the two fixtures to be played the next week must be won, or else we could forget about promotion for another year. That weekend involved a Friday start for the delights of Newport and then down to Bournemouth for a Monday evening game. It is not necessary for me to state which director left home Friday midday to return on the next Tuesday morning. But in fairness the chairman did see the Newport game, having made his own way down on the day of the match. So, off we trooped, more in hope than expectation.

'John Bond was as aware as anyone of the stakes and he called for a supreme effort with just ten games left to try and salvage something from the pending wreckage. John Jackson and I, and the travelling Burnley fans, sat through an abysmal 90 minutes at Newport with the miserable game petering out to a goalless draw, except that Newport compounded the felony by scoring a late goal and denying so much as the faintest hope to the permanently optimistic mathematicians to cling to, and no probable sequence of results were left to redeem us.

'John Jackson was desperately disappointed and left for home more depressed than I had ever seen him, and he had to withstand an unacceptable level of personal abuse and vilification, in part from some who should have known better. However much I disagreed with him, it turned my stomach to witness some of it and it eventually had some bearing on my own departure.

'Late on Saturday night, we arrived in Bournemouth, where gynaecologists are redundant, and it was a subdued weekend with the players going through the motions of light training and quite clearly everybody was ready for home. I remember taking a long walk on the front and wondering where the hell we were heading from here. It was no surprise that we lost the match, and sat watching in the directors' box was Ian Branfoot, one of the six applicants for the manager's job after, I repeat after, the chairman had unilaterally promised the job to John Bond. In the boardroom was a delightful gentleman of whom I had heard, but had never met and this was Alec Stock, who in a ten-minute chat made me think that the best men in football are those that make the least noise.

'John Bond was jeered and barracked most vehemently throughout the game and was clearly blamed by the locals for an unfinished stand and an unhappy balance sheet; and it was more than noticeable that he did not show up in the boardroom after the game. For my part I could not have been treated better and the other interesting duty I had to perform was to go on to the pitch before the kick-off and present a memento to a Burnley fan in commemoration of his feat in completing a visit to every ground in the Football League. Now then, that is a fan, but I shudder to think what his wife makes of it, if he has one.

'John Bond made another serious error of judgement that night and did himself much harm in my eyes. He invited me to be present in the hotel for a pre-match talk to the players and he astounded me by making a strong personal criticism of the chairman and went on to say that I was the only director with whom he could establish a working relationship. I have already made the point that lurking within him is a politician, but this was a misjudgement worthy of the worst kind of rabble rouser and had the very opposite effect of what he intended. Worse still was the manner in which he told Brian Flynn, holder of some 60 international caps, that he was dropping him for that match. I found it incredibly abrupt and for me it should have been done in a private face-to-face discussion. But then I am not a football manager.

'This displayed the poorer side of John Bond as a man manager which I found very disappointing but I chose to keep my feelings to myself as I felt unable to intercede between chairman and manager especially without much support at board level, apart from the very ill Alan Hutchinson, who to my great regret, and the club's great loss, was destined to play no further part for us.

'I did not know it then but the fixture at Bournemouth[31] was to be the very last competitive game in which John Bond would take charge of the team.

---

31 It was another 1-0 defeat.

'It was a long and quiet journey back to Burnley, arriving back at around three o'clock in the morning, and the manager was terribly disappointed and distinctly upset by the reception he had been given by the Bournemouth crowd where he had managed prior to his time at Norwich. The coach back from any fixture is no place to discuss the game much less to plan the future, and to describe it as morose would be doing it a disservice. Something had to be said and it was arranged that I would meet with the manager and John Benson later that week and I would try to involve some other directors, which at least showed I had not lost all my optimism. No other directors were available when it came down to the brass tacks, and so I met Bond and Benson on my own, now a new experience I might add.

'No permutation of possible future results would bring us promotion now and the atmosphere in the club was morbid and worse, while the town varied between anger and an ominous indifference, an attitude most unusual for the once soccer-mad town of Burnley and its surrounding districts. The malaise affected John Jackson too and he became untypically quiet and restrained in his appearances on matchdays. The end of the season could not come quickly enough for any of us. However, one of us was aware that the close season would be a very busy period in which crucial decisions had to be made.

'The antennae of professional footballers soon sense discord and rows within a club and they had heard for themselves the manager giving his opinion on the chairman, and an atmosphere so poisoned translates itself into bad playing results as sure as night follows day. Eight of the final ten league fixtures were lost. Anybody involved in football and anyone with a modicum of common sense will tell you the effect that sort of run has on season ticket sales for the next year.

'The personal relationship between chairman and manager degenerated into an all-time low and I found it truly appalling as

I sat in the middle. Frankly, part of me felt for both of them to an extent, but more importantly my beloved Burnley Football Club was being crucified. I could not be altogether sure whether it was merely to get away from it all, or Bond's ostensible need to look at players that we could not afford to buy, that motivated him to miss the final eight games after the Bournemouth debacle. I had not used that word "debacle" since the Crewe nightmare, but we were now so well and truly in the madhouse with a club full of recriminations but devoid of solutions, and with me finding myself more isolated than ever.

'Fantasy and panic make strange bedfellows and lethal cocktails and one followed the other in chaotic fashion. The board now was notable only for its inertia and lack of regular contact and this at a time when so much needs to be decided behind the scenes. Supporters, sponsors and players were all in varying degrees ready to wash their hands of us and a great deal was grinding to a halt.

'My own business was feeling my absence and I was very worried by it all, losing sleep and pondering on what next move would be best for the club and for me. In eight short months I had seen the club torn apart and even at that stage it was clear for me that the next season was unlikely to be any better on the field. And: the prospects of sustaining a reasonable level of income from the gate and sponsorship were declining by the day. Drastic measures were needed or the alternative was to face an unacceptably long spell in the lower reaches. They tell me that if you sit on a poisoned dart, you soon discover your real friends and I felt that I had landed on a quiver full.

'Towards the end of the season, Martin Dobson had been given the opportunity to manage near neighbours Bury and although he was contracted to us and an invaluable asset to the club, no reasonable man could stand in his way. Unknown to Dobson I had obtained from Bury a letter to release him if Burnley were to offer him a position and, in fairness to Dobson himself, neither could this be made public and thinking back to the Colin Sanderson scandal, which wrongly cost him his seat on the board, I kept this knowledge from Jackson. What a hell of a state we must have been in for me to do that.

'By this time, I was seriously thinking that John Jackson could not possibly hang on to the chairmanship and that it was very probably coming to me. There is no doubt that I would have taken it had it been offered, in order to enable me to get on with the job of doing what I knew was needed so urgently. I was by now more and more aware of the prophecy of John Bond that I would not be allowed to function as managing director, a view that was repeated quite unsolicited by Bill Fox, chairman of Blackburn Rovers, whose view was that a chairman/managing director relationship was quite impractical at a football club. But: my view remains that it is perfectly workable to have such a relationship but the chemistry between John Jackson and me did not lend itself to it.

'Duck your head here Derek, but I have to put on record that I was finding my visits to Ewood Park were becoming more and more frequent and I looked on it as a refuge of sanity with a set of directors who did credit to their club and were the most hospitable around.

'Numerous people were encouraging me to engineer a coup to oust Jackson both from the chair and the board, but at the time I reckoned that the cure was worse than the disease. Mad schemes were proposed and I tried to give a good hearing to all but the most idiotic so long as the intention was for the good of the club. I visited the homes and businesses of one or two likely investors and future directors, and undoubtedly, I was in a position to muster a large degree of support if I had opted for an all-out war, and a boardroom fight to the end. I, and I alone, know how close it came and there are times when I have regretted not carrying it through to its ultimate conclusion.

'Such manoeuvrings were not going to escape the attention of John Bond for long and I suppose that he wished for it to happen, as he probably thought his chances of survival were better with me in control. In reality, it would have been the opposite. As I mentioned, I had the letter from Terry Robinson, chairman of Bury, agreeing to release Dobson. Robinson was over the proverbial barrel as his approach to Martin had been outside the protocol on poaching from other clubs, and I absolutely knew that Martin would have come like a shot, provided a certain director had packed his bags. All this came out long after the event, but my judgement was 100 per cent on that one.

'It was even more justified as Dobson and Casper would take their new charges to promotion on a shoestring, concurrently making a great deal of money for Bury on the transfer market. A wise man always backs quality and to me, Martin represented quality, and Frank was as shrewd a coach as I had seen in his short spell in charge pre-Bond. How full of "if only" is life, if you let it. The moral I learned to my cost is to grab it with both hands when the chance is there. It rarely comes twice.

'The busiest time for the administration of a club begins with the end of the playing season, but here we were effectively paralysed with a board that hardly ever met other than to engage in mutual recriminations, a manager who missed our final eight games and was clearly demoralised, no sponsors to be seen and a bank that had once tried to throw money at us now in a state of panic. It had by now capped our account borrowings and was imposing impossible conditions, while at the same time withdrawing their shirt sponsorship. The sponsorship that had previously been used as a lever to win our account when they were providing us with such generous banking terms that only a fool would have declined.

'For many years the club had banked with one of the "big four" and had been supported at a cost, it must be said, through good times and bad. As a matter of courtesy, I had shown them the terms offered to us, hoping against hope that they might match them, but knowing it to be unrealistic. In all probability at that time, they were glad to be rid of a football club account.

'Now the sudden restrictions of our borrowings, at the very time the bank was withdrawing our shirt sponsorship, hit us very hard at the worst possible time. Its immediate effect was to box us into a corner in our negotiations with the Maxwell factor at Oxford who were in talks with Billy Hamilton. Maxwell had gone to the chairman and Jackson had quoted a fee of £175,000 which was fair to all parties, and he told me we should expect between £150,000 and £175,000 if the fee had to be determined by tribunal, telling me that Gordon Taylor was of that opinion.

'The bank would not budge one penny and threatened to stop our wages payments. In retrospect I should have financed them myself for the interim period and I regret not doing that. There was a weak excuse, as the board had determined that directors were not willing to open that particular door. I spoke to John Jackson by phone and we agreed that we had to settle for a beggarly £77,500 which I managed to increase to £80,000 by accepting deferred payments. This was outrageously inadequate for a player of Billy's ability and I tried to persuade him to stay but he was determined to go. At the end of his contract there was nothing we could do to dissuade him.

'Among my souvenirs is a letter from the self-same bank, in which money was put up for us, but on the grounds that it MUST be spent on players, and not dissipated, yes the word was "dissipated", on day-to-day running costs. I immediately wrote back at length to try to explain the manner in which the club was financed and explained the importance of timing in transfer sales. It was to no avail.

'Football found its proper perspective when the dreaded news came that Alan Hutchinson had died. As John Jackson so rightly noted in his annual statement to shareholders, the loss to the club was nothing compared to the loss to his family. Selfishly for me, I had lost the one true friend on the board, and Burnley Football Club would never be the same again. His association was far too short and this only served to highlight the extent of the tragedy.

'Life had to go on, and a couple of weeks before the new season was due to start, the chairman seized upon a newspaper article written under the name of John Bond which was extravagant to say the least and contained some inflammatory observations including a statement that "the game had gone" and indicating that all enjoyment and interest in it was a thing of the past. At a time when the commercial manager and I were trying to drum up interest and encourage the sale of season tickets, it was a masterpiece of bad timing. Journalists are always in need of a new line and I tend not to take too much notice of the popular stories that make news one day and forgotten the next.'

Having read the offending newspaper piece by Bond, chairman John Jackson was incensed. In the *Burnley Express*, Keith McNee reported his findings under the heading 'CLARETS SET TO SACK BOND':

'John Bond's reign as Burnley manager could come to an end tonight after only 14 months. The three-man board of directors will meet and Mr Bond's resignation threats are certain to be discussed.

'The 51-year-old Burnley manager revealed today that he is not prepared to stay on for a second season unless Mr Jackson is removed from the board.

'He said, "Close friends of mine have known my views on this football club for some time. All I want to do is manage the club in my own way, as I have done at my previous clubs. Let nobody get the impression that I have lost my enthusiasm for the game of football. I am still as prepared as ever I was to try to make Burnley a First Division club again. But I am afraid that is an impossibility when there is friction between myself and the chairman. I am afraid that is the case and it just has to be sorted one way or the other. The game has gone and the only thing that would entice me to a match if I leave Burnley would be to watch my son Kevin playing for Manchester City."

'Asked what his attitude would be should Mr Jackson lose his place on the board, Mr Bond said, "In that case, I would be prepared to continue. I still firmly believe in Burnley FC, but there are enough problems in soccer without some people making them that much harder."

'Mr Jackson told me today, "All the matters including Mr Bond's threats to resign and the team's performance over the last six months will be discussed at the board meeting tonight."

'Derek Gill, who has been very prominently involved during the summer on Burnley FC matters, was not available for comment as last night he attended a Canon League football dinner in London. But he is certain to be at tonight's board meeting and I understand that Mr Bond has been invited to be there.

'Although there have been hints that Mr Jackson is himself under some pressure, I feel that it would be very difficult for any football club board of directors to accept the sort of comments that Mr Bond made about his feelings on the game.'

'John Jackson was livid,' continued Gill in the diaries, 'and if he had been looking for a reason to sack the manager, he believed he had one now. He convened a highly secret meeting but leaks from it were in the press in no time at all and when John Bond was called to the club to explain himself, we were besieged by reporters and photographers who must all have been psychic. The night of the summons to the manager there was a formal board meeting, something of a novelty in those days, and novel too was the introduction to the board of Basil Dearing, a local solicitor, and close friend of John Jackson. If you get the impression that I was now even more isolated, you would not be far wrong. The chairman addressed the meeting in his best barrister's accent and demanded an explanation from the manager about the offending article and how he proposed to carry on in the future.

'Without question, John Bond articulated his side of the affairs on both the newspaper article and the dismal performance of many of the players he had introduced to the club. He was very open in his admission of his errors and took the line that having made them, they were irreversible and this was not the time to change in midstream. It was not John Bond that declared that Joe Gallagher was fit for professional football and he never put forward excuses, some of which were available to him if he had chosen to use them. I am fairly sure that he knew that words alone were not going to save him and after artificially conclave-like deliberations by the directors, he was told that he had effectively terminated his own employment. He left the boardroom with dignity and I will be surprised if he ever sets foot in Burnley again.'

* * *

The board meeting minutes told the story of the end of Bond's employment, 'The manager entered the meeting at this point and was asked by the chairman to give an explanation to the board regarding certain articles which had appeared in recent national newspapers. Mr Bond said he had not spoken with the press. The manager said he would not be held responsible for what had been written. The chairman then asked the manager if he had asked the press for an apology or asked them to retract the comments he was reputed to have said. Mr Bond said he had not made such a request to the press because he had never made the statements in the first place. The manager was then asked to leave the meeting for a while.

'The directors then discussed the management position for some time and it was unanimously agreed that he be asked to resign his position with the club on the grounds that he had terminated his own employment. Mr Bond was then asked to re-join the meeting and the chairman on behalf of the board then asked Mr Bond to resign his position as manager of the club, in an amicable manner.

'Mr Bond replied by saying that he would relinquish his position as manager provided that adequate compensation be made to him. Mr Dearing asked Mr Bond what figure he had in mind. Mr Bond would not quote any figure and said the directors knew full well what was due to him in accordance with his contract. The chairman then informed Mr Bond he would be relieved of his duties as manager of the club forthwith. Mr Bond replied by saying that he was not sorry with the outcome of the decision and said he would not leave the club for less than £50,000. Mr Bond then left the meeting.'

One thing is certain; Bond did not receive £50,000 as part of any settlement. Basil Dearing was asked to deal with the industrial tribunal but following that entry in the minutes there is no further mention. How much Bond actually received therefore is a matter of conjecture.

The day after the sacking, Keith McNee, in the *Burnley Express,* again reported on the situation and contacted Bond at his Cheshire home. 'THE SADNESS OF JOHN BOND' was the header and the story continued:

'John Bond spoke today for the first time about his dismissal as Burnley FC boss, his first sacking in his 15-year managerial career. Fifty-one-year-old Mr Bond stormed out of Turf Moor last night after being informed by the board of directors that his employment with the club was being terminated. This followed some very strong comments he had made over the weekend in which references were made to the fact that he could not manage the club effectively while barrister John Jackson remained chairman. After a two-hour meeting he left Turf Moor and said, "I have absolutely no comment to make."

'But today at his Knutsford home he told me, "I am very disappointed about what has happened last night. I have never been sacked before. Whether I will stay in the game is a matter which will be decided by other people. At the moment I don't want to say anything further about what has happened at Burnley."

'There have been hints that Burnley will face a hefty compensation pay-out to Mr Bond but I feel that in view of the events that led to his sacking, the amount may turn out to be modest. Mr Jackson told me today that he did not want to make any comment to add to the board statement issued last night. But he did announce that Burnley solicitor Basil Dearing was appointed to the board at last night's meeting.

Gill's notes continued, 'There were vastly more legitimate reasons for ending his term as manager than an article in a red top newspaper and as it was but a few days to the start of the new season, the timing was imbecilic. But we were in the boardroom of Burnley Football Club, and by definition were not creating a precedent.

'The year of the John Bond management had been an unmitigated disaster for the club and the man himself but it would be totally wrong to place all the responsibility for it on John Bond alone. This would be both cowardly and dishonest but regrettably the exaggerated fiction has increased over the years with subsequent poor performers always ready to put the blame elsewhere, particularly when the subject of that criticism is not there to answer back.

'Then it dawned on us that there was a football season about to start later that very same week and it would be a good idea to get someone to run the football team. Take it from me, this had not been thought through and there was no option but to ask John Benson to take the reins. He was not expecting this turn of events and in his honest and straightforward way, his first question to me after being offered the job was to enquire if the appointment was for no better reason than we had not got the funds to sack him and bring in another management team. He actually said to me that Martin Dobson was the obvious choice and in our shoes that is what he would do.

'Saturday was soon here and a new temp was at the helm, but this time it was not a quarter-final at Tottenham and a 4-1 sensation was hardly on the cards. It was Plymouth Argyle.

'And we were in the fertiliser.'

11

John Bond states his case

JOHN BOND was gone, but even the manner of his 'sacking' was worthy of a Brian Rix farce when he found himself locked out of the building on Harry Potts Way prior to the meeting. To keep the press at bay and from coming up the stairs and banging on the boardroom door, the directors had locked the main reception entrance. Milling outside were all the reporters and photographers with Bond among them waiting until a key could be found and he could get in. In some ways it almost summed up the chaos and disorganisation of the season.

Years later, Bond was given two platforms to say what he thought and give us his side of the story. The first was in a small publication produced by former player Paul Fletcher designed to raise funds for the penniless club a couple of years after Bond had gone. In *BFC and Me*, Bond was given a page and wrote an article under the headline 'What went wrong, my side of the story':

'When I joined Burnley Football Club as manager I had only one thought in mind. The First Division. My only real knowledge of this great club, steeped in tradition, was of my playing days, battling at Turf Moor in front of capacity First Division crowds against McIlroy, Adamson, Pointer and Miller. The club had a playing pitch, stadium and training facility to match anything in Europe. I had been promised support without interference from chairman and directors, so how could I fail. But I did. And I remember my stay at Burnley as the biggest disappointment in my football career. So, whose fault was it?

'Certainly, as manager I take a large share of responsibility. But not all of it. Strangely, even after a few months at the club, I still felt like an outsider. Looking back, I feel no one could be blamed for this; it was just the history of the club. I realised that I was the first outsider to be appointed manager. Before me the post had been filled from within the ranks. Alan Brown, Harry Potts, Jimmy Adamson, Brian Miller, Frank Casper had all established themselves as players before becoming manager. All were northerners and had learned the way this successful, town club had survived among the big, city clubs.

'Then, suddenly, this southerner arrives to manage. Obviously wanting his own way and using management techniques both tried and tested in the upper divisions. The club at the time was in the middle of transition. The great Bob Lord era was over and a new, young chairman, John Jackson, headed the board. His inexperience as chairman, coupled with a relatively new board of directors, added to my determination to have my own way. A formula for disaster. The only remedy was success on the field and that's when fate, bad luck, call it what you like, took a hand.

'Firstly, the Hamilton-Reeves partnership ended in mid-season when Kevin was tragically injured with an injury that effectively ended his career. Trevor Steven was sold to Everton in the famous Burnley tradition of selling. Each year, a product of the youth policy was sold but after Trevor Steven there were no other younger players coming through. I then made an error when I bought Mal Waldron from Southampton, and my other buys were struggling for success on the field. All, except Tommy Hutchison, a great player and good pro, who although he never really felt accepted at the club, was voted Player of the Year, for two consecutive seasons.

'Amongst the gloom, every now and then, I could see what this team was capable of. We kicked off against Port Vale at three o'clock and at 3.30pm we were 6-0 up. Brian Flynn was playing as well as at any time in his career and I knew that if only I could combine a few good results with a slice of luck the team would believe in me, and the directors would believe in me.

'But it was not to be and I left the club with great sadness in my heart. Hindsight is a wonderful thing and I can clearly see now a few mistakes I made but each one was made with a true desire for success for the club.

'I have no animosity towards Burnley Football Club or anyone associated with the club. It was simply a plan that did not work, a relationship because of inherent traditions, that never had a fair chance. I hope the club one day returns to its rightful place in the top flight of British football. I am only sorry I was unable to lead the way.'

In 2004, Phil Whalley interviewed Bond at length. I thank Phil for this: the result of the 30 questions that he asked. Bond gave his responses:

'My perceptions of the club were nothing but good. The tragic thing about it, in many ways, is that I played at West Ham and we used to play at Burnley and it was a club run along the same lines as West Ham. It was a coaching football club. There was always a lot of coaching going on and the people there were interested in coaching. And they used to play the sort of football that we did at West Ham, to knock it about and play, and there were always expressive footballers playing at Burnley. So, I have nothing but admiration for them and nothing but good to say about them. They were a good little club, although a big club in terms of ambition and support. It wasn't particularly the area I wanted to be as a person, I never wanted to live in the town, but overall, I met a lot of good people who knew their football.

'John Jackson gave me no real impressions about the state of the club and had no real bearing on me going to the club. He asked me whether I'd like the job and it seemed with me having just retired from Manchester City, that it was a good opportunity. I never looked on Burnley as anything other than a top club. The fact that they weren't in the top league didn't mean anything to me, and they certainly had that potential. You had only to walk into the ground to see that. So, John Jackson didn't have any bearing on me going to the club, he just offered me the job and I thought, yes, it's a good idea.

'It was strange though, the way he left it, he didn't want me to take over until June, but things happened when a few people got to hear that I had been appointed. Whilst he hadn't disclosed it to anybody, I knew I was going to be the manager. There were a few words coming out in the press that they didn't want any big-time Charlies and when I heard that it didn't exactly fill me with joy and happiness. But again, when I went and took the job, in my first game at Hull, as I walked from the tunnel to the dugout, a section of the crowd booed me and I thought that was exactly what I didn't need.

'They'd already sold Trevor Steven when I took over so I was told then that he was going to have to go and they'd agreed a fee with Everton. He was a good prospect and he felt he had to leave. So that was all set up and I just did the deal, but I squeezed a bit more out of Everton. But there were people there like Martin Dobson who was a good player, or had been a good player, but he was on his way out I felt. And I always felt he was one of those that didn't want foreigners or people from a distance at the club. I think maybe he thought that he himself might have got the job at the football club, so he didn't want people like me. It wasn't an easy ride for him or me from thereon in.

'Burnley had players that were okay but they weren't good enough. They'd just got relegated and it wasn't a good side so I needed to get players in. I suppose my massive mistake was getting too many in too soon. You can reel off the players I signed and quite a few of them didn't really do their stuff and that lumbered Burnley with a few players that weren't up to it. So that was a mistake on my part and I admit that. I can be quite an impetuous person and signing players didn't bother me as long as I thought that they could make the club better. But it didn't make the club better because they weren't up to it. Take Gerry Gow, he'd done a fabulous job for me at Man City, but unfortunately that was where he should have finished; he had very dodgy knees and it just didn't work out for him at Burnley.

'My assessment could have been more thorough. I know you're talking about people like Lee Dixon and Brian Laws. Laws was a half-decent player. He was okay but there was more to me letting Laws go than me just thinking that he wasn't that good. I just didn't want him at the football club and if a manager doesn't want a player, he tends to get rid of them. I'm not on my own regarding that. If your face doesn't fit you say "on your bike".

'Lee Dixon, in all fairness, had potential and he had ability, and letting him go, which overall could have looked a mistake from Burnley's point of view, probably hastened his development into a better player. It probably made him have a look at himself and made him realise that he had to do something with himself, and in fairness to the boy he went to a smaller club but ended up at Arsenal and had a fabulous career which was absolutely marvellous and I was thrilled to bits for him. I wasn't sour about the fact that he proved me wrong and made himself into a great footballer. There's plenty of people who've done that from different football clubs. It's probably happened to most clubs at some time or other. So, I let Dixon go.

'An "us and them" division probably did develop in the camp. The people who had remained at Burnley were feeling a little as if they were having their noses pushed out of joint, but that wasn't something I did casually, that was something that I wanted to do. I felt that at the time it was too much about Burnley and the Burnley players and that maybe a lot of them were getting soft rides at the football club. The club wasn't doing too well and it needed to change. But I probably made the changes too quickly. It would have been better getting one or two in, leaving it at that and then building up gradually. But that approach isn't uncommon to me. Every club I've been to I've tried to bring about a big change fairly quickly and I've always taken my own staff in as well so I know exactly what I'm doing and who I've got working under me.

'It's difficult to put your finger on what was wrong at the club. The lady that made the cakes and the sausage rolls and so on was a darling and I thought if only everyone was like her. But there was a snideness about the place, an air about the place that said, "This is our town and we don't want outsiders." There was a lot of noise from players that had been playing at the club about the state of the place. They'd finished playing there but they were slagging people off who weren't Burnley people or who hadn't previously been connected with the club. And it was there within the club.

'It was there for me but to this day I still play golf with Brian Flynn and Kevin Reeves and we got on famously, as I did with people there like Billy Hamilton. If it had been left to me, we could have made Burnley a good team again; they weren't prepared to go behind people's backs. They got on with it; they may not have thought that I was the best manager they'd ever come across, but they went along with me and we got to know each other and the atmosphere became better. But there was always that element in the background; Burnley people who thought I shouldn't be managing their football club. I'd feel it if I went round some of the bars and restaurants, I didn't feel at home.

'In fairness, it was a bit like that at Manchester City when I left Norwich which was a very homely place. The sad thing is that I always remembered Burnley as that sort of football club when I used to play against them for West Ham. I used to like going there and I used to enjoy playing against them. But it was not like that when I was the manager.

'I know that you do have managers and chairmen who like their staff to live in the town or close by and that sort of thing has been going on in football for as long as I've been involved. But I always thought that was silly. The fact that I lived an hour's drive away out of Burnley didn't make me feel any different or want me to do any different job than if I'd been living next door to Turf Moor. I wasn't really interested in Burnley as a place; I was interested in Burnley Football Club and if the club did well, that was all I wanted to do.

'The apprentices feared me? That's nonsense really. That's never been a real interest of mine. I always wanted to coach the finished article, not youth players. I never really had much contact with them; maybe at pre-season when we'd have all the players together and work as a whole group but then as the season got underway the youth team would go with their manager and the first-team would go with me.

'But, of course, if you're the manager, you're in charge. You won't achieve anything if the players run things and do what they want to do; you won't have a cat in hell's chance. You've got to have discipline at the football club and the apprentices have got to be prepared to clean the pros' boots properly and make sure the dressing rooms are clean. I like the places that I'm in to be clean; I don't want to go into the football club and find things grubby and dirty. That's their job and if they don't do it right and properly, I'll be on their backs.

'But it never occurred to me that they were frightened of me, they might seem a bit iffy about me if they'd seen me coming down a corridor, and then they might have been a bit nervous. But I've been through those sorts of things myself at football clubs, you know, when you meet directors and businessmen and you're a bit wary of them. But that goes on at all football clubs, it's not something that just comes with Burnley. Possibly the boys would walk round another two streets so that they'd miss me but I'd go along with that. I wouldn't mind that so much because that's what makes them know what they've got to do, and what they've not got to do, in order to achieve things and do something.

'But something that was a massive problem at Burnley was the "them and us" attitude which was behind what happened when I brought in John Sainty to work with the youth team. If you really knew John Sainty, you'd know that he is one of the easiest-going people you'll meet and an outstanding coach, so I brought him in because I thought he'd be a good coach with the kids. But, after reading Martin Dobson's article in the paper, it seemed that he got them to think things that really weren't there and he fed their minds with different things. I think that was really sad. Burnley at the time I went there needed a complete and utter clear-out, and start afresh. I went half the way. We got it going a bit but there were people in important positions who were making snide remarks behind your back; that's what happened at Burnley. You had to clean the club of things like that and start afresh, be it with all Burnley people, or people from outside Burnley, but it all had to be cleaned out.

'Now, bringing the kids along in a family-like atmosphere, encouraging them and so on, is exactly the way to do it, but my first job when I got to Burnley was not to get the youth team set-up sorted out with a view as to what was coming through in five or six years' time. My priority was to get that first-team going as quickly as possible. Burnley had just been relegated, they were struggling, and it was my job to get Burnley on the way again. But we probably went about it a bit too quickly and too strongly and with too many newcomers. But the intentions were to try and get them on their way quickly so we could then get on with getting the other things sorted out. Maybe if we'd got it going a bit quicker, then the younger players that left would have been there a bit longer.

'Financially what happened was that I spent money on what I thought were the right things to enable the club to get on the right track. That included paying wages that would motivate them and reward them and I wouldn't have it any other way. In football, it's not up to the manager to say what they want and what they want to do at a football club. If the club can't afford what you want, then that's where you need a good strong chairman. John Jackson liked the glory of being chairman of a football club. I know that for a fact. And he'd go along with you, he'd say, "Yes, okay, we'll take him, you can have him, get him in." And he'd make money available that probably wasn't there. And that would be wrong, but every manager in the country would take that opportunity, to spend money they haven't got if the club allowed them to have it, and I think that is what I did.

'It's up to the chairman. The manager can say that he wants a player and the chairman will tell him whether or not the club can afford it. If the chairman says the club can afford it then the manager will have the player. You could ask every manager in the county the same question and they'll give the same answer as me. The funds of the club are down to the board and the financial people at the club, not down to the manager.

'So yes, the board at Burnley backed me financially to a large extent. One or two of the bad buys I made were not down to the board. They were down to me, players like Gallagher and Waldron. We paid excessively for Waldron around £105,000. I thought he was a good player and we got him at the club and he couldn't play! It still goes on to this day. You think you know someone; you're looking at a player, sitting in the stands watching them, and then you get them to the football club and he can't do this or that and you wonder why you bought them. It's happened to most managers but unfortunately happened to me too often at Burnley.

'I can't spend money that I haven't got. If there isn't the money and I want players, I can't buy. But it wasn't like that. John Jackson was like me. He wanted Burnley to take off. He thought I was the one who was going to make it take off. He gave me licence to go and get players whether or not the club could afford it. I wasn't bothered about that, if we'd been a raging success, no one would have worried about whether or not we could have afforded it. It didn't work out that way, but the financial side of things was none of my business.

'John Jackson never really openly came out and said that we couldn't have any more. We got to the end of the season and things had not worked out as well as we had expected, we'd finished around eighth. He didn't like how the club was going on, he didn't feel the club was doing as well as it ought to be. There were a lot of snidey remarks and an "us and them" situation. And then I did an article about him in the *Daily Mail*. I went to a board meeting on a Monday after the Saturday game. He started talking about me and all of a sudden, he slammed a paper down in front of me. He didn't like it and he said, "I'm sorry but you're going to have to go." It was pathetic really and that was that. It was a relief, to be honest, he put me out of my misery. It wasn't something that I was willingly going to walk out of, but it certainly wasn't something that I was enjoying.

'John Jackson wasn't the fellow that I thought he was when he interviewed me for the job. He was without doubt one of the nicest fellows I have met outside the game. Inside the football club, forget it. He was not open with me and I didn't think he was sincere with me. He was a fabulous fellow to be with if you wanted a social night out but when he was inside the football club, he was a different person. As different as chalk and cheese. He was an incredible man to understand, to get to know, but at the club he was going behind your back. I had a couple of friends who used to come with me everywhere at the football club, and we socialised and got to know John well. We had some of the best nights of our lives out with him. But when you got back to the club, he made your job harder, made it more difficult. He did allow me that year to do basically what I wanted, but when that wasn't working out it didn't suit him. He had taken over as chairman, he wanted to be the chairman of a Burnley that had just won promotion, but it wasn't like that and it didn't suit him.

'I don't think promotion was ever on during the season. It was about getting the right set of players together who wanted to succeed. It was what I tried to do at Burnley, to get a group of lads together quickly and to try and succeed quickly. It can be done; I did it at Bournemouth when I got a lot of players in that I knew.

'I did well on small budgets at Norwich and Bournemouth. If I'd been left alone, I'd have done well at Burnley, I have no doubts about that. But you've got to understand what the club wanted, and what I wanted, Burnley to get back up again. Burnley were sinking and needed to be pulled back up to where they wanted to be, not where they were entitled to be. I always saw Burnley as one of the stepping stones to things happening. Burnley were a good football club; they played the game the way I loved it being played. I know that from the times I used to play against them. It was something that I admired and that was the way I wanted to go when they offered me the job. That was why I took Burnley on at that particular time and I desperately wanted to get them back on that level again.

'The more I think about it, the more I realise that it was never going to happen because there weren't enough people around prepared to give me the time and space to get things done. Given the time again, maybe I wouldn't have taken the same sort of players on, or some of the players that I brought to the football club. I certainly wouldn't have signed Malcolm Waldron. But I was there to get instant success; that was what the club were looking for and then to build on it from there.

'I think, yes, I promised too much too soon. If I'd gone into it a bit more carefully and a bit less flamboyantly, it would probably have been better for everybody, including myself. But that situation was not what I wanted; they got me in the club to get Burnley back up there again, that was my brief.

'Kevin Reeves was a massive loss. He and Billy Hamilton had a tremendous partnership. If you haven't got a decent striker, you can forget it, you won't have a team. We were blessed. I got Kevin Reeves in who was an international player, a good player, as good a target man as you could wish to have. And then we had Billy Hamilton, as honest as the day is long. The two of them went together perfectly. Then, all of a sudden Reeves has got this thing. At first, they thought it was a tumour, but it turns out he's got an arthritic hip and that was him out of the game. It was terribly sad and it took the stuffing out of the club. If we could have kept those two together, we might have been in business. Reeves made it all tick and that's why he was just a few years previously, he was a million-pound player.

'There were other disappointments. I was disappointed with Willie Donachie. I rated him as a great player at Manchester City but he wasn't a great player at Burnley. He didn't do his stuff at Burnley. And he wasn't too old and went on to play quite a few games for Oldham.

'Steve Daley was another disappointment. Me and the chairman flew out to the US to sign him. But he was an overrated player really. Manchester City paid £1.4m for him but he didn't do that well at City. In truth he probably wasn't a First Division player but I thought that at the level Burnley were playing at that time, he would do well, he'd be a player.

'Martin Dobson: the best thing I can say about Martin Dobson was that he was a wonderful player. As long as things were working out for Martin Dobson, he was a good lad. But I didn't like Martin Dobson. All of a sudden, he's got to battle for his place and fight a bit, and he didn't like it one bit. He didn't like the fact that I didn't see him as an automatic choice. His attitude was, "Who is this fellow coming in that doesn't play Martin Dobson? Who is he?" And I had all the respect in the world for Martin Dobson and for what he'd done at Burnley. He was an outstanding player and I loved the way he played the game. But I didn't know he was like that. All the others had been getting some stick, and he shouldn't because he's Martin Dobson? That was the problem with him; he was too fond of Martin Dobson.

'Yes, I took the captaincy away from him. As I've said, he was an outstanding player, and I can understand that others, especially the younger players, looked up to him and I admired him for the way he played the game. But I didn't like the way he played it at Burnley sometimes, and I was the manager, so I did what any other manager in the game would do. I left him out. I dropped him. And it's a problem sometimes when you leave players out. Players don't like being left out, but some of them knuckle down and show you that you've been wrong about them, which is certainly the reaction you are looking for.

'Did I have the backing of supporters? I think if I'd succeeded, they'd have come along but they were ready to say "I told you so" if it went wrong. And to be fair to them, they finished up right and I was wrong.

'Their feelings about me coming to the football club were right and the people who brought me to the football club were wrong to do so, because it absolutely didn't work out. Burnley and I did not go together in way, shape or form.

'I do understand that people did want me to succeed, not because I was me, but simply because this was their football club; and there were a few people at the club who were a delight to see every day. But I felt they were a minority. And it didn't do me any favours when ex-players criticised me in the press. They weren't Burnley fans but had just played at the club and stayed to live in the town. The papers would ask them about me and I was slagged off. And I didn't need that.

'But there were a lot of people around Burnley who I loved and to this day remain great friends but the best I can say to you is that Burnley and I were not made for each other. It's sad, really because it was such a good club but the impression that I got was that too many of the people there were defensive and hostile to anyone they saw as an outsider. There was a director there who used to come in and see me daily and talk to me about the chairman and some of the directors. He'd even ring me up to talk about John Jackson. He didn't like Jackson. He'd say that the rest of the board were of this opinion and that opinion, but then when we got to the boardroom, he'd turn completely against me. He'd follow the chairman every time. That sort of thing used to happen a lot.

'I took a lot of stick at Burnley but it did not affect my family or life beyond the football club. We used to get on famously with John Jackson's wife; we had some fabulous times around at their house. They were amazing people in some ways. So, I wouldn't say it affected my family, but I did become fed up of having to work with John Jackson and the whole thing had turned very sour by the end.

'The things that have been said and done since then have been too unkind but then people were being fed by a lot of ex-players. There's been a lot of nonsense and a lot of nasty things said about me and my time at Burnley and that has soured me with the place. Really, though, I like Stan Ternent, funnily enough. I admire the way he stood up to be counted when things weren't going well. There was an element in the club that wanted him out and he stood up to them and I think that was strong and brave of him. I still look for their results and I look at Stan Ternent and think he's done such a good job, a fabulous job. Yet it doesn't take them long to get on the old bandwagon does it, of criticising and giving him stick.

'I think that the impression I used to give of myself as a person didn't help. I can be brash and flamboyant but I can also be hurt quite easily. Ask anyone who knows me well and they will tell you that I'm an entirely different person to the one that used to be depicted in the press. The media have always painted Ron Atkinson and myself as champagne drinkers, but I don't like champagne. And yes, maybe I used to sit in the stand and have a cigar when I was watching the game, but so what? Plenty of people have done that; it didn't make any difference to how I looked at the game.

'I think it's sad but I wouldn't go back if I was asked to do a half-time draw but I have nothing against the people of Burnley. I wouldn't disagree that if there is animosity towards me it is based on leaving the club in a bad way in terms of finance and morale. I have said a number of times that I made mistakes. But, as good as some of the younger players might have been, the team I inherited was not good enough. The fact that they'd been relegated the year before suggests that.

'The mistake I made was to try and build the club up too quickly. If I had gone about it a bit more carefully, got just a few players in, say Reeves and Tommy Hutch, and then waited to see if we needed somebody else, then that might have been better. But the whole intention of my approach was to try and get Burnley back to being a top club, where they could be if we got the right players in. That was my sole intention. I didn't go to Burnley to try and destroy the club.

'Rightly or wrongly, what happened at Burnley has been laid at my door and some of the more aggressive elements at the club have seen me as an easy way out, to blame me for everything that subsequently happened. I do think that Burnley supporters are quick to get on the back of their manager, and this hostility towards me has continued. When I was at Shrewsbury, we drew Burnley in the FA Cup and they threatened me, told me not to come to the place, I mean, what's that all about? It hardly made me think well of the place; it made me think, "To hell with them. If that's how they want to be with me, then that's how I'll be with them."

'I wanted to be successful at whatever I did. Failure didn't do me any favours, and that's what I was at Burnley, a failure. I'd gone from Norwich to Manchester City and was one of the top six managers in the country. I was on a shortlist of three for the Manchester United job when it went to Dave Sexton. I was offered the Benfica job while I was at Manchester City but I turned that down. I didn't fancy it, as everything was going swimmingly for me at that time: I was recognised as a top manager. I was not sacked at Manchester City, I resigned because of all the nonsense that was going on there at the time.

'I can't say that it had been in my plans to go to Burnley after leaving City but when John Jackson came to see me, we had a meal together in Manchester and he offered me the job. I didn't look at Burnley as a Rochdale or a Bury; I looked at Burnley as a big football club. John Jackson desperately wanted to be the chairman of a First Division club; what would be better for John Jackson and Burnley Football Club than that? So, he flung money at me. I didn't spend it wisely, I made too many mistakes at the football club. But rather than sitting down and working out how we could get things back to some sort of normality, he's making remarks about me that I didn't like. So, I had a go at him and we parted company. It wasn't the best thing I ever did in my life but more than anything it was a bad thing for Burnley. It would have been better if the Burnley episode had never happened, for both sides.'

12

What the papers said

FOR THIS chapter we need to turn the clock back 12 months to the time of the appointment of John Bond. If you remember, he and John Jackson met in Manchester and he was offered the job there and then and told to say nothing. I wrote to John Bond several years ago and asked him about it. He was moving house, pressed for time but still had the courtesy to send a short reply:

'Dear Dave, I'm in the middle of moving house so you can guess this is a very busy time. But in answer to a couple of things you asked. I spoke to John Jackson in Manchester in the early part of the year and he told me after that, I had the job, but we couldn't let it out until the season had ended, and to go away and say nothing to no one. I presume he must have told the board I was the man because when the season ended, I had to wait a few weeks, then went and met the board, and was told that I was the new manager.'

'Manager's job is up for grabs' said the *Evening Star* leader on Wednesday, 18 May, when Keith McNee reported on the possibility of a big-name appointment.

The newspaper wrote, 'Burnley could go for a big-name manager in their bid to bounce straight back into the Second Division. That was made clear by chairman John Jackson last night after he saw the Clarets plunge back into Division Three after being beaten by Crystal Palace after only a season in the higher flight. He said, "There is no truth in any suggestions that we have someone lined up and waiting in the wings but we will take stock of who is on the market. With managers like Dave Sexton, John Bond, Tommy Docherty and Jimmy Frizzell currently looking for jobs we would be foolish to make an appointment without seeing who applies and what they have to offer."

'He added, "Frank Casper is a leading contender for the job which will be advertised from this weekend. We will be seeking a manager or player-manager and despite what has been hinted in certain quarters no players will be bought or sold until the new manager is appointed. We have come to a very sad point with relegation confirmed last night but we will bounce straight back into the Second Division. That is certainly the intention."

'Meanwhile Mr Casper, who took charge of Burnley team affairs after Brian Miller was sacked in January, was travelling back from London with the players today. He told me, "I am disappointed that the board of directors have decided to advertise the job. I firmly believe the players want me as manager and as I have said all along, I will be applying. It has been a difficult and trying time since I took over in temporary charge and I think it should be remembered that I have had to keep going without the assistance of a first-team coach. There has been added pressure on the players through not having a permanent manager. I am fighting for my job now and for my family's future. I just want it all sorting out so I can get organised for next season. Believe me I have strong feelings for Burnley FC and I am desperately eager to continue to help them."

'Skipper Martin Dobson who is likely to be playing again for one last season in 1983/84 told me, "The players want Frank Casper to get the job on a permanent basis. Obviously, the appointment is out of our hands because managerial decisions are not made by players. But the feeling in the dressing room is that Frank has a lot to offer our club and a few months is not sufficient time for him to prove himself."'

Casper's and Dobson's words fell on deaf ears. John Jackson never had any intention of appointing Casper. There was always the strong suspicion that neither was John Jackson ever particularly fond of Martin Dobson. It is pure speculation that Bond and Jackson had shared their views about Dobson so that Dobson was very early on earmarked as part of the clear-out. With Dobson also promoting Casper's credentials in the press, again it is speculation, but it would hardly have endeared him to Bond.

A year on, it was all over, with local man Granville Shackleton reporting in the *Burnley Express*:

'The 14-month reign of John Bond as manager of Burnley Football Club ended on Monday night. He was sacked by the board of directors after he was kept waiting outside the locked doors of Turf Moor. His departure was in complete contrast to his arrival last year when there was almost a carnival atmosphere to mark the appointment of the first manager at Turf Moor without previous Burnley connections.

'Bond's insistence that he could not do his job properly and that the club could not be successful until the board sorted itself out finally brought matters to a head. The three-man board of chairman John Jackson, managing director Derek Gill and vice-chairman Dr D. Iven called Bond to Monday's meeting. They had already been in session behind locked doors for an hour before Bond arrived at Turf Moor and the door was still locked five minutes after the time he had been told to report.

'Finally, his assistant manager, John Benson, was able to get a key to allow Mr Bond and himself into the foyer. The door was locked behind them, leaving a posse of pressmen and photographers waiting for the decision. That decision was inevitable, in a situation which had become one of whether John Jackson OR John Bond stayed, but not both.

'Shortly after ten o'clock and more than two hours after Bond had gone into the meeting, club secretary Bob Bradshaw came down the stairs from the boardroom and read out the following statement:

"It is with regret that we have to notify you that the employment of John Bond as manager of Burnley Football Club has been terminated. John Benson will take immediate charge of team matters."

'The pressmen were then hustled out of the foyer as Mr Bradshaw returned upstairs where the directors were still in session. At the same time John Bond dashed out of the door to his silver XJS to speed off to his Wilmslow home. He brushed aside reporters with a final, "I have absolutely nothing to say."

'And another chapter in Claret history had been written.'

Just one year and two months had elapsed since the triumphant appointment with its loud fanfares, brash statements, beaming faces and rash forecasts, to the late-night humiliating departure and the realisation that this had been just a futile exercise with a horrible ending. The club that had been solvent was now financially strapped, the family ethos ripped apart and the future now without any clear direction.

In his 2004 interview with Phil Whalley, Bond had referred to the ex-players who had 'slagged' him. They had given their views in the *Daily Mirror* in May 1987, just a few days before the fateful Orient game. Penniless Burnley were down at the bottom end of the old Fourth Division after a terrible season and ready to fall victim to the new rule that the bottom club would be out of the Football League and down into non-league football. The blame game was in full flow, scapegoats were needed and fingers were pointed. Reporter Keith Meadows wrote:

'John Bond was last night slammed by the stars for pushing Burnley down the road to extinction. The big names from the little Lancashire club's glory days are stunned and angry at its current plight. For Burnley, who still graced the First Division only 11 years ago, are now 270 minutes, three games, away from becoming the first casualty of automatic relegation from the Fourth Division to the GM Vauxhall Conference.

'And ex-Turf Moor internationals like John Connelly, Jimmy McIlroy and Brian Pilkington, and recent ace Steve Kindon, fear an even more unthinkable fate. For all believe that losing league status will lead to the death of a club whose stadium puts most grounds in the country to shame. But the shame is now all Burnley's. They dropped into the 92nd spot on Wednesday night and they are favourites still to be there, and nearly £1m in debt, come the final day of judgement a week tomorrow.

'Jimmy McIlroy, capped 55 times by Northern Ireland and, like many other former Burnley greats, still living in the area says with bitter irony, "Who would believe that a club that faced Manchester United, Spurs and Hamburg, would now be awaiting the three most crucial games in their history, against Southend, Crewe and Orient."

'The ex-stars are almost unanimous in tracing the major role in the club's decline and fall to the management of John Bond, now boss of Birmingham, and the chairmanship of John Jackson, as recently as 1983/84. John Connelly, 20 England caps and a flying winger when Burnley won the league title 27 years ago said, "The appointment of John Bond, by people who hadn't a clue how to run a football club, doomed Burnley. He brought in old players on long contracts and his name will never be mentioned with any favour in this town. I'd tell him to his face if he walked into my fish and chip restaurant. His track record is abysmal and I am flabbergasted every time he gets another job in the game."

'Kindon, another speed merchant in two Turf Moor spells, blasted, "This was never a club for a flamboyant fellow with gold rings. He received over £300,000 from Everton for Trevor Steven and went for crocks and old guard players like Gerry Gow, Tommy

Hutchison and Steve Daley. He spent money like it was going out of fashion."

'Kindon points to a big overdraft when former dictatorial chairman Bob Lord stood down. Connelly adds, "We ex-players have been involved in fundraising and hope to collect £20,000 towards new players. But our efforts will be wasted if Burnley go out of the league; I believe the club would fold. The big ground has been a noose round their necks and Bob Lord made a terrible blunder in building two new stands and then having to sell players."

'Kindon disagrees, "Lord did nothing but good for the club. This was the last of the Lancashire small-town clubs to deteriorate."

'Brian Pilkington, former Burnley and England winger, described the club's situation as pitiful and very sad, "Bob Lord won't just be turning in his grave; he'll be spinning in it. Burnley had a superb set-up when I was there and they are the homeliest club that I've ever played for. But this is all down to bad management from the directors over the years. And John Bond put players on long contracts and couldn't get rid of them."

'Harry Potts, Burnley manager until eight years ago, said, "When I was sacked in 1979, we were in the Second Division and had a good team. Naturally, it is very depressing to find them at the bottom of the league but where there is life there is hope and they still have matches to save themselves."

'A more recent Turf Moor hero, Trevor Steven, sold to Everton for more than £300,000, said, "It's very tragic. I'm hoping they get the results to survive and then make a fresh start."'

No wonder John Bond took umbrage at all this. Only one player was put on a long contract, Joe Gallagher, and, ironically, Gallagher was about to play in the Orient game after which he would be feted in true hero fashion. Connelly's comment that Bond's track record was abysmal was inaccurate; he had success at Bournemouth and Norwich and took Manchester City to an FA Cup Final. Steve Kindon's comment about spending money like it was going out of fashion made no mention of it being money he was allowed to spend by directors. Pilkington's comment that he couldn't get rid of players ignored the fact that he disposed of both Mal Waldron and Steve Daley not too long after he signed them. A waste of money yes, but quickly got rid of.

On Saturday, 21 January 1989 the *Lancashire Evening Telegraph* headlined with 'BOND BLASTS BACK'. The night before, Bond had appeared on Granada TV's *Kick Off* programme and answered questions put to him.

The newspaper reported on Bond's appearance, 'John Bond, the man Clarets fans love to hate, admitted last night that he made mistakes during his short stay in charge at Turf Moor. He faced the cameras to defend criticism of the disastrous 12 months four years ago that saw Burnley crash from the Third Division to the Fourth Division for the first time in their history. On Granada TV's *Kick Off* programme, he confessed he made errors but said he had no guilty feelings over anything he did.

'Bond, in the TV station's Manchester studios, faced a grilling in a live link with the members of Burnley's supporters' club at the club's Centre Spot.

'His biggest blunder, he said, was in sacking Frank Casper as coach, and bringing his own men in[32]. Bond was also forced to admit that it was a mistake selling Brian Laws and giving a free transfer to Lee Dixon, both defenders now starring at Nottingham Forest and Arsenal respectively. And he admitted it was a mistake to sign players such as Gerry Gow, Dennis Tueart and Joe Gallagher who he claimed was not fit when he joined the Clarets.

'But first he reacted to an accusation made by Burnley veteran Leighton James who claimed in a newspaper last week that during his time at Burnley, Bond had been out of touch with the man

32 He did not sack Frank Casper. That was done by the board of directors before he arrived.

in the street. Bond retorted, "Burnley were not exactly top of the First Division when I took over. They were in the Third Division. And maybe it was other people who were out of touch as well as me. And maybe it was down to people who had passed before I went there."

'Supporter Michael Rumney asked, "Despite your lack of success as manager, why do you always blame directors when you leave a football club?"

'Bond replied, "Well I wouldn't like to say that. If you were to speak to Sir Arthur South at Norwich, Harold Walker at Bournemouth and Peter Swales at Manchester City, they would not agree with you. I think I have had my fair degree of success within the game and I think that at certain clubs I have done well."

'Another fan, Derek Adamson asked, "You had Brian Laws and Lee Dixon at Burnley and released them both. Do you not consider this a serious misjudgement as they are both playing for top First Division clubs?"

'Bond said, "Just let me tell you, I hold my hand up about that, I am prone to making mistakes as you or anyone else is in life you know. At that particular time, we sold Brian Laws and I thought we got good money for him. I'm not saying we got the earth but we got fairly good money. Dixon? I didn't see it that way and I just let Lee Dixon go."

'Duncan Wood asked, "You brought three other Johns to the club, Benson, Doherty and Sainty. Do you think your loyalty to these three contributed to your downfall?"

'Bond replied, "Well I didn't see it that way. I think John Sainty was a great coach with me at Manchester City and I don't think he lost his way when he went to Burnley."

'Presenter Elton Welsby interrupted and pointed out that Bond had told him earlier that using the benefit of hindsight, he would have taken somebody with him who knew the club. Bond said, "Well I think that's the thing I did wrong. Frank Casper was in charge I believe just before I took over and maybe I should have kept Frank with me. I had no grudge against him. It was just that I wanted to keep my own men with me and maybe that was a big mistake not keeping him at the club because I do believe you do need somebody who has been at the club and who does know the club."

'Maria McWilliam asked, "You left Burnley with nothing, not even its once proud youth policy." Bond said, "You know as well as I do the players Burnley had when I took over. And I must tell you with all the talk that has gone on, I bought players in, the cost to the club of bringing players in was £308,000. And I'll tell you what they got back. They got £150,000 for Reeves in compensation and including that they pulled in £575,000[33]. You ask me how they found themselves in so much debt. I will ask you the same question, because I don't know."

'Paul Grace asked, "Why did you offer lucrative contracts to players that then left the club in dire financial circumstances especially as some hardly played for the club?"

'Bond said, "I will sit here now and hold my hand up and tell you I made mistakes with the likes of Gerry Gow and even the likes of Dennis Tueart. I certainly made a grave mistake with Joe Gallagher. But something you don't know is that it wasn't entirely down to me. When we got Joe down to the club doctor, I didn't think he was fit. We took him to a specialist in Manchester but the doctor came back and said he was okay. I didn't agree with the doctor but by that time we had to keep him."'

Fair play to Bond for facing questions. Communication was one of his strengths. John Jackson, meanwhile, said very little of his time as chairman. That is certainly no criticism. It is reasonable to think that he realised he had made mistakes and he certainly came

---

33 It's difficult to see how Bond arrives at this figure, unless he is including the Trevor Steven sale fee, a sale that was nothing to do with him, plus what they got back for Mal Waldron and the sale of Brian Laws.

to the conclusion that Bond was an unsuccessful appointment. Their relationship was a strange one, however; almost best friends outside of the club with each of them saying what a fabulous social companion the other was, but inside of the club each unable to get on with the other. Jackson explained this strange phenomenon in terms of wearing two hats, his social hat, and his chairman's hat.

Not until 1988 did Jackson make any real comment on his time as chairman and even then, it was a very short one in the Paul Fletcher booklet *BFC and Me*:

'1948: fan, Strong, Woodruff, Mather, Attwell and Brown. Forty years ago, I slept contentedly certain that these now legendary players would combine to create a team that would keep us at the top. 1988 and continuing status, fan. A combination of the finest support in the division, a united[34] board, and a settled policy that would keep us at the top. But still I dream, this time of promotion.

'In between: I first became a director and thereafter succeeded Bob Lord as chairman of the only club that has ever mattered to me. Burnley. When I became chairman in November 1981, there was no time for dreaming. The harsh reality was that we were close to the bottom of the Third Division, at our lowest ever position, under severe financial pressure, with dwindling gates, and a disenchanted public.

'The next four months were filled with instant decisions, the reduction of entrance prices, the recognition of the supporters' club, the re-organisation of both our finances and equally important our public relations. The results on the field were dramatic; only one defeat in 35 league games, combined with a meteoric rise up the table. Nothing could go wrong. Promotion was achieved at Southend. The championship was won. A bright future awaited. Perhaps on reflection it was all too easy.

---

34 By this time Jackson was no longer a member of the board. 'A united board.' Perhaps a pointed reference to the board that he was on that was anything but united, and when he was convinced that Bond and Gill were planning a takeover behind his back.

'Thereafter it went wrong with a vengeance. Despite two cup runs to remember, culminating in a night of glory at Tottenham, and two memorable games against Liverpool, we returned to Division Three. The nightmare events of the following two years and the reasons for them have been the subject of ill-informed comment from almost everyone but me and so it will remain. For the sake of the club, my only comment is, as we from Burnley say, "Only them as knows, knows them as knows."

'Let's remember the good times of the past and look forward to the good times of the future.'

The piece was short, cryptic and left people wanting more information about what really went on during those two nightmare years, for that is indeed what they were. Not until 2004 did Jackson agree to reveal his thoughts on what took place, in the first Burnley anthology that I wrote, *No Nay Never Volume One.* I was delighted when he agreed; the John Bond year at Burnley was, and remains, one of those subjects that sets people talking. It was also before I had met Derek Gill and seen his diaries. The 2004 article he wrote included what he wrote in 1988, so I have not repeated that part:

'The compiler of the various reviews of the John Bond season has suggested that the story would not be complete without some observations from the then chairman. Further, I have been asked to fill in a little background about my appointment, initially as a director and thereafter as chairman. In spite of remaining virtually silent for nearly a quarter of a century, I believe that the matters I now mention are now history, and it is time to reveal my thoughts about the year [it was these thoughts that prompted Derek Gill to take out his old diaries and update them].

'It is not my intention to reveal that some of our legends have feet of clay[35] but it is my intention here to show that a number of myths have absolutely no basis in fact. The only relevant factor,

35 I suspect he is referring here to Martin Dobson.

which is still present, is the obsession that I have with Burnley, which has affected my life and family for almost 40 years and still does.

'As I believe will be accepted by all, I am a lifelong supporter. I began behind the goals in 1947, moved to the enclosure where I was happiest and eventually moved to the stand. I felt I was near to God when Jimmy McIlroy bought my parents' house when he moved to Burnley, and my peripheral contact with the players continued when I sold my first home to Jimmy Robson sometime around 1967.

'In the mid-1970s I decided to try to buy some shares in the club and I discussed the matter with Jimmy McIlroy who told me that a friend of his, John Cook, the son of a former director had some shares for sale. I bought a sufficient quantity to qualify for the board and recall paying £5 each for around 100 shares. Although a recently qualified barrister, I spent more time trying to persuade Bob Lord to invite me to join the board than I did persuading juries that they should accept my client's version of events, and finally in late 1976 I succeeded. I was offered, and immediately accepted, the position of director.

'It is impossible to overstate Mr Lord's knowledge of football, and impossible to overstate the precarious nature of the club's finances at that time. Bounced cheques were not uncommon. During the next few years, I served an apprenticeship in every sense of the word. I learned a great deal about what to do and what not to do. It is now accepted that Mr Lord controlled virtually every aspect of the club's affairs. On most important matters, the directors were informed rather than consulted. The financial position and the club's resources were such that Mr Lord was content if the club merely stayed afloat. Consequently, and inevitably, we were close to bankruptcy and close to relegation when he decided to retire.

'The first myth to explode is the suggestion that I bought the club. What actually happened was that a consortium of four raised £52m in total to buy Mr Lord's controlling interest[36]. The apparently low price reflects two factors; the first was the dire financial position and the second was the distaste the general public felt for football in the early 1980s. The members of the consortium bought an equal number of shares and I was elected chairman. I in no way controlled the club; indeed, my position as chairman depended upon the support of my colleagues, a fact that John Bond was later to discover and even try to exploit. Consequently, after I became chairman, I felt it my duty to implement the views of the board, that is, to govern by consent. This view was later to cause me considerable problems. But more of that later.

'During the year, the board were obviously worried about the poor performances in the league. A meeting was arranged between Brian Miller, Frank Casper, George Bray, Doctor Iven and myself. The purpose of the meeting was to ask the management if the board could do anything to help. Brian assured us that he required nothing further from the board, and he was confident that his management team was capable of improving the situation. The discussions at the meeting were in themselves uneventful, but the attitudes showing by various people were later to affect important decisions made by the board. During the meeting Frank Casper made no contribution at all. At the time I understood that he agreed with everything Brian said and was giving support, albeit silent support. But was that the correct appreciation of events? Was it possibly the appropriate role for an assistant manager to play at a club, which inevitably appointed the assistant when the manager left?

'After the meeting we allowed the position to continue until after the fixture at Bolton. By then it was obvious to everyone that changes were necessary, and we replaced Brian Miller with Frank Casper. We invited Brian to stay at the club, but he

---

36 There is another report that the shares were bought for £35,999.84.

declined. Ironically, many supporters, including two who were later to become directors, urged us to replace Brian Miller. Later, I smiled when a board containing these two same supporters re-appointed Brian. Imagine my feelings when the club approached the Orient game.

'The decision to dismiss Brian was taken before the Tottenham cup tie. Bad timing? If we had delayed the inevitable, lost at Tottenham, then acted, the timing would still have looked awful. Did winning at Tottenham make the timing wrong? I don't believe so. No one could foresee those two own goals[37].

'Thereafter followed a dismal period under Frank Casper that ended in relegation. To this day I cannot understand the reasons why a team that included Martin Dobson, Billy Hamilton, Mickey Phelan, Brian Flynn and a young Trevor Steven was relegated. Whether it was because the players were not as good as we thought, as John Bond said, or because the leadership on and off the field was inadequate, as others have hinted, perhaps no longer matters. At the time the board had to decide upon the manager's position, and we came to the conclusion that promoting from within, someone whose only claim to the job was that he was assistant to the manager, was no longer acceptable. I must say that nothing that has occurred in the 20 years since has caused me to think that the decision was wrong. The production line that produced Harry Potts and Jimmy Adamson had come to an end.

'Thus, the board decided to appoint an outsider. I turn to the two most important myths that have surrounded the John Bond era so far as I was concerned. The first is that I had a particular influence on his decision to come to Burnley, and thereafter he was "my man" who I allowed to spend unlimited amounts of money.

'The applicants for the job were not as numerous as the press reported. The shortlist included John Duncan and Frank Burrows,

---

37 In the 4-1 win, two of the goals were own goals.

who were our second and third choices. Another candidate who was shortlisted was a former north-west manager. He didn't perform too well at the interview stage; he couldn't remember the name of the coach that he wanted as his assistant.

'During the discussions after the interviews I strongly supported John Bond and I voted for him. The unanimous vote of those present was cast in his favour and I offered him the job. As I am sure he will confirm, I didn't influence his decision at all.

'Immediately after his acceptance, I was excited. I was ambitious for the club. In my first year we had gained promotion and I was looking forward to the future. An ego trip? Perhaps a little harsh but not entirely unfair. Although the finances had improved, we were by no means out of the mire, and only Trevor Steven's decision to move on made any money available. As to Trevor's transfer, John Bond obtained from Everton 50 per cent more than the next best offer, which was from Terry Venables[38].

'The arrival of JB [Bond] had an enormous effect on the club. It would be unfair to minimise in any way the tremendous and dramatic uplift in morale. Burnley, nicknamed "Grumpy Town" by Tommy Hutchison, was back in the limelight for good reason. Whatever else John Bond was, he was charismatic and the club was alive and vibrant. At the time, and immediately after the appointment, the almost unanimous view of the town and the supporters was that we had made an exciting and courageous decision.

'As we expected, JB brought in new players and as we also expected a new assistant manager, John Benson. Although John Benson later failed at Burnley, many who knew him, including me, who knew him at Burnley and later at Wigan, rated him very highly. I often wonder about the support John Benson received

38 It's difficult to see how John Jackson arrives at this statement. Everything was sorted before Bond arrived at the club.

from some of the players during the year he was manager. I say that because Tommy Hutchison later told me that he himself hoped to replace John Bond and become player-manager. Tommy told me that when he didn't get the job, he was never thereafter able to support John Benson as much as he could have done. If only that had been known at the time, the history of Burnley FC may well have been different.

'The signing of new players, although anticipated, caused what turned out to be insurmountable problems later. The players split into two groups, the old brigade and the newcomers. John Bond was later to accuse me of always siding with the old brigade. I didn't intend to let it show but Kevin Reeves and Tommy Hutchison apart, I didn't see much value or improvement in the signings and valuable money was spent.

'After the euphoria, which began when his appointment had worn off, it became clear to me that John Bond was not the right manager for Burnley. I had totally underestimated the hostility that would be shown towards him by some members of the playing staff. In addition, I had not considered the parochial attitude of many people with whom John Bond was expected to work on a day-to-day basis. It no longer matters as to fault or the assessment of reasons, the time arrived when I no longer wanted John Bond to remain as manager.

'I turn to the next myth: that is that John Bond spent money that the club couldn't provide and that I let him spend it without any restraint. The truth is that JB never spent money that had not been made available to him by the board. However, how it became available is an interesting story.

'As I have explained, I felt it my duty to carry out the views of the majority of the board and at the time we had as members of the board two very successful businessmen, Derek Gill the financial director, and Alan Hutchinson. It was the financial director's view, supported by the majority of the board, that if we could make money available to the manager, we should do so and the manager should decide how it was spent. The view was, that businesses ran on overdrafts and we should use available overdrafts and other resources to buy players. "Let's get stock on the shelf," was a phrase I heard being used during the discussions.

'I disagreed with the financial director. I believed that football was not quite like other businesses. My experience in football has taught me that clubs could have a poor season both on and off the field, not necessarily reflecting badly on the board, the management, or the players. I believed that we should have retained money for a rainy day. Lawyers are generally more cautious than successful businessmen and I had seen enough rainy days at Burnley Football Club[39].

'It may well be that if Kevin Reeves had not been injured, and if Gow, Gallagher and Mal Waldron in particular had succeeded, John Bond would now be a hero.

'At that point I should have resigned as chairman. I believed we had the wrong manager and the club was pursuing unwise policies. If I had resigned, John Bond and the financial director would have been delighted and that was the main reason why I stayed. What happened thereafter was a financial disaster. John Bond would ask for money, the board would authorise it, and the money was spent. I had no enthusiasm for the manager and I showed it, and no enthusiasm for the policies. Not surprisingly the relationship between John Bond and myself was awful and deteriorating.

'Subsequently I have learned that discussions were ongoing between the financial director and John Bond without my knowledge of a nature that I now feel was unhelpful. It is important to remember that I was chairman only because the majority of the

39 This, of course, is at complete variance with John Bond's statement that the chairman "flung money at me".

board gave me their support. One matter of particular importance that I was made aware of at the time was a possible takeover of the club. An approach was made to John Bond. Thereafter, John Bond approached Mr Gill and a meeting was arranged to discuss the matter. Mr Gill later told us about the meeting but did not feel able to tell us the identity of the potential purchaser. In the event, nothing developed thereafter.

'As the season progressed, the relationship between John Bond and myself deteriorated, if that was possible. Publicly I had to support him and no doubt that is the reason why to this day, many people think he was "my man". I am confident that John Bond will confirm that this was as far away from the truth as could be imagined. In the circumstances, I take it as a great compliment that he did not approve of me as a chairman when he was manager.

'I would add this about JB: lawyers are able to, and are required to, separate personal from professional views. My decision not to support JB as manager was made wearing my professional chairman's hat. My personal view of JB as an individual outside the club was quite different. Outside the club, I enjoyed his company; he was charismatic, loyal to his friends and great fun to be with. My family enjoyed his company and did so on numerous occasions. Another example of the problems that arise when business and pleasure is mixed.

'In the next 20 years after the Bond and Benson era, Burnley appointed as managers Martin Buchan and Chris Waddle with no success. They reappointed Brian Miller and Frank Casper with no success. It was not until Jimmy Mullen, who was relatively new to the club, was appointed that success returned. It would appear that the lessons we should have learned took longer than necessary to sink in.

'Although my brief does not extend to mentioning other matters, I cannot let the opportunity go by to mention some events and some people. Perhaps like an Oscar acceptance speech, I will miss out some important events and some very supportive people. As to games: Southend and Tottenham were outstanding. As to people: the support of Dr Iven, Albert Maddox and Brian Miller, both at the time, and continuing to date, has been rewarding. It may well be, and I hope it is, that they believe as I believe, that whatever decisions I made, I made them believing they were in the best interests of Burnley Football Club.'

Look closely at the views and recollections of Derek Gill, John Bond and John Jackson. Each has his own version of what went on. A later chapter will attempt to make some sense of these varying accounts. To a degree, the journey that these three took is a reminder of the first stages of Dante's *Inferno*. 'Abandon Hope All Ye Who Enter Here' it says over the gates to Hell, and just inside are the uncommitted, those on the journey who are neither good nor evil. Then it is on to the first circle of the abyss where reside those souls who do not warrant damnation.

Abandon hope all ye who enter here might have been the inscription over the Burnley Football Club boardroom door at the beginning of 1983/84, for it was a doomed journey that they were undertaking with no hope of salvation. None of our characters ever warranted damnation. They were just three men who were fated not to get on together.

13
A shameful relegation

ROY OLDFIELD was the club groundsman at the time of the John Jackson chairmanship and the John Bond season. I am using parts of his account of 1984/85 which we wrote together in *Mud, Sweat and Shears.* Roy liked Bond and he liked Derek Gill. He knew Jackson less well, but found him a refreshing change from Bob Lord, not that Roy disliked Lord. On the contrary, he had huge respect and affection for him. But Jackson was just – different. You wouldn't have found Lord, for example, driving the dumper truck to clear the snow off the pitch in winter, as Jackson once did. You wouldn't have found Lord governing by consensus. You would not have found Lord taking part in a half-time penalty shoot-out with the opposing chairman as Jackson did during the Alan Stevenson testimonial.

It was a long, hot summer; it would be a long, drab season. Make no mistake, this would be a grim, joyless relegation with not quite one of the poorest-ever Burnley sides, but almost. The previous relegation did at least have the magnificent cup runs to lighten the gloom and financial security. But what was about to unfold was simply shameful at a club bereft of any ideas as to how to stop the rot. The popular line was to heap all blame on Bond; that it was his legacy, that he had spent all the money. But there was far more to it than that, something that Gill was able to acknowledge. Jackson too realised that the Bond appointment had been a disaster. Where the board were culpable was in not dismissing him as soon as they knew it was a flawed appointment.

Bond was now gone; the 'formal execution' as Gill called it, had taken place. Roy was sad to see him go as he got on well with him; Bond was unfailingly courteous to him and always appreciated the extra work that he had to do when the team trained on the pitch. Say what you like about Bond but he was personable, approachable, sociable and communicative. When Bond departed, mindful of how cold Roy was, sometimes working on freezing days, he bought him a beautiful warm sweater. Roy, now passed away, continued:

'Here then was the new season at Turf Moor but there was no money and a boardroom that continued to malfunction. It was a recipe for disaster. All this is now so hard to look back on with several years in the Premier League to be proud of, commercially successful, and well respected within the football community.

'With supreme irony, while Burnley were about to have such a dreadful season, just a few miles away, several ex-Burnley players discarded by their club were taking Bury in the opposite direction to success and promotion. Football can kick you in the teeth sometimes and at Burnley this fact of life was about to unfold with a vengeance.

'There were so many ex-Burnley players over there it was untrue. With supreme irony managed by Martin Dobson, released of course by John Bond, coached by the discarded Frank Casper, and Ray Pointer, inspired by the mercurial Leighton James, sprinkled with former Burnley players, while Burnley plummeted to new depths, this bunch of cast-offs took Bury to a fairy-tale promotion. Burnley director Derek Gill took note and had already earmarked Dobson for a return to Burnley as manager should he ever become chairman, an ambition he had. The other Burnley players there were Kevin Young, Terry Pashley, Wayne Entwistle,

Winston White and Joe Jakub. Their success rubbed yet more salt into the festering Burnley wound.

'James Bentley in his fine book *The Forgotten Fifteen* set the scene to the season, or at least one of the scenes. Burnley was no longer a mining town but there were still plenty of ex-miners around, and these were hard times in the industry. Not only that but the last major cotton mill had closed down so the once great industry of Burnley was now a relic. This was a fading and derelict town in 1984; a few new industries were arriving but overall, there was a pall of gloom over Burnley. Rejuvenation was a long way away and if Burnley people needed good news, it was not going to come from the football club, once its pride and joy, playing against the best teams of Europe.

'Bentley wrote, "The country was in the grip of industrial action the like of which had not been seen since the previous decade. Whenever the phrase 'miners' strike is used these days, it is always a reference to the dispute between Margaret Thatcher and the National Union of Mineworkers and secretary Arthur Scargill, that ran from March 1984 into 1985. The national strike was called by Scargill as rifts developed between miners who wanted to strike and those that wanted to keep on working. Years later they have still not healed in many communities. The pervading image of the strike all these years later is undoubtedly what became known as the Battle of Orgreave. The coking plant in South Yorkshire was the location of a mass picket by thousands of striking miners on 18 June, watched over by a similar number of South Yorkshire police. It was like something from the civil war, was one recollection."

'Meanwhile, under the wooden stand at Bury, Martin Dobson, having just been allowed to leave by Bond, planned for the season that for him and his team was to be a triumph on a shoestring. At Burnley, with a boardroom that still smacked of opulence, John Bond hadn't quite left and was still trying to hire players for the new season. He had just announced that he accepted two-thirds of the blame for the failures, angering supporters even more.

'Out went a whole raft of veterans he had signed and others he deemed not good enough, seven all told, and the local newspaper described all these changes as too sudden to take in. This had once been such a stable club where things changed slowly and gradually. Now it was as if there was a revolving door. On top of that was the bombshell sale of Billy Hamilton, sold to Oxford United for a fee far less than he was worth.

'Then, as Gill described, Bond went, just days before the start of the new season. Fans were left reeling, astonished, open-mouthed and wide-eyed. Their club was in a shambolic state with no money and when the board appointed John Benson as manager, he was the fourth in just 20 months. Keep in mind that Tommy Hutchison would have loved the job had he been asked. If supporters then thought that Benson could steady the ship, how wrong could they be?

'The team that at the beginning of the Bond season was rated as favourites for promotion was about to sink like a stone into the Fourth Division. Former club historian Ray Simpson summed it up. It was beyond comprehension, he wrote. It was shameful. In his extensive history of Burnley Football Club, *Clarets Chronicles*, Simpson summarised the sorry tale:

'"Benson's Burnley won just two of the first 11 games. Player of the Year Derek Scott fractured his leg in the 3-2 defeat against Rotherham. The ghost of John Bond continued to hang around the club as the former manager announced he was to sue the club, alleging breach of contract and claiming damages for wrongful dismissal. He would indeed have his revenge but not in court. The writing was on the wall and with firepower a glaring problem and precious little money to solve it, the Clarets lay a lowly 15th in a poor division with a quarter of the season played.

'"Brian Flynn, the Welsh international, was made available for transfer at his own request and a 5-1 hammering at Reading was the final straw for one Burnley fan who wrote to the *Burnley Express*, 'When you have been brought up on caviar, you cannot be expected to watch tripe.'

'"Benson argued that a good side had not become a bad one overnight. The results, however, begged to differ. Six defeats in seven games poured oil on the troubled waters of a reported £300,000 debt, blamed by all and sundry on Bond's disastrous transfer dealings. Even a 9-0 FA Cup victory over non-league Penrith, with hat-tricks from Wayne Biggins and Alan Taylor, failed to lighten the mood.

'"Such was the growing concern that former Burnley player Jimmy McIlroy, now reporting for the *Burnley Express*, penned a front-page leader in the local paper following two humiliating Christmas defeats to York and Bristol City, 'To believe that things can only get better is to believe in miracles. I have to concede that nothing short of a miracle can stop the rot and the unthinkable, Fourth Division football next season.' But in Burnley miracles were in short supply.

'"Burnley started the new year with another home defeat as the icy weather accentuated the shakes that supporters were already suffering. The month-long hiatus and the enforced winter break initially seemed to benefit the team with a convincing 7-0 win over Rotherham. Back-to-back wins over local rivals Preston and Bolton made it just one defeat in five games as the sunshine of spring replaced deep winter. But the month of postponements left Benson's men with a punishing schedule of two games a week through March and April and this had a devastating effect on the players. Just one win in 15 games saw the crisis deepen.

'"Burnley skipped into the dreaded bottom four following a home defeat to Bournemouth that attracted only 2,655 fans. Looming large was an end-of-season decider against Swansea, now managed by John Bond. Swansea were one of a handful of teams fighting to avoid the drop along with the Clarets. Taylor's goal allowed Burnley to breathe again in a dramatic 1-0 win at Swansea but a dreadful home defeat to Bristol City by the same scoreline undid all the hard work and kept the nerves jangling. An emergency board meeting 48 hours before a trip to Walsall, a game that would decide Burnley's fate, a meeting at which John Jackson announced he was to stand down but retain his place on the board, only served to increase the tension.

'"Despite a heroic 3-2 win at Walsall, there would be an anxious six-day wait until Swansea and John Bond finished their own fixtures to clear up the final relegation place. Burnley held its collective breath knowing that John Bond's side needed just one point from their home game against Bristol City. The blackest week in the club's history so far was sealed when that game ended in a 0-0 draw. The immediate aftermath saw John Benson fall on his sword and Frank Teasdale took over the chairmanship of the club just four months after being appointed as a director."

'How ironic that John Bond played such a role in Burnley's relegation. Football does this. The man that supporters vilified, and have continued to disparage ever since over the years, then played the final part in this disastrous season. One horrendous display in a 4-0 defeat at Bristol Rovers had been described as a pathetic joke by manager John Benson. Now down at rock bottom, fans wondered if things might improve; after all, they couldn't be relegated any lower than the Fourth Division. Or could they? The club's troubles were far from over but at that point nobody knew it. Nobody knew how low they could sink; how close they would come to utter failure and humiliation. But, hope springs eternal, and there is no hope as optimistic as that which belongs to a football fan.

'If it was one of Burnley's worst ever years then the same could be said for football in general. It was a time when football, by and large, was played in conditions where spectator comfort and safety were not yet under the spotlight. Public perception, that is to say the way that non-football fans viewed it, was, according to the *Sunday Times*, that it was a "slum sport, watched in slum conditions, by slum people".

Many of us looking back can take exception to being described as slum people, but the slum stadium description was apt enough. The jury at the Hillsborough disaster trial in Warrington judged that the stadium was inadequate and unsafe. The ladies' loo, back then, at Doncaster Rovers was a bucket in the corner of an old brick hut with an earth floor. The men's urinals at Turf Moor were a disgusting, foul-smelling disgrace and for good measure were right next door to the food shack round the back of the Bee Hole End terraces. The season 1984/85 has often been described as football's most troubled, faced with growing hooliganism and confrontations between rival football gangs, the Bradford City fire and the Heysel Stadium disaster. They were not good times. Derek Gill's diaries certainly record the trials and tensions of the season, but we shall leave those until the next chapter.

Mud, Sweat and Shears revealed more, 'Gill had been able to forecast that the club would face overheads of £237,000 in the 1984/85 season. Budgeting difficulties, he knew, lay in the lottery of gate receipts that were allied to playing results and progress in cup competitions. But to offset the vagaries of attendances was the Billy Hamilton money, spread over a 12-month period and the insurance proceeds of the Kevin Reeves retirement. On top of that were the possible sales of quality players such as Michael Phelan. A financial godsend was the League Cup tie against Manchester United. Of course, Burnley were thrashed but gained something around £50,000. Derek Gill was on holiday and phoned several times for updates of the scores, but in truth all he wanted to know was the attendance at Old Trafford from which he could compute the probable financial take.

'The good fortune of this windfall was enormous but Gill was always wise enough never to anticipate such bonuses or to include them in any predictions. He knew full well the age-old football truism, that a failing team produces declining attendances, this then reduces income; and this is a self-accelerating downward spiral. Prophecies of doom thus become self-fulfilling.

'Thus, the search was on for more directors who might bring with them, if not a little bit of investment, then at least some enthusiasm and know-how. Gill surmised that only anyone who was crazy would join. In the meantime, groundsman Roy Oldfield knew little of all this, and why should he, as he toiled away in all weathers feeling less and less appreciated. Years later he might well have appreciated knowing that Derek Gill felt that at times, Roy got a raw deal.

'Two would eventually join the board in January 1985, Frank Teasdale, and Lancashire cricketer Jack Simmons, although it must be said neither was crazy. There were no fools on the board, said Gill; each man in his own sphere was an accomplished expert. It was only when they were together that they could not cooperate.

'New funds came into the club when those with a bit of money could become vice-presidents, at a fee of course. The club needed all the help it could get especially with the bank pulling away its previous generosity. The season had started with the club up the creek without a paddle and although it now had a paddle in the shape of the worthy John Benson, it was still being carried along in a current of poor results, dwindling gates and mediocre players.

'Roy had heard some of the rumours and whispers and stories of boardroom unrest, but what could he do. All he could do was get on with his job and ignore the caustic atmosphere. But he had great respect for Derek Gill. "He was a man you could talk to. He listened and was very fair."

'Benson from the outset was of the belief that Martin Dobson was the obvious choice to replace John Bond but for that to happen it needed Gill to become chairman. To do that it would need Gill to remove John Jackson as chairman, and at this point he was not prepared to do that.'

The whole football season was marred by two terrible events. As Burnley were heading down, Bradford City were heading up. Sadly, they played in what one might agree was one of the 'slum' stadiums written about in the *Sunday Times.* The Heysel tragedy was the second catastrophic event.

Mud, Sweat and Shears explained, 'They'd had a great season at Bradford and the cameras were there on 11 May to record the Division Three trophy being presented at the last home game. More than 11,000 people had turned up to watch the game and as the interval approached, John Helm commentating noticed fire starting in the main stand. Within a minute the flames spread so that people scrambled to get out of the stand. Helm at this point comments that he hopes the whole stand won't burn down but within a minute it is clear that this is exactly what will happen. The fire is now raging and smoke and flames billow upwards while more people try to escape. In less than two minutes the fire is spreading alarmingly and there is raw panic.

'It was when the roof caught fire that the next stage of the horror began, as felt and bitumen and timbers fell on to the trapped spectators below. Exits were found to be blocked and Helm continues to describe the scene as the cameras show the appalling scenes. Supporters are now being dragged out of the inferno; the images are distressing as people with burning clothes are lying on the pitch with others trying to beat them out. Within just four minutes, a disaster and tragedy of an unimaginable scale had developed, killing 56 people and injuring hundreds more with awful burns.

'Liverpool had travelled to Belgium and the Heysel Stadium for the European Cup Final on 29 May. In a season that had already seen dreadful scenes of hooliganism at grounds across the country, this football disaster now gave football a simply awful image. Poor segregation, Liverpool fans spilling into areas not designated for them, flimsy fencing, inadequate policing, fans in attack mode and finally a collapsing wall all added up to another horrendous incident.

'With 14 Liverpool fans found guilty of manslaughter and sentenced to three years in prison, Heysel is sometimes seen as the nadir, the absolute rock bottom of the hooligan problem; 1980s hooliganism, by now labelled the English disease, was rampant throughout the decade, with 1985 seen as the worst of times. How ironic that in the 2016 Euros, the organised Russian mobs that ran riot referred specifically to the gang warfare that had pervaded English football 30 years earlier.'

It was proposed that all football fans should have ID cards, but they never saw the light of day. The objections were too plentiful.

Only once in the notes that Roy kept of his daily efforts to keep the pitch in a playable condition did he refer to the state of the team, when he noted that it was the worst he had ever seen. His time at Turf Moor dated back to the early 1970s and the team that Jimmy Adamson put together that he said would be the 'team of the '70s'. Roy had then seen the decline of the late '70s and the very early '80s, but this was now, he said, as bad a team as he had ever seen. There were many matchdays, as he sat on his old pitchside wooden bench in front of the Cricket Field Stand, that truly saddened him, watching this inadequate team flounder.

Jimmy McIlroy, in his local newspaper role, wrote that it was a team devoid of understanding. All three departments, defence, midfield and attack, looked inadequate and incapable of obtaining results:

'It goes without saying that when a side is down, it seems to take more than its fair share of setbacks; though to be fair, a lot of the disappointments that have come the Clarets' way are of their own making. It doesn't help matters to hear the mindless chants from a section of the Burnley fans of "Benson out" or "Bring back Martin Dobson". What's needed is blood and sweat, fellows who are prepared to run until they drop, to rectify mistakes, chase hopeless balls. In other words, simply refuse to be licked. If there is a message to be passed to the people who hold the fate of this once great club in their hands, the players, the staff and the directors, it is, "Get your fingers out and set about restoring some lost pride."'

His piece had no effect whatsoever. There was no surprise in that. This was now a board incapable of arresting the rot, of stopping the inevitable and fast approaching relegation to the Fourth Division for the first time ever.

'Wednesday, 22 May: manager finished today,' Roy Oldfield wrote in his diary. Another season over, a boardroom in turmoil, supporters wondering how it could be any worse and asking who would be the next manager. For directors, in particular Derek Gill, the question was where would the next money come from to pay the bills?

Tim Quelch adds to the story, 'After Bond there were no radical solutions and the opening game against Plymouth Argyle (1-1) attracted just 4,664 to Turf Moor. Benson's team included newcomers Peter Hampton, Kevin Hird, Barry Powell, Neil Grewcock, Alan Taylor and Neil Whatmore unfit, the makeweight striker in the Billy Hamilton deal. Brian Flynn could only make it to the bench. Neil Grewcock took the honours, giving a fine display of wing play.

'Burnley won one, drew four and lost two of the opening league games and succumbed to Manchester United 7-0 on aggregate in the Milk Cup, after Mark Hughes scored a hat-trick at Old Trafford.

'Up front, Grewcock has been a major influence. You wonder what he has been up to in the last few years. When he gets the ball, he goes straight at defenders and more often than not beats them to get into good positions. Unfortunately, his shots and crosses could be better, but at the moment there is no one really to cross to anyway. If only Billy Hamilton had stayed.

'Wayne Biggins, and, at times, Alan Taylor tries hard but they do not have the aerial power to cause big defenders any problems. Taylor's ball control has let him down too often and the midfield players do not seem to have any understanding with him when they hit a pass. The forwards don't look as if they can do the business. Whether a fit Whatmore will solve this problem remains to be seen. Whatmore, in fact, scored only once in nine games and was offloaded on to Mansfield in March having spent a period on loan with them.

'Flynn was dropped and transferred at his own request to Cardiff for £20,000 after appearing in the disgraceful defeat at Reading (5-1). Burnley had actually led at half-time. Flynn's sale enabled Benson to purchase Geoff Palmer and striker Les Lawrence, but by now the crowd had lost faith. Only 2,916 turned up for the midweek victory over Brentford, a new post-war low. Mid-table obscurity became the new target. Crushing defeats were experienced at Bristol City and York, both of them 4-0. Band Aid asked "Do They Know It's Christmas?" Burnley could have asked the same question.

'As expected, Burnley went out of the FA Cup at Second Division Wimbledon. [Roger] Hansbury put in a transfer request and this brought Joe Neenan to the club. The icy January weather provided much needed respite for Burnley's dwindling supporters. Amazingly, it seemed to rejuvenate the team. Immediately after their enforced break Burnley took Rotherham to the cleaners 7-0 with Kevin Hird scoring a hat-trick. It won Burnley the Fiat Performance of the Week award of £500 and a new strip for Barrowford Celtic boys' team. Thereafter, the magic disappeared.

'Trying to restore the magic, Benson arranged a pay your own five-day break to Majorca. He insisted it was not a holiday but training in a different environment. It did the trick. Just the prospect of the trip lifted Burnley sufficiently to overcome Preston 2-0 and on their return from Majorca, they overcame Bolton at Burnden Park 3-1.

'Life did not get any better though. Burnley promptly lost their next four games and did not manage another victory for 11 games. The die was cast. The board reduced admission prices to £1 for the final three home games which helped swell the gates to around 4,000 but did nothing to help the team's form. Apart from a home victory against Cambridge and an away win at John Bond's Swansea, the results remained dire. Benson described the 4-0 defeat at Bristol Rovers as a joke, but no one at Turf Moor was laughing. Even a final-day victory away at Walsall could not stave off relegation to the Fourth Division, another new low. Top-20 pop group Simple Minds warned "Don't You (Forget About Me)". But after the Bradford fire and the Heysel crush, many of us wanted to forget all about football.

'Chairman John Jackson resigned and so did his expected successor Derek Gill, leaving new director Frank Teasdale in the hot seat. Benson left the club by mutual consent, so the managerial merry-go-round was given a further spin. The inexperienced Martin Buchan, assisted by Tommy Cavanagh, were the board's final choice as replacements. Derek Scott and Mike Phelan both refused to re-sign, Scott moving to Bolton for £20,000 and Phelan to Norwich for £70,000. Hutchison rejoined Bond at Swansea. In came goalkeeper Joe Neenan permanently, Ray Deakin and Jim Hegarty.'

If anyone thought that Buchan would be the answer and that there would be a quick exit from the Fourth Division, they could not have been more wrong. Near ignominy and oblivion was just two seasons away. An unthinkable seven years in the bottom division was about to follow as a now penniless club eked out an existence, with the fans' fingers pointing at Bond set to continue.

14

The boardroom soap opera

IN HIS March 2005 notes, Derek Gill recorded, 'The meeting at which the formal Bond execution took place saw the addition to the board of Basil Dearing, a hardworking local solicitor. I regarded him as a capable man who would bring a bit of much needed energy into the place. Around the turn of the year, we took on two others, one of whom was destined to become chairman within months, and the other, although willing, found himself unable to devote much time to the club. The first of these was Frank Teasdale, whose claim had been canvassed by John Jackson for many months and for those months I was against his appointment.

'But he did a great service to the club, fronting in my absence a meeting with Multipart that resulted in a beneficial shirt sponsorship for us. I had initially taken the view that he was very lightweight and flippant, almost acting the village idiot part. His performance with Multipart caused me to reconsider and for a time he gave every indication of becoming a first-class director. However, the manner in which he turned at me behind my back in gossip and insult with John Jackson led me to think I had been correct the first time.

'Jack Simmons was the other new boy and after initial enthusiasm found the commitment impossible for him, due to his cricketing roles.

'I was well aware that John Jackson now had friends on the board, but in my innocence thought that my obvious commitment to the job, and my knowledge of the inner workings of the game, would neutralise any biases. I could not have been more mistaken.

'I am ever more amazed that I battled on within the board of a club, a ship without a rudder if ever there was one. But what a fine man was John Benson, disparaged by Frank Teasdale among others, making his job so much more difficult. No set of directors ever won a league, but there have been plenty over the years who have had the opposite effect and we were a prime example. Would I and the club have been better off if I had just packed my bags there and then and returned in due course to say, "I told you." That will never be known.

'What I do know is that I would be better off by some distance if I had never set foot in that lousy boardroom.'

* * *

Gill's original diaries read, 'The close season was not totally barren and we had made a few free transfer signings and at least had a full squad in place to start the new season. There were four free signings comprising Alan Taylor, Kevin Hird, Peter Hampton and Phil Malley. No one can argue with any fairness that this did not represent sensible dealing at the level we were required to play.

'My personal disappointment was the decision to release Willie Donachie but I had learned my lesson from the sale of Brian Laws when I stuck my oar in to no effect. These signings comprised the final legacy of John Bond and if anyone wishes to argue financial irresponsibility, let him come forward. Between them, these four appeared 437 times excluding any entries as substitutes and does give some credence to John Bond's view that any mistakes were behind us, and the best bet was to battle on regardless. This is precisely what I resolved to do but only after a great deal of agonising, as by this time I was on the verge of leaving the club out of frustration as much as anything else. I was nominally the managing director but unable to put into place the policies that I believed to be necessary. Responsibility without authority, a lethal combination.

'Relative to our status at that time, our facilities behind the scenes were most opulent, having been approved and gloried in, by the late Bob Lord. These had been way out of bounds to ordinary mortals even being ludicrously named after the chairman himself by his fellow directors, supposedly to his surprise, according to the telling of the tale by the travelling commercial manager, Jack Butterfield. For any reasons, it was both pleasing and sensible for John Jackson to open up this cloistered area to sponsors, and a new breed to be flatteringly described as vice-presidents, at a fee of course. Naturally this attracted a goodly few who could raise and were sufficiently interested to invest the annual subscription, which localised the best rumour factory in the town, and gave open house to some of the loudest mouths around. But it did have the benefit to us of aiding pre-season funds and consequently the income from season tickets which might have been a total disaster managed to raise almost £60,000, which at that time was a real boost, even though it was around 25 per cent down on the previous year.

'It was no secret that the club was going to be very hard-pressed to keep its finances stable without selling one or more of the better players, and it was even less of a secret that our signings did not have the marketability of those on contract at the same time, the previous year. It is a classic vicious circle known to every football club outside the top few, and even they can fall victim to it when things do not go their way. Then the dilemma is simply that income will not meet costs without player sales and if the better players are sold, then income will drop still further. Therefore, clubs like Burnley are hostage to fortune both on the field and to the backing of their local communities. The per-capita income for

Burnley, relative to its catchment area, was a great deal lower then, for many of the reasons I have tried to explain, and put simply we needed all the help we could get.

'The poison remained un-sucked and it is difficult now to resist the odd wry smile when I recall some of those who turned against the club and were nothing less than obstructive to our needs. These were the self-same who thought that they should be wheeled around on sedans to the best seats when the big cup ties were being held, such a short time before. It was also more than instructive to note the numbers who awarded themselves the right to free entry tickets on matchdays, and I was less than impressed by certain senior managers of substantial companies in the area who attended at the expense of their PLC employers, and imagined themselves to be experts in waiting. They were ever ready to offer "why did you not do this" or "why did you not do that" when anything went wrong. Or, when the dice dropped our way, it was "oh, I always knew that". It was strange that those who rarely put their hands in their pockets had the most to say. One might ask, "Who needs enemies?"

'The arrival of Plymouth Argyle to open the season was almost upon us and the management of the team had yet to be resolved. Most managers have the luxury of losing about half a dozen games before the ritual vote of confidence, the prelude to imminent dismissal. But we were nothing if not different having sacked our incumbent during the week prior to kick-off. Up the creek without any kind of a paddle is an understatement and there was no other option other than to throw John Benson into the hot seat there and then. Mindful of the unhappy experience of Frank Casper as caretaker manager when we had dismissed Brian Miller, it was decided that the only course was to offer the position permanently to Benson and then hope like hell.

'John Benson is a man out of the top drawer and I would trust him with any confidence and I would also know that whatever job he was given, he would do it to the best of his ability. I think that he was more popular with the players than his erstwhile boss, and judgement becomes secondary when one simply has no alternatives.

'It was left to me to speak to Benson and I had a long and frank exchange with him confident I was in discussion with a man capable of separating issues from personalities, and who was tremendously forthcoming about his concern that he might not be able to do this difficult job to satisfy either the board or himself. In a most honest manner, he told me that he would have preferred to continue to act as a number two, and be prepared to give it his best shot as assistant to whoever we chose to bring in. Looking at the contracted players at that time, the board reasoned that there was nobody to step up. John Benson, however, told me that, in his opinion, Martin Dobson was the obvious choice despite not having the slightest suspicion that I had a letter from Bury guaranteeing his release. John Benson is a very straightforward man and asked me simply whether or not he was being offered the job because we thought he was the right man for the job, or because we could not afford to meet the balance of our commitments to him which had almost two years to run. I spoke honestly about our dilemma and we quickly had a rapport from which the spoken word was as good as a contract.

'Based on mutual trust, Benson could get down to work and he tried tremendously hard to succeed. Not being a fool and also more than alert to the insecurity of his tenure, he made a most unusual proposition to me, which says more about the man and the relationship I had with him. Being as close as he was to John Bond, he could hardly be insulated from the boardroom manoeuvrings or rumours thereof, and he was one of the group that thought I was destined to become the real boss of the club. This might have been tacitly understood but was certainly not a subject for conversation and I always avoided getting into that type of discussion with him and indeed tried to be evasive even when the gossipmongers were in full cry.

'Benson knew that my long-term ambition was to bring back Martin Dobson as manager if ever I was in a position to do so; and I suppose it is true to say that many others had come to this conclusion with only Dobson unaware of it. Mindful of this, Benson concluded that his reign would be a short one and that if managerial changes meant that he would be out of work, he suggested an amendment to his contract, the like of which I have never encountered before or since.

'I have no intention of disclosing his salary except to say that it was modest and that in all probability less than would have been demanded by a replacement. The proposal was that he would reduce his earnings by 20 per cent for two years, in exchange for an agreement to guarantee him no loss of net income for a third year, in the event of his dismissal. He reasoned that this would give him breathing space should he need to get himself established elsewhere, and which he also said would be outside football. We both knew how fleeting employment was as manager of Burnley and I agreed, giving Benson and the club the time and opportunity to concentrate on the real issues of the day.

'After leaving the board, I was abused and ridiculed by two directors about the Benson arrangement who separately based their abuse on the grounds that I had agreed to make payments to a past employee with no benefit to the club. The desiccated explanation of what finance men refer to as DCF (discounted cash flow) gave the impression to me of being way beyond their understanding, but in essence it is simply a statement of the obvious, that money paid out at a later date is preferable and less costly on interest alone than cash paid forward. With interest rates and use of money combined, there is no doubt that the Benson arrangement was beneficial to the company, and if any of my successors wish to be enlightened further, I can supply them with plenty of financial references to check it out.

'There were two impediments preventing me from pushing at the board for the return of Martin Dobson. Firstly, there was antagonism between Dobson and chairman John Jackson, which alone made it impossible without the removal of the chairman, which I was unwilling to instigate. Then there was a serious and monstrous extra-contractual arrangement with Dobson that had been entered into by the then Football League vice-chairman, Bob Lord, no less. For the good of Dobson, I will not go into the detail but it is sufficient to leave it on the basis that money promised to Martin when he signed for Burnley from Everton, the same Everton whose conduct over the Trevor Steven transfer was so immaculate that I blush to mention it, had not been paid. It was an arrangement that had Lord been sitting in judgement on any other club would have caused him to come down in righteous indignation like a ton of sausages. Martin had long since left our employment before I was able to conclude something for him and I treasured his personal letter thanking me for my part, as had Brian Laws before him. On men like that I rest any case I might wish to put.

'The new season was with us, and now committed to Benson and, with John Sainty also having left after his short stay, we had to follow the logic of Benson's appointment by allowing him to bring in his chosen assistant and the choice fell on Ian McFarlane who interestingly had been the preferred choice of another well-known manager[40] who had been interviewed in Monty Python fashion the previous year. McFarlane joined us early in the season and pleased most people by immediately moving into Burnley, something that neither Bond, Benson or John Doherty had been prepared to do. And, with parochial mentality in the town, was destined to be a permanent negative for them. They were disparagingly referred to as the "Manchester Set", as if they had come from another planet[41].

---

40 In his 2005 interview with Phil Whalley, Gill revealed that the interviewed candidates – Bond had already been told that he was to be the new manager but to say nothing – were Jimmy Frizzell, Ian Duncan, Ian Branfoot and Stewart Houston.

41 Much later into the 1990s, it amused Gill that some of the most vociferous objectors to where Bond and his staff lived were perfectly happy that Jimmy Mullen, who took the club to two promotions after the horrors of the Fourth Division, resided in Blackpool.

'P for Plymouth day arrived. We set off with five players making their debuts and the ground was in a most subdued state. Having once told the press that I would never feed them a bad line, I went back on this undertaking on a little matter that seemed quite harmless at the time, but had its amusing consequences. Like my own boys, John Jackson's son preferred to watch matches with the real supporters and in his case, he enjoyed standing behind the goals where one of his delights was to imbibe in a meat pie at half-time with his pals.

'Amongst the more important matters discussed at board meetings was the seriousness of meat pies being cold or unavailable on many occasions. Nobody dreamed that this was a matter of interest to the press but we were acutely aware that there would be more than a passing interest in the size of the crowd after all the sensational publicity we had attracted during the week. Clever sods that we were, or rather I, with the chairman's connivance, decided that we would add 2,000 to the published attendance, thinking that the miserable gate that we expected would fuel the discontent even further.

'As if to prove that we did not get everything wrong, the gate on a perfect day was a derisory 4,644, but the press reported it as 6,644.

'All good stuff of course except that John's lad and his pals were unable to buy their pies at half-time and the way the match was going, that would indeed have been the highlight. Needing every penny that we could take, the chairman questioned the catering manager on the unavailability of pies behind the goal area. But he was utterly lost for an answer when he was told that this was the result of the gate being much higher than expected. Somewhere in there, there must be a moral. The match itself was drawn as Burnley managed a late scrambled equaliser which was received in a sort of eerier quiet by the few spectators that had endured the game to the finish.

'Well before the season began, I had prepared budgets for the year and one of the difficult assumptions I had made was for an average gate of 6,000. The indifference of the crowd was more potent than any level of abuse or jeering, and we all feared for a drastic drop in revenue. Budgeting expenditure in the football club was not difficult once elementary systems had been put in place to replace the primitive wet finger in the wind records that had passed for financial control before my time. It had been back on 5 March 1984 that I issued a preliminary budget indicating total overhead costs of £237,000 and the published accounts for that year show that these costs were kept to £219,860, with most of the savings made where I least wanted them; namely, on scouting costs. I would take anybody on at Burnley Football Club on any test of financial management with one eye closed and both hands tied behind my back.

'The budgeting difficulty therefore does not relate to anticipating expenditure, but to the lottery of gate receipts which ally closely to playing results and the degree of progress in cup competitions. To me then, the obvious method of presentation is to assume elimination from the cup competitions at the first hurdle and arrive at the worst position which might then result. In doing so, there is created an awareness of the doomsday scenario and with good time in which to institute any corrective action. In our case, as with all the lower-division clubs, this means a realisation of the optimum time for the transfer out of any valuable player. Basing my projections on these parameters and for this particular season being faced with the possibility of no shirt sponsorship, I had to conclude that a loss of £209,000 for the year might ensue and which could only be reduced by transfer receipts. To break even we needed the utterly unrealistic average attendance of 13,600 and our position could not have been clearer. With the bank taking an ever-hardening line, despite the undeniable fact that they themselves had done much to push up borrowings, and had suddenly withdrawn their shirt sponsorship, we were placed into a far more difficult spot than could have been imagined, so very recently.

'Having agreed to take the Billy Hamilton transfer money over the normal 12-month period, I was sure enough of reasonable stability so long as the insurance proceeds for the forced retirement of Kevin Reeves came through. Still in the background was the possibility of having to sell one or more of the better players, of whom Michael Phelan was by far the most valuable, but also capable of commanding high fees were Wayne Biggins, who had done so well since coming from the non-league scene, Vince Overson with his aches and pains well and truly behind him, Derek Scott who had finally tired of seeing players better rewarded by moving around, than remaining loyal as he had done, and Brian Flynn still under 30 and widely respected.

'Disturbingly, for a net-selling club, the transfer market was going through a quiet period and there was little confidence in the game overall[42], so that consequently the values of these players were far removed from the mad figures now so common. But it was still not contaminated by agents and associated conmen, so that civilised dealing remained the practice of the majority.

'Ironically, I did not realise just how high profile we were and myself in particular, until I made an unannounced and surprise appearance in a publication, which might be said was the crown of my career. Nobody bothered to tell me of course, but to his intense amusement a friend of mine sent me a copy of his schoolboy son's comic called *Match Weekly,* in which a fictitious sort of poor man's Roy of the Rovers played at Burnley in a cup tie, and yours truly made a highly unrealistic approach to sign a star player. We were daft enough, without a doubt, but even Burnley drew the line at signing

42 A reference to the hooliganism and general malaise in football with the 'image' of the game at a low ebb.

players from schoolboy comics. This came back to mind when TV news, no less, carried a piece in February 1993 announcing the retirement of the aforesaid Roy of the Rovers. Would you believe that his shirt sponsor was the same TSB who had dumped us so unceremoniously? Oh, how the would-be mighty were fallen.

'Next on the schedule for our delights was a rerun of the previous year's League Cup fixture with Crewe Alexandra to visit us on the first midweek Tuesday night, varying only from the disaster of the previous year in that the first leg was at our ground. Before the pitifully small crowd that barely exceeded 3,000, we were two goals down in no time at all and "déjà vu" was just not in it. Mercifully, new signing Neil Grewcock reduced the deficit after an individual effort that took him almost the length of the field, and we were relieved to lose only 2-1, which fairly indicates the depth of the gloom which was pretty much all pervasive. We had nowhere to turn and wandered off to Doncaster for a Friday night fixture which was duly lost 2-0. The return half of the Crewe fixture had to be faced the next week and we were more than normally uptight for this one.

'In all circumstances I thought that John Benson was most positive and by that only measure we appreciated how Burnley played much better and led Crewe by the only goal at the end of 90 minutes. And even better, glory be, we managed to score twice more in extra time to get us into the hat for the second-round draw when by the rules of the competition we were assured of a draw on a home and away basis with a club from the top divisions. Our greatest hopes were realised when the news came through that we had drawn the biggest financial fish of all; it was Manchester United. It could have been better only if the first leg had been at Turf Moor, as even our eternal optimism was hard put, to imagine that we might win this one. The best hope was that we could keep the margin at Manchester down to reasonable levels so that the game at Burnley might at least have some semblance of interest, beyond the rare opportunity to see some of the game's top players in action.

'I estimated that the draw would be worth some £50,000 to us, and so it proved, even though the first leg was lost 4-0. The second was just one goal better for us but the essential side of it to us was the boost to cash that would pacify the bank. Crucially for us there was a breathing space in which to take the long road to stability which had once been tantalisingly within our grasp, but lost through the weakening of the team when transfer deals failed to produce the essential balance, and matches began to be lost with ever-increasing frequency. And then as we always see, the attendances fall off and the downward spiral accelerates and the prophecies of doom become self-fulfilling.

'The board now was comprised of John as chairman, with David Iven[43] vice-chairman, myself as managing director (now there's a laugh) and Basil Dearing attending to any legal affairs. Prior to him joining the board I had not looked on Basil as a hardened football man but on joining he always discharged any jobs quickly and efficiently and was never afraid to give an opinion on all aspects of the club's affairs. He and I would never be particularly friendly or close, but I began by respecting what he tried to do and felt that matters in his domain could be left safely in his hands. He was clearly a hard worker in his own profession as a solicitor and he was willing to meet to discuss club matters before normal daily working hours. However, this idea of his never took off as indeed it was bloody hard work to get the full board to meet at all, let alone at such a novel hour.

'On balance, however, I have to go on record as saying that Colin Sanderson was a better director for the club and I remain regretful of my part in his resignation a year earlier. Probably this is because I felt that Basil was a Jackson man, and as was to be the

43 Frequently referred to as 'the lodger' by Derek Gill.

case with Frank Teasdale, I suspected that there was too much talk to which I was not privy, and in the ultimate, was to be the major factor in my eventual resignation.

'The trial marriage of a board with just three of us, supplemented as it happened by the lodger, who stayed in place so long that gravitation laws needed rewriting, to explain that he outlasted us all, had become discredited and the search was on for more director fodder. I suppose our standing was now at a rating so low that it would preclude anybody with half a brain from wanting to join us, but this did not stop us from imagining that being a director was still a prize to be coveted. Who better than I to know this, when I recalled my own reaction to the stunning possibility of this place in the sun? The ideal candidate was seen to be one that combined blind support for Burnley, and as near crazy as one could get away with. It would also be a great bonus if we were able to find someone with the time, diplomacy and knowledge to deal with Lancashire County Council, as the licensing authority, who seemed to delight in giving us as hard a time as was humanly possible, without in any way minimising the importance of the safety of spectators.

'My summer had been spent almost entirely devoted to the administration of Burnley Football Club and I was over-ready for a holiday once the season got underway and I had completed all the pre-season work and preparation. I knew that in any board disagreement which might be construed as being personal between the chairman and me, there was no doubt, I suspected, where the sympathies of David Iven and Basil Dearing would lie. This was all the more ironic as John Jackson and I still retained the ability to differentiate between issues and personalities.

'John had long canvassed the claims of Frank Teasdale, another friend of his and who was very close to John Gilbraith. The family company that bore the Gilbraith name was our most reliable and best sponsor and if consideration was due in any quarter, it was surely the Gilbraith connection that headed the queue. If we were to invite Teasdale there was an overriding necessity to avoid offending John Gilbraith, as when all was said and done, it was his firm that was coming up with the sponsorship money, and the company retained the Gilbraith name.

'Frank Teasdale had done a great service for the club in introducing me to the management of Multipart and helping to persuade them to take on the shirt sponsorship vacated by TSB. There is no doubt at all that this could not have been achieved without the Gilbraith involvement which was handled with real dexterity by Teasdale on behalf of the club, and when I sat in session with them, I was content to watch Frank effectively conclude this crucial function for us.

'For me at Burnley Football Club, it was a new experience and from that moment I was ready to approve Teasdale's appointment which I have to confess to previously opposing. I had judged him from a distance as being lightweight and difficult to take seriously but I was now ready to put up my hand and say that I was wrong. Another Jackson man maybe, but one with whom I felt sure that I could work productively for the good of the club. The approach, if there was to be one, was put on ice, while I went off on holiday.

'My holiday had taken me to Barbados on a post-season cricket trip with the Lancashire county club, demonstrating that I could never get away from sport. It meant that I missed the glamour trip to Old Trafford. Not quite being on the same wavelength as an evening trip to Scunthorpe or Notts County with the reserves, for which I would be and was the one and only volunteer, I hardly need add that there was no shortage of volunteers for this one. I kept in touch with three telephone calls for the latest score and soon the more important news about the size of the crowd from which I could compute the probable financial take to us; much the most important aspect when it was quickly obvious that we were going to lose quite heavily.

'Taking part on that tour was everybody's favourite Lancashire cricketer, "Flat" Jack Simmons, whom I knew to be a Burnley supporter from his days sitting near to me in the Hundred Club, which was an exclusive part of the main stand area, doubtless so named because it seated about 80 supporters. I also knew that Jack knew the Gilbraith set and got on well with them as indeed he did everybody that he came across.

'Jack and I spent much of that holiday discussing the club and I do not think that he suspected that in my way I was assessing the chances of getting him to join us along with Frank Teasdale. There was no doubt that he was another Burnley fan and when I invited him to come over and see the set up, he agreed without hesitation. On my return to the club, I mentioned Jack as a possible to John Jackson who welcomed him when he was assured that he was genuinely Burnley. After both Teasdale and Simmons had the chance to fully understand just what they were letting themselves in for, they eventually joined the board, in January 1985.

'How little could a decent and unscheming man like Frank have imagined that just four months later he would be thrown into the chair, I can only guess. And despite certain matters to which I will return in due course I could only wish him well.

'Writing this now some time after he took the chair, I was pleased for him that all the hard work he must have fulfilled and the uncouth abuse that he endured has at least paid off for him, in seeing the job through to a stability for which he has to be given much credit[44]. Lucky he undoubtedly was with unimaginable increases in gate revenue, but those who were so ready to abuse him and blame him when gates were on the floor should have the good grace to now give credit. When all is said and done, there is no crime in being the recipient of a large slice of good fortune,

---

44 Gill was able to see that Teasdale stuck it out, oversaw the survival of the club and the win over Orient in the last game of 1986/87, and then saw them get to Wembley in the Sherpa Van Trophy, the year after. No mean feat.

and then the real test comes in the manner in which one's good fortune is put to use. On that score I am not so sure he scores so highly, but more of that anon.

'The playing season stuttered on in a desultory sort of way and the vibrant atmosphere of the early Jackson days had been replaced by a ponderous indifference throughout the club that translated itself into a sort of demoralised apathy among supporters and the crucial fundraisers. The bandwagon jumpers on the town council, unquestioned legatees of the best seats on better days, put in their own two penn'orth by demanding a fee of £2,000 for their consent for a lottery stall in the town centre. Needless to say, there was a surfeit of knockers and freeloaders still expecting royal treatment.

'During October came the first home game to be played before fewer than 3,000 spectators including the aforementioned and the pre-paid season ticket holders, and with the apathy affecting the playing staff as it will always do in these circumstances, our results were up and down with more emphasis on the downs. Another relegation had not entered our heads, unthinkable surely, as the bloody Third Division was bad enough. We used to talk stupidly about the excellence of our facilities compared to our peers in that league, but conveniently forgot that many of them had the disconcerting habit of defeating us where it mattered.

'Despite the relatively recent Casper experience, the fate of a manager invariably hangs on playing results and Benson having estimated all this, like the sensible man he is, continued to work very hard and, of the four managers with whom I had experience, spent by far the most time with the reserve team players, and went so far as to register himself as a player with the Central League side. He turned out on the field on numerous occasions when he felt he could be of most use and encouragement to the youngsters and trialists. Score him where you will as a manager but I tell you, and nobody is better placed than me to know what was going on, he considered being manager of Burnley to be a great honour and he gave it his very best shot from the first day. In between playing for the reserves and his midweek first-team duties, he rarely missed an opportunity to get about and look for free transfers or bargains. I would defy anybody to work harder. A very good number two, I would conclude for John Benson and it was his misfortune to be thrown in at the deep end of a club in paralysed turmoil.

'Repeating my earlier assertion that there were no fools on the board, we knew that we could do no more than dig in, at least until the insurance money for Kevin Reeves came in. Obviously, this meant that even glaring team weaknesses could not be corrected by new signings, and the collapse of income from the gates, lotteries and sponsorship implied that we would be compelled to use the Reeves money for day-to-day running costs when it finally arrived. This would fly in the face of the TSB edict that our overdraft should be spent on new players and not dissipated on the running of the club.

'Players normally completed their contracts at the end of June, with the year obviously depending upon the contractual length in each particular case. One of the arts of establishing playing contracts is to ensure that there is never the possibility of a mass exodus at any one time, and thereby ensuring that renewal negotiations can be conducted without undue pressure on the club. Throughout these years we had maintained a known wages ceiling for playing staff, and although signing inducements and kick-backs were excluded, it was a principle that we kept to this wages ceiling and did not allow it to be breached.

'But: by now the year-old chick incorporated into Joe Gallagher's contract was about to hatch and come home to roost. It will be remembered that Joe had negotiated an inflation clause into his agreement that meant he had to be paid an extra five per cent or so, for the second of his four-year deal. Having originally adopted the attitude that next year was a long way away, and we had supposed that we might simply upgrade the others on the top rate, we found that the overall cost of maintaining the principle exceeded the limit of the top wage commitment. As a result, for the first and only time, I was in an embarrassed relationship with our key players such as Phelan, Flynn, Hutchison, Scott and Overson. I never remember having to lie to any of them because the question was never put to me, but it remained a betrayal of an undertaking that their wages were the best that the club was paying to any player. The absurdity of it all was the lunacy that Joe, although registered with the club, was not taking part in any competitive matches, with the entire club at odds with the medical expert, on the issue of his fitness.

'Signing goalkeepers from schoolboy stories was still to come, but the tragicomedy of having your highest-paid player barred from training and doing no more than keep his head down and draw wages was not far removed from fantasy. Joe was so apart from the club that he did not even attend Turf Moor on home matchdays. His calm and composure in view of it all remains a matter of astonishment.

'I have already tried to show that John Benson was nothing if not a pragmatist and on taking up his job I had acquainted him with the limits of wages costs payable in total and to any individual player. Quite rightly he argued that either Gallagher should be paid up or he must be made to play for his money. Still snookered by the medical opinion, John Jackson and I brought Joe to the club on a Saturday prior to a home match and put it to him that he was not fit for professional football and we were fully entitled to terminate his contract by giving him the necessary six months' notice. Joe is bright and knew how to stand his ground, possibly knowing that he could produce an independent medical opinion via the players' union to confirm his fitness.

'The manner in which he was being ostracised within the club must have placed him under great strain, but his outward calm was remarkable. The question was, how much would he accept to terminate his contract "by mutual consent" and John and I made an offer of a capital sum very close to one year's full earnings. He seemed to imply agreement but resurrected the alleged promise of an ex gratia payment that he claimed had been made to him, and which had first come to my attention after his first appearance for the club in the opening match of the Bond season at Hull. Put in a nutshell, it came down to Joe agreeing to confirm his unfitness if the termination payment met his demands. For me, he did not have a leg to stand on, and for football purposes certainly only had one, however it was viewed.

'I prepared a three-page letter-cum-agreement for him to sign when he was to meet John and I later, but now having gone home and thought things out, and presumably taken advice elsewhere, Joe would not budge from his requirement, which if I conceded would have given him more than his entire contract was worth. I therefore wrote the appropriate letters to terminate his contract and then inevitably found it to be subjected to appeal at the Football League headquarters in Lytham.

'I was confident that the documents I had prepared and the undoubted evidence that could be called from any professional football watcher would prevail, and this unhappy marriage would be ended, hopefully with as few recriminations as possible. I was in the office when one of our directors appeared and the subject of Gallagher came up. I could not believe my ears when he calmly announced that he had rung the Football League and told them to ignore my letter. For probably the only time, I exploded in front of the office staff as what he had done was to undermine me and worse, make the presentation of our case to terminate Gallagher's contract dammed near impossible. The Football League must have thought we were crazy and that the right hand did not know what the left was doing. On the latter they would be correct. How I now regretted the loss of Alan Hutchinson and Colin Sanderson, with whom at least I would have had some sensible dialogue. For me came the dreaded realisation that although I was nominally the managing director, there existed more than ever whisperings behind my back. If I could have obtained the authority, and had the strength to do it, I would have shifted the entire board out of the place and kicked it into shape with a new crew.

'To this day I do not know if this director acted unilaterally or in conjunction with other directors but I attended the appeal hearing with John Jackson, anticipating the worst. Gallagher was represented by Gordon Taylor of the PFA, and he took John Jackson apart in the presentations.

'The preamble to this case meant that our presentation was fatally handicapped before one word was spoken and even a highly skilled and supremely articulate barrister like John Jackson had little chance. Our credibility was nullified as a result of my letter and its subsequent repudiation by another director's phone call. John had decided to base our argument on the fact of previous agreement to the termination of his contract, and that the only area of difference lay in the determination of the amount of compensation due to him. How easy it would all have been if we had had the backing of our own medical evidence.

'Pure farce, nothing less. To have alternative or superior viewpoints put to me by supposed colleagues, and then following these through in a business-like way by requiring me to retract my original letter is one thing, and although it might have caused me some slight internal embarrassment, it would not have left the club looking so silly at the hearing.

'In my heart of hearts came the bitter realisation that my days at Burnley were numbered.'

15

A scapegoat is needed

IN HIS diaries, Derek Gill said, 'Recollections of my final few months are easy to recall. Enough was enough and my decreasing interest was noticed and by now other members of the board had been made aware that I would not be prepared to carry on at the club if behaviour within the board did not change and I repeatedly pointed out to them the dangers of the administration of the club being concentrated almost entirely in my hands. Indeed, the computerised records were being prepared through my private business and it was rare indeed if a day went by without my presence in the club.

'The absurdity of it all demonstrated itself on most matchdays when my attendance at away fixtures became irregular to put it mildly and John Benson went out of his way to let me know that the players were commenting on it. It was serving to confirm the lack of respect for the board as a whole and throughout the entire club there was little attempt to disguise this. Relegations do not arise solely from results on the field; they are largely pre-determined by cock-ups behind the scenes.

'When a labour of love turns to drudgery, time starts to drag on, and deteriorating interest shows through in many unexpected ways. I found myself engaged in my own business when Friday afternoons came round and filling my diary with

Friday appointments which precluded me from making overnight trips. One of the enjoyable perks of football directorships is the ability to visit other clubs and enjoy boardroom facilities. These can be particularly pleasurable when there is an interest in the result, but one that falls short of making or ruining the weekend.

'Of all the clubs that I had visited I enjoyed Blackburn Rovers, our nearest and greatest rivals; a statement that will undoubtedly not endear me to some Burnley fanatics. Consequently, I got into the state of never needing much of an excuse to miss Burnley's longer away trips and toddle over to Ewood Park with my wife who was equally at home and at ease with the wives of the Blackburn directors. Inevitably, I was the butt of some bantering but it was all good-humoured and I never left the club without feeling grateful to them all. To me it gave the impression of being run exactly as I would have tried to run Burnley if the opportunity had come my way. Long after I left football it was only necessary for me to pick up the phone to be given the same friendly hospitality and I stopped asking for tickets only because I did not want to cross the line between welcome and toleration. I will always be in the debt of Terry Ibbotson, Rob Coar and Len Neale, whose friendship was so genuine. How I wish they had been Burnley supporters.

'Shortly after Frank Teasdale became a director, my wife Kathleen and I picked him up and took him to Ewood for his first visit as a director to a match not involving Burnley. Even that managed to rebound on me. Kathleen explained to Frank how pleasant it was at Blackburn with all the directors seeming to pull together, giving such a good atmosphere throughout the club. The comparison with Burnley could hardly have been more marked and as if to underline it, the next news saw me being quizzed by John Jackson, wondering if my wife was a Blackburn Rovers supporter. I went so far as to tell this to Rob Coar, to which he made the obvious comment, that it was no wonder we were in such a mess.

'The jury were out in the [Joe] Gallagher appeal and no genius was needed to anticipate the outcome. John [Jackson] was required to leave to attend to his own affairs and I waited for the verdict which upheld Joe's appeal against dismissal and reinstated him as a registered player. On behalf of the club, I accepted the decision, having no alternative whatever I might think about his fitness or the "agreement" with him. I undertook that he would be instantly returned to the fold and treated on an exact par with the remainder of the players. Joe hardly looked impressed with my commitment which I relayed to John Benson at the earliest opportunity.

'Benson's reaction was perfectly predictable, and faced with Gallagher's wage costs out of his budget, he immediately determined to use him on the field. For once, my private ideas on a player's capabilities coincided with those of the manager who had no doubt that a fit Gallagher would be far too good to be anything other than an automatic first-team choice. It so happened that Michael Phelan, easily our best player, was soon to be injured and a defensive vacancy occurred. We were due at Preston and our then modest expectations were on something of a high with two consecutive home victories behind us. Bravely, Benson threw Gallagher into the gap, and every pre-match prognostication was confirmed. Joe did everything that could possibly be expected of him but as soon as he was exposed to turning in one direction, his immobility stood out. We got away with it for 80 minutes and were leading by 3-2, but then the inevitable happened and we surrendered a late goal to leave the match in an unsatisfactory draw.

'Joe was tried again for the next fixture but the same difficulty was apparent and he had to be substituted. Nothing should detract from his ability as a player and there remained no doubt at all that a fit Joe Gallagher would have stood head and shoulders above the other defenders. But: everybody apart from our medics could see that the man was handicapped beyond repair. Incredibly Joe did play out his full contract[45]. The remainder of the season saw him engaged in Central League games, apart from two other appearances necessitated by injuries to preferred choices. He was one who never stepped remotely out of line and kept strictly to himself any thoughts he might have harboured about his rather weird situation.

'After I had left the club, Joe contacted me at my home regarding the alleged promise of the "ex gratia" payment but had to accept that it was out of my hands, and in any event would not have been paid even if I had remained at the club. It was two years more before I had occasion to speak to him again and this time it was in the sponsors' lounge at Turf Moor after the famous Orient game that had resulted in Burnley retaining their league status against all the pre-match odds. The wine flowed freely that night and everyone was in party mood apart from Joe. I mentioned to him that he seemed subdued and he agreed, with the stunning rider that he was saddened as this had been his last match and his playing career was finished. I knew that he was only 32, calculating in a flash that this must be so, as he had been 28 when we signed him on the four-year contract. In all innocence I asked if he had been offered a new contract and if not, there was plenty of time for him to get fixed up elsewhere.

'"What, me?" says he. "Who the hell will take me with my knee?" Game set and match to Joe.

'Back in October/November 1984, Benson was faced with the consequences of the retention of Gallagher and the effect on his playing staff budget. Of still more importance, the entire club financing was beginning to flounder, and we needed to anticipate further deterioration of match receipts, resulting from

---

45 Gallagher played just once in the Bond season, five times in the Benson season, not at all in the Buchan/Cavanagh season, but he played 41 times in the 'Orient Season' for Brian Miller including the very final game which just had to be won. With supreme irony, it is for this that he is written forever into the Burnley history books as a hero.

unsatisfactory playing results, plus the lessening of bank interest. I was containing costs across the board (apart from the drinks cabinet) and at the end of October our financial statement disclosed a surplus for the first five months of £48,492. As my reputation among some later bead counters has been questioned, I have to confess that it might have been £48,491 or even £48,493, as the figures were displayed only to the nearest whole pound. However, I trust this is near enough for the thrust of my argument. I knew that this positive balance could not be sustained by normal trading, but we were still not in receipt of the proceeds of the insurance claim for the Kevin Reeves injury. By now we were in no doubt that the claim had been substantiated and the only outstanding matter was to wait for the wheels to grind slowly through, and the cheque to come to hand. But as anyone who has ever had to deal with insurance claims of this type will know, there is no certainty until the cash is banked.

'To our discomfort, shoes were leaking at the bank and feet were not so much cold as frostbitten. I will always contend that the bank's refusal to give us some very marginal leeway at the time of the Hamilton transfer had lost us the best part of £100,000 and it was blindingly clear that any further deterioration in our relationship with them would have severe repercussions on us. Therefore, I brought forward discussions for the review of our overdraft facility. The bank laid out ideas for the utilisation of the Reeves insurance money and specifically ruled out "dissipation of funds" on day-to-day requirements and insisted that funds would not be utilised for training, or improvements to club premises, etc. The bank considered that the proceeds should be applied in the acquisition of players [and told us]:

'"If the funds were not to be spent on players, then perhaps you may consider a reduction in the facility."

'I responded at length by letter explaining that our income comprised three basic elements, namely: one, match proceeds, gate money, sponsorships. Two, profits from lotteries, etc. Three, transactions in the transfers of players both in and out. In further amplification I confirmed the damned obvious that the first two elements could not cover normal running costs and concluded … and here I quote precisely:

'"… that the essence of the exercise is to retain the better players as long as possible, but to work in the knowledge that if and when maximum borrowing is approached, then outgoing transfers, being as I said one of the three main elements of income may need to be implemented. The art is in the timing and you may be assured that the club will not permit itself to get into a position whereby we are forced into a sale, such as was the case with Billy Hamilton. And consequently, fail to receive the optimum price."

'At least that managed to prevent a reduction in our overdraft facility and the bank wrote noting our intention to strengthen the playing staff but omitted any reference to dissipation of funds on running costs. I suppose that I won on that one but there was no possibility of allowing all the insurance money to go on new players. We restricted our outgoings to the very modest signings of Geoff Palmer from Wolves and one Les Lawrence, then trundling the rounds at Rochdale. Les was signed for a small fee and was one of the first I saw to turn up with some sort of financial adviser, or life assurance salesman, depending on the point of view one wished to adopt. It did not matter to us as his wage requirement fell easily within our limits and there was no question of signing-on fees or anything so exotic. He did, however, hold another insurance policy of which I was totally innocent and this was some sort of individual policy from which he could draw if he was unable to appear because of injury. It came to light later when it was necessary to certify certain periodic absences due to injury, but the rub on us was the dawning that in his situation, he was on better money being injured than when playing for us. I will not infer that there was any impropriety about this in his case, but from our standpoint it was a nonsense. It was just another for your education I thought, and I could not help but wonder how many others still lurked beneath the surface, waiting to be discovered.

'Palmer's signing was straightforward enough except that he lived in the Midlands and did not give the impression of being too eager to move into the locality. So, I agreed with him that we would meet petrol costs for three months only until he got himself to the area. He was just 30 years of age and we could reasonably expect a few years from him. He was one who just got on with the job, he was no bother of any kind, but never moved house and I was not surprised to see him transferred back to Wolverhampton after one year, by which time I was yesterday's man. But to the best of my belief, Geoff gave good service while he was with us.

'Now and again, however, it was necessary to turn attention to other matters, even sometimes to football matches, but the board was made aware that the bank no longer looked on us as flavour of the month, and day-to-day income needed a boost. The decline had to be arrested and, as it was unthinkable that the board itself might have some responsibility, a scapegoat had to be found. The spotlight fell on our young, enthusiastic and likeable commercial manager, Wayne Dore.

'There cannot be many aspects of business that are worse than needing to labour on, when one's interest and commitment is on the wane. I regret that for a time I found myself in that category. My heart could never totally abandon Burnley Football Club, but at the same time I could have abandoned that board of directors with the greatest of ease. There were times when I thought that I could pick a few names at random from the telephone directory and not do any worse. Worse than incompetence is indifference, and when indifference combines with arrogance, there is only one way to go which is down. And that is precisely where we finished in every sense of the word.

'The board seemed to find difficulty in reconciling the depletion in commercial receipts with poor playing results, which were no doubt themselves influenced by the unhappy atmosphere in the club, the direct result of the shambles of a board. I felt, and had often said, that one of the worst features of the board arose from it being comprised entirely of professional men, with Jackson the barrister, David Iven the doctor, Basil Dearing a solicitor, and me an accountant. Of this motley crew I was the only one engaged in an industrial capacity and it struck me that barristers and doctors especially, and solicitors to a lesser extent, were in contact with ordinary mortals at stressful times, and there was a danger of appearing patronising or worse.

'Of that board it is probable that I was the only one who had ever been in the position of having to carry out the dismissal of a senior manager on a face-to-face basis. And, I had not forgotten the disgraceful way in which we terminated the employment of Brian Miller. Consequently, when the board decided that Wayne Dore was the cause of all our ills, I volunteered to be the one to break the news to him. Naturally, this was a job they were all more than happy to leave to me. I went to the club the next morning and spent some time with Wayne, going through all his outstanding jobs, and it was impossible to avoid comparison with the neat and organised state of his office and the administration that I had once found in the secretarial and earlier commercial departments of the previous regime. He was the sacrificial victim offered to placate certain of the local "Mafia" and the freeloaders who still had some influence with my colleagues, and he was made to carry the can for the lack of success and interest in the parts of the club for which he had neither responsibility or authority. I put it to him that the drop in commercial revenue was so serious that the board had no choice but to take this drastic step, and mentioned among other issues that we were unhappy with him living in Blackpool. This was more or less to confirm that what Tommy Hutchison labelled "Grumpy Town" must indeed be populated by "Grumpy Town" men.

'Wayne was shocked and immensely disappointed as he had high hopes for some of his initiatives and by way of an exercise in industrial management relations, he rightly noted that there had not been a single prior word, direct criticism, or any previous warning to him. He went on to actually thank me for talking to him and explaining the club position and went on to say that I was the only director at Burnley for whom it was possible to have any respect of any kind. I could do no more than wish well to the man, and was glad to give him good references for when he successfully applied elsewhere. I relayed to the chairman the remarks about respect.

'On to the scene had been brought the arch fundraiser, Jack Butterfield, having of course been previously at the club as a successful commercial manager when there was a First Division team in place[46]. I had met Jack on a couple of occasions when Burnley had games away to Tranmere Rovers, whom we seemed to draw in cup ties with great regularity. I was aware of him without being a confidante, or so much as a friend, and I had some indication of his abilities from my first exercise for the club and fact finder for John Jackson and his board. The organisation at Tranmere was in evidently good shape, and had made an impression on me, particularly as Tranmere, then very much a basement club, were existing on meagre gates. It was well known that Mr and Mrs Butterfield retained connections in Burnley and would welcome a return to the area. His name was under discussion at the club and I arranged to meet him on neutral territory when a position was offered to him and accepted, subject to obtaining his release from his contractual obligations to Tranmere. This was speedily

---

46 Butterfield had been integral to Bob Lord's need to raise money to keep the team well paid, and provide them with the best travel and hotel facilities, including luxury summer voyages on the *QE2* in the mid-1970s.

and cordially arranged between the Tranmere boss Ken Bracewell and myself.

'All too aware of our internal mayhem and unwilling to entice a man away from a secure position, I went out of my way to put every possible reason to him for turning down the job and I well recall mentioning that my own tenure was by no means assured, although the reaction to this was neutral, as it was with many others who somehow imagine that a football directorship fulfils life's ultimate ambition, and that no sane person would ever surrender it voluntarily. He possessed a wealth of stories from the Bob Lord regime and one in particular deserves repeating, if only to give an indication of life in that era.

'Jack had come to Burnley as a player shortly after the war but unfortunately his career was finished prematurely as a result of a badly broken leg. This had left him with some residual problems causing discomfort, if not outright pain ever since. However, back in the Lord days there was the practice on home match Saturdays for a gang of four comprising Lord, manager Jimmy Adamson, assistant Joe Brown, and Jack, to repair to the non-Catholic club for a ritual game of snooker and it was always considered to be in the worst possible taste for the chairman to fail to be on the winning side. Now whether Jack had drawn the short straw and in playing with the chairman had missed a ball that he ought to have potted, or whether he was the enemy and had potted a ball any sane man would have missed, I do not know, but either way Jack incurred sufficient displeasure to be poked with a cue on his injured leg by the delightful chairman, causing him great pain. There must always be times when anyone has had enough and Jack complained. Clearly unused to having his authority questioned, the chairman proceeded to poke the leg again, only harder this time. Nice chap that Bob Lord[47].

---

47 There is the unconfirmed story that Lord once sacked one of his employees for having the temerity to beat him at snooker.

'1984 was preparing for the history books and our main hope became a forlorn hope that not many would be read[48]. Beginning at Preston on 3 November, there was only one league match won until the end of January, a miserable run that ended astonishingly with a 7-0 victory over Rotherham on 2 February. Between times we managed just one draw at home with four other games lost. We were reduced to thinking that a gate of 4,000 would be a bonus and having tasted Manchester United in the League Cup, we clung to the hope of a money spinner in the big one. Draws for the first two rounds of the FA Cup were as helpful as possible with just Penrith and Halifax Town standing in our way.

'Fortunately, we progressed through both rounds and then waited anxiously for the third-round lottery live on TV, the Saturday afternoon of the Halifax game. What the gods would destroy they first drive mad, so it is written. No, not Manchester United this time, or even a chance for Spurs to avenge their hammering of not so long ago; oh no, nothing like that. No disrespect intended, but the worst possible draw for any club had to be Wimbledon away and of course that is what we got. This was the Wimbledon that visited Turf Moor in 1975 as a non-league club with Burnley in the top handful of the First Division. As every Burnley schoolboy knows, Wimbledon won, to write a page in history as the first non-league club to win at a First Division ground. Maybe on that logic we might just do the same to them but our blind optimism had faded long since.

'The match itself was played before just 3,381 spectators and we lost it by 3-1, leaving us with minimal takings. The costs of travelling and hotels are deducted from the match takings and then each club shares according to percentage agreements laid down for all participants before the competition starts. Even though I have no recollection of the proceeds I have no doubt that ours would be nowhere near enough to cover the wages for that week.

---

48 And here we are writing one. And with his own diaries.

'Into this oasis of joy on the next Thursday came our two new directors, Frank Teasdale and Jack Simmons. I have confessed earlier to having misgivings on Teasdale and it was probably my fault that he was not appointed a month or two earlier, but at all events, now, here he was and I was overjoyed to witness the enthusiasm that he was bringing to his appointment. Jack Simmons's appointment had to be viewed differently. He was with us for the contacts that he could provide and to help in plans that I hoped to bring forward for the development of activities outside football. In particular, we had a large unused gymnasium that might lend itself to other activities, that might not bring massive revenue but could surely help to develop local interest by association with the club[49]. That this did not work was not due to any lack of effort by Jack or myself as we examined numerous options. But elsewhere on the board there was not much interest and my enthusiasm, to put it mildly, was not what it was.

'Frank was like a breath of fresh air in the place and I could not have been happier to have him with me. He had an early complaint which will sound strange now, but initially his ardent request was for a "proper job, give me something to do". I frequently sat with him on the team coach and we talked incessantly about the club's prospects and problems, and I felt ashamed that I had delayed his appointment by my unjustified doubts about him.

'There was an early away trip to York with our Central League team at which we were able to compare notes and I wrestled with him the problem of how to construct a board that would meet the approval of the chairman and vice-chairman, who remained happy to let me take on the entire day-to-day running, but the latter I rated as being there as an impediment to real progress. I

---

49 Groundsman Roy Oldfield recalled in his book that the only take-up was by the tennis club, and there was extra work for him when he had to clean up the mess they left.

had been close to resigning in late 1984 when all the joy and fun had gone out of my association with the club, and had suffered a real body blow with the fiasco of the Gallagher termination that never was, but I had determined to get out into the sun for a couple of weeks in January and perhaps take stock then. In fact, I had gone so far as to confide in a close friend that I was torn with the knowledge that there was a real danger of the administration of the club falling back into its prior mess. It was a point that I made endlessly to the board, but to which no one paid much notice.

'Back home refreshed, I put resignation thoughts behind me and came to a decision on the way I would tackle my personal, and, if I may be so arrogant, the dilemma of the club. For a few weeks I had kept it all close to my chest and happily re-beavered myself back into the swing, and as if by magic there were better playing results in February, which always makes everyone feel that bit or, indeed, that great deal better. In five games up to 2 March, we managed three victories, the last two being against local rivals Preston and Bolton Wanderers, and we had sneaked a few places up the league table. Frank Teasdale was still rightly pushing for his proper job, and I was holding off partly because it was the job of the chairman to allocate board responsibilities. In addition, I had also come to the conclusion that the correct course of action for me, and I genuinely believed for the club, was to challenge John Jackson for the chairmanship.

'I had long since accepted that the Jackson chairman and Gill managing director arrangement was a failure and no matter what else may happen, it needed consigning to the rubbish bin. Nothing could bring back Alan Hutchinson as the logical candidate to compromise, if you wish to put it that way, and for the life in me I could not imagine any other board member ready to step into the breach. My personal choice was as simple as it was stark; either I carried on under John Jackson, or I tried to replace him. I am well aware now that it is easy to present this as a naked bid for power, but I know now the innermost thoughts in my mind, and it is to my own conscience that I have to answer. That gives me no trouble at all on the issue of Burnley Football Club.

'In the weekend of the League Cup Final at Wembley, we had a home game which was less than the proverbial bundle of laughs for us as we had got back into our losing ways, with three games in a row going down to defeat, and this particular one ending in an unsatisfactory 1-1 draw, before a horrific attendance well below 3,000. The boardroom was quiet and depressed as well it might be. I was taken aback at about six o'clock after our visitors had left, when I was asked by David Iven if my wife and I would represent the club at Wembley the next day, when Norwich and Sunderland were due to meet in the League Cup Final. John was either unable or unwilling to go and we were certainly not going to be the only club in the entire league to be unrepresented. But in any event, the idea of the Gills doing the honours in the box really did tickle my fancy.

'Off we went on the Sunday morning for a touch of how the other half lived. We had a minor glimpse when seated next to the juvenile chairman of Derby County for the pre-match luncheon, Maxwell Junior [Robert's son, Ian] no less. He was explaining the mammoth signing fee it was necessary for him to pay to his star centre-forward. All I was thinking about were the gate receipts of two pence half-penny for our fixture the previous day.

'But more than that, I was thinking about what the hell was going on at Burnley and was it really me here in this box, and am I soon to be away from it all? I can remember little about the game apart from it being refereed by Neil Midgley whose friendship I have retained to this day, and whose companionship has given me great sport on winter trips to the sun[50].

---

50 Norwich City won 1-0.

'Sitting in front of my wife and I were Bill and Marjorie Fox and they invited us back to their hotel for the evening where we had an enjoyable meal with my thoughts wandering again to the Burnley board and why the hell did it not have men of that calibre. The evening was not without its lighter side as it was far too late for us to drive back to Burnley, as we had intended to do, due to our late arrangements, and we needed a bed. A room was booked for us along with an early start next morning but we had no hand baggage or anything resembling the standard requisites for an overnight stay. I can recommend one hotel in London for its discretion if the need arises[51].

'Home and back with my feet on the ground, I was ready to take the step upon which I had decided and, on this issue, at least our sieve-like board kept an absolute news blackout, and I went to the extent of not even mentioning it to my immediate family. A strong reason for this was that I knew my wife would have been far from keen for me to become chairman, as she imagined that I would lose even more sleep over this wretched club, if indeed that was possible.

'My strategy was simple in the extreme. I handed to each of my co-directors my intention to oppose John at the next board meeting and gave my reasons for the step I was taking. I stated that I would not discuss the matter any further with them as I was not going to get into a whispering campaign. And I told them it was something I felt was needed for the good of the club and that it transcended personalities. At the time of that letter, I had decided that I was going to forget about resigning and that my alternatives were to serve the club as a totally committed chairman or to revert to being finance director and limiting my involvement to that function, possibly even relegating it to a reporting role. It is arguable that my temperament would have made this unlikely as

51 Clearly the hotel staff thought they were having a mucky weekend.

I had been in complete charge of my own business for years. I had gone so far as to put this to John Jackson, before I ever became a director, trying to honestly assess my own character and my ability, or lack of it, to work on a committee.

'Unknown to the board then, here was a personal business development which was to bring my main business into another factory which stood less than five minutes' walk from Turf Moor and for which I already had a managing director. It would have given me all the freedom I needed to pull my weight even more than ever at the club.

'All five directors including John Jackson were handed the same letter and I tried to dismiss it from my mind until the next board meeting.

16

Resignation and reflections

GRANVILLE SHACKLETON, sports editor of the *Burnley Express* during these torrid seasons, wrote passionately and tellingly of all the problems that were destroying the club in 1984/85. The two articles that follow are from the back end of the season and give the picture of exactly what director Derek Gill was leaving behind.

The first, from April 1985, read, 'Burnley Football Club is now at the lowest ebb in its history. This morning, a club that was once feared in this country and on the continent lies in 22nd place in the Third Division of the Football League, the lowest it has ever been at this late stage. Tomorrow, when bottom club Cambridge United are visitors to Turf Moor, and unlikely to bring more than a car load of supporters, we could see a new record low gate at this ground, even worse than the paltry 2,655 who watched the game with Bournemouth last week.

'The dreadful performance at Wigan on Easter Monday left young, middle-aged and elderly fans all agreeing; this present side gave the worst performance any of them had ever seen from a team representing Burnley. Over the last two miserable seasons following the managerial sackings of first Brian Miller and then Frank Casper, this once proud club has put up some bad performances on the field. But never anything as bad as the disgraceful shambles at Wigan, where the last thing the club needed was to see players, representing the club, throwing in the towel as they did at Springfield Park on Easter Monday.

'Fourth Division here we come seemed to be the attitude and the shocked fans left the ground in disbelief at the lack of fight and even interest by the players they had travelled to encourage. Some of the fans that I spoke to told me they had confronted chairman John Jackson after the match. They said he hadn't been able to come up with any answers to Burnley's problems, but praised him for facing up to them, and giving as good as he got.

'I applaud his courage but I also feel that, in his normal vocation as a barrister, had he been faced in a court of law with having to defend these Clarets, even his ability to put over a case would have failed to mitigate the errors.

'The board, of which Mr Jackson is chairman, appointed John Bond as manager following the sacking of Frank Casper. It turned out to be a disastrous move and one that ended last August with Bond's sacking. John Benson, Bond's number two, took over at the invitation of the board early this season, and now he faces an almost impossible task of keeping the Clarets out of the Fourth Division

'He has repeatedly slammed the players for their attitude on the field and it has made no difference. He has called them, "Puppets on the opposition string," and commented after the Wigan game, "It is a terrible indictment, but staying in the Third Division means more to the spectators who pay to see them, than it does to the players who are paid to play for the club."

'He has more than once said during the past months that if he felt his resignation would help, he would hand it in. As far as I am aware the threat of being fired has never been, at any stage, even hinted to him by the board. In the time available to do something about strengthening the team, Benson has brought full-back Geoff Palmer and striker Les Lawrence to the club for a total of about

£20,000, and goalkeeper Joe Neenan, and more recently midfielder Mark Rhodes on loan.

'Had he been given more money, maybe he could have avoided the team's present plight. No one will ever know, and neither did we ever get the chance to know whether Brian Miller or Frank Casper would have succeeded had they been given more time, or the money John Bond was allowed.

'We just seem to have been going round in ever-decreasing circles since the Clarets were relegated to the Third Division almost two years ago. And now the prospect of Fourth Division football at Turf Moor next season looms large and it may already be too late to do anything to prevent it. What a dreadful mess we've got into and whoever carries the can, it won't alter the fact that Turf Moor is now in a mess of its own making.'

A month later, Shackleton penned this article:

'The Clarets are still hanging on to a Third Division lifeline, fighting desperately to prevent themselves being relegated to the Fourth Division for the first time in their history. But even if the club does finally survive, it faces an almost impossible task of selling itself to a dispirited and apathetic public. It has got to be done, but how? In my view it will not be done without changes, even if only of attitude, in the boardroom and in the management of the club. The board meets tomorrow night, when it could well be that John Jackson resigns the chairmanship while staying on the board.

'But I believe that of equal importance in this vital meeting should be a decision that would bring Martin Dobson back to Turf Moor as soon as possible to become player-manager of the club. I have the greatest respect for John Benson as a man. He is as honest as any I have ever known and desperately eager to make Burnley a successful club despite all the problems he has had to face. But the Burnley public generally does not like him, while it thinks the world of Dobbo. And Dobbo loves Burnley so much that he would jump at the chance to leave Bury, where he has won them promotion from the Fourth to the Third Division.

'But: and this is vitally important, Martin Dobson, even with the public behind him, would fail as Benson has done if he received no more help from the board. The influx of new directors during this present season only seems to have increased the traumas in the boardroom and it is no secret that the chairman and the managing director, Derek Gill, do not see eye to eye. This was made public at the last annual meeting of shareholders when a question about their relationship in board matters was virtually ruled out of order.

'Pleas from the present manager for more financial help from the board seem to have mostly gone unheeded and all the time we have been sliding down the Third Division. All this season we have wanted at least one more player who could hold the midfield together but the transfer deadline came and went in March without any success in getting that man.

'True, we got Mark Rhodes on loan from Rotherham United just a few minutes before the deadline but, with respect, and despite his fine game in the victory over Swansea last Saturday, Mark was not really the type of player we desperately needed. Benson knew the man he wanted long before the last-gasp decision to sign Rhodes on loan until the end of the season. The manager would not make his name public in fairness to him and his club. But we never got him because, it can only be assumed, the board were not prepared to lash out money.

'Everybody knows Burnley have grave financial problems. But so have other clubs who have at least tried to bolster their sides whether they were facing relegation or going for promotion.

'It is little more than two years since Burnley were taking on the might of Liverpool at Turf Moor and beating them 1-0 in the second leg of the Milk Cup semi-final. It was not enough to reach the Wembley final and further disappointment came when the Clarets lost at Sheffield Wednesday in the quarter-final of the

FA Cup. But since then, it has been nothing but disappointments with the board's decision to bring in "outsider" John Bond proving to be in complete contrast to all the high hopes. Now it seems an opportune time to go back to the old tried and trusted system of appointing home-grown talent, to put this club on the road to recovery.'

* * *

Derek Gill's diaries pick up the story, 'There were two developments from co-directors. Firstly, came notification from Jack Simmons that he would support me and I accepted this with gratitude but declined to discuss it further, as we each understood where the other stood. Then to my amazement Doc Iven came and told me that he wanted me in the chair. I could not have been more surprised as I had taken it for granted that he would wish to retain John. The temptation now to approach Frank Teasdale and Basil Dearing was enormous, and probably the only thing that prevented me was a sudden call to visit a major customer in America. This meant that I missed two crucial games but at least prevented me from breaking my word and canvassing Frank or Basil.

'John and I had a stroll together before an away game and there was not the slightest antagonism in either direction and I mentioned to him that after the vote, if I was not to be chairman, I would certainly be standing down as managing director. He took this as agreed and understood.

'How far things had been discussed between some or perhaps all of the directors I never did find out and, while thinking on my feet, contemplated confronting him with the intentions of Doc Iven and Jack Simmons. The implications were clear as could be and the best John Jackson could hope for was to retain the chair on his own casting vote. That, I would suggest, is something that most sensible people would not entertain. In essence, I was certain that the change would take place and I was ready to put in place the changes I wanted. My recommendation for vice-chairman was to be Frank Teasdale and I would have insisted that David Iven became life-president. Jack Simmons would continue and be encouraged to bring non-football activities to fruition.

'For John Jackson I was ambivalent and while I would have preferred him to resign, I certainly would not have pushed the issue, as apart from any other consideration, his was the best knowledge of the intricacies of the Football League regulations and politics. I would most certainly not have wanted there to be any sense of a palace coup and if John had chosen to leave the board for professional reasons, it would never have been disclosed by me that he did so on a vote of his fellow directors. Words are easy I know, but he would also have been granted as a matter of course all the facilities due to him as a former chairman. In the end it did not happen but had it done so I am sure there were two other possibilities for the board who could have made positive contributions.

'Push soon came to shove and the crunch meeting began. I knew which way I was going and was numbed when each director in turn was asked by the chairman for his vote. David Iven was first and was as good as his word and supported me by giving his reasons. He was followed by Frank and Basil in turn who each made the same response in three little words. "As it is."

'And what about Jack? Unavoidable other business kept Jack Simmons from the meeting[52] and it was down to me to vote for myself. John did not call upon me to vote saving himself the embarrassment of having to rely on his own casting vote, always assuming that I would have voted. That it was unnecessary was clear enough by his reaction which displayed beyond question that he knew the outcome in advance of the meeting, and I have

52 And on Jack Simmons's absence from the vote, you could say that the history of the club was altered. One man, one vote, and one absence that was so critical.

to admit that my mind was in a whirl, with more balls in the air simultaneously than I could handle.

'Then came the hammer blow or the triviality that took me off the board and out of Burnley Football Club. In my frustration I made a remark borne out of that frustration, and which I cannot now remember, but it was enough to sting John Jackson into a riposte in which he said there was even a view on the board that I was "paranoid". I had known John for around four years and knew not to take everything at face value. So why all the fuss about this remark?

'What was getting to me was the realisation that the undercurrents were still in full flow and that as ever I seemed to be the last one to find out. I therefore went to the extreme of writing to the directors with an Oxford dictionary definition of "paranoid" and stated that if this was to be the way, I would resign. I had not really put my mind to the question of who would say such a thing, and thought that it might have been John having one of his games, and would later laugh it off. Never did it cross my mind that the originator would be Frank Teasdale, but eventually he came forward and admitted to it.

'This, the Frank taken to Blackburn by my wife and I, then to be quizzed by the chairman as to where my wife's allegiances lay. This, the new director I looked on as a breath of fresh air. Most damning of all, and the one that really hurt me was that it was to this same Frank that I had transferred all the 100 qualification shares that he needed, when no other board member would help him. Frank: hell, he was the one on whom so much would depend and from whom there would be no secrets, and no bar to him taking the chair in his own right, if and when he gained experience, and it suited us both and more important might be in the best interests of the club.

'Suddenly, they were all out of step except me, and when that happens it is necessary to look in the mirror.

'Very hard I looked too and what I saw was a man frustrated to distraction with a situation worsening by the day and crying out for leadership. Leadership that I thought I could provide but was prevented from exercising. In my private business we had taken on additional premises and there was a need for me to spend more time there; a place where any sane person would have seen his primary duty, regardless of the unpaid hobby job.

'I hope that I am being sufficiently honest in my appraisal to look realistically at why I was at odds with the entire board, none of whom I regarded as fools. Passing of the years has long since erased any bitterness or antagonism in me, and there are therefore times when I look back and think I was foolish in the extreme to resign over what in the end was something and nothing. I have asked myself whether deep down, I wanted to replicate Bob Lord, a man for whom I had no time whatsoever, and just be the unquestioned dictator? I hope not but cannot in all honesty rule out that thought. After all, I know from my early 40s with seven dependent children, I had walked away from a secure and highly paid job to dip my toe into the independent water and did not rest until the business that I had bought into was mine 100 per cent. I had told John Jackson before I became a director that I was at my worst in a committee room. I just find it impossible to suffer fools, and have to admit impatience with ditherers and hangers-on. The undercurrents that were always in the club had not been totally foreign to me, as I had often had semi-secret talks with Alan Hutchinson, even to the extent of suggesting to him that he should challenge for the chairmanship.

'So just where did I see myself in relation to my co-directors? With John Jackson it was unlikely that there would be much change in our love-hate marriage. My view of David Iven remained that he should vacate his position as a voting director and accept the position of club president, to be retained for the rest of his life. Jack Simmons: I was not the least surprised when he left the board at the earliest opportunity. And the great white hope was Frank Teasdale.

'To my regret I found the past tense all too appropriate. With Frank and I working in harmony, I would never have contemplated resignation. The others could have been towed along, if need be, and there was always the chance of other good directors joining, once the place achieved some semblance of permanency and harmony. Frank was, and to me still is, likeable and cheerful, the essence of all things to all men, an attribute that the hard world of football would doubtless temper, in its own time. On the face of things, he was the one with whom it was so easy to get on with, and whose devotion to the club was transparent, and one whose judgement could be trusted. But the single "paranoid" jibe hit me so hard that now I can hardly believe how badly I reacted to it. There had been the earlier triviality about my wife being a Blackburn supporter, which we treated as a huge joke, without reading the warning signs if that is what they were. But "paranoid" from a supposed colleague behind my back caused me to conclude that I was lumbered with yet another director not to be trusted.

'Did I really want to soldier on in these conditions and spending half my time looking over my shoulder, or with my ear to the ground listening for boardroom tittle tattle or worse? I spent some thoroughly miserable hours pondering the issue and flew the Atlantic with nothing else on my mind. You ask yourself if football is worth the loss of sleep that I was enduring and the answer to that one does not require the brain of Britain to resolve. I cannot begin to guess how many times I spoke of my impending resignation to other directors, and to try to say that I was serious about it, which seemed necessary as none gave the impression of taking much notice.

'To this day Frank insists that he told me not to resign and I would never accuse him of being untruthful, but I have no recollection of it. Jack Simmons and David Iven say the same but it was indicative of my frustrated state of mind that I was unmoved. Perhaps Frank was right and I was indeed paranoid! But if I was, it was not for the reason which he said, namely that I was only interested in gaining power for myself.

'The occasional interlude from boardroom madness was played out on the football pitch where the ultimate disaster befell us. It was relegation to the basement of the Fourth Division[53]. In all our worst nightmares we had not anticipated this one, and at this even our miserable board must take some of the responsibility.

'In the final analysis, it must be left to others to judge for themselves whether or not my motives were no more than a bid for personal power in the club; and in this respect there is no argument that I had reached the point at which I knew that without the power to act as I saw fit, I saw no point in continuing with this enormous personal frustration. I wanted the power, to give me the ability to act for the good of the club and not for personal selfish gratification. I can maintain that to this day with total conviction, despite the undeniable fact that I would have been greatly honoured and felt much pride, had I been elevated to the major role. Power for its own sake is both demeaning and corrupting and I would hope to have been able to resist both.

'Nothing could get me away from the stark realisation that the question was academic and my alternative course of action was to carry on in the financial director role, simply reporting. I had to examine my conscience and admit that I was temperamentally unsuited to that type of job. There was plenty to occupy me in my own business which was now weighing ever more heavily in the equation. And the club, devoid of any conceivable attraction, was on its knees with the relegation to the bottom rung and another

---

53 It's astonishing to think that this had been a leading First Division side just ten years earlier.

spell of recriminations, infighting and abuse. I was effectively doomed to be on the outside of the real decision-making and knew that I could not live with that. The pettiness of the off-stage back-biting by a supposed colleague had finally made the game not worth the candle.

'With a heavy heart I wrote out my resignation from the board. Even at this ultimate development I had to tell them for the umpteenth time that the club wages were processed through my works computer. If I stopped the service the staff would not be paid. And still the useless buggers did nothing.

* * *

Gill's notes of March 2005 added more to this story, 'For me, the early summer of 1985 was a strange and empty time. My resignation had been described as "sensational" by the local scribblers, and with the club at a lower ebb than ever, I did have a degree of guilt at leaving it. One or two of the erstwhile loudest mouths joined the board, and there was an inevitable time when fingers from the boardroom were pointed in my direction. I attended a few Annual General Meetings, which bordered on the school playground. At such times my ambivalence was at full power and I felt irritated at having no part, yet more than happy that I had no association with the current crew.

'I had sometimes been tempted to think back to the "paranoid" jibe by a man I wanted to trust, and there appeared to be an obsession among the board that I was sat at home sticking pins into effigies until my day arrived again. This went to a ridiculous level when I sold a minority interest in my business to a major PLC venture capitalist business. To some it could only mean a bid to return to Burnley Football Club. It led me to pose the question, "Who now was paranoid?"'

* * *

Gill's diaries take up the story again, 'The resignation of a director was required to be submitted in writing and by one of the odd articles of the Burnley club constitution it did not take legal effect for one month. It may be remembered that my very first board meeting had coincided with the resignation of two directors from the Lord era. It had surprised me to see them both at that meeting and taking a full part in it, even though they were yesterday's men, as soon as the meeting terminated. This was not how I was going to act. I was going to do no more than hand in my resignation and leave the premises. And then: in all my time at Burnley Football Club I had been on the end of a good few surprises, but the final one took first prize.

'My resignation was public knowledge when John Jackson calmly told me he was quitting[54]. I would have been less shocked if he had announced a vow of celibacy and joined a silent order of monks. I mumbled something about whether he was quitting the board or just the chair and he confirmed the latter. For a time, I considered withdrawing the resignation and standing as replacement chairman. With the benefit of hindsight, I wish I had done just that. David Iven has insisted subsequently that if I had been prepared to wait just 48 hours the ultimate prize for a Longside supporter would have been mine. That I will never know for certain but my regret at not putting it to the test is aggravated as a result by not knowing. It is a continuing and no doubt permanent irritation with which I must live. It has regrettably caused me to lash out on one or two occasions when I now wish I had kept quiet.

'Why then did I not withdraw my resignation and fight for the authority to do the job? The simple answer is that I had no stomach for continuing with the same board and did not fancy

---

54 And who could blame him. What a thankless job it is being a chairman. A job where willing men stick their head above the parapet and that in itself makes them the target for blame and abuse when things go wrong, from fans and the press, and they are a sitting target at AGMs.

my chances of getting the measures through that were needed to change it. Being the boss of a divided board was no worthwhile prospect to me and I reasoned on my feet that John and I might do no more than swap roles, with the same disruption for the club. Furthermore, I was never going to submit myself to the level of abuse that John had suffered through certain sections of the press, about which I had complained on his behalf to no avail.

'With just one member on the board with whom I could have felt at total ease and whose judgement I could trust, I would have carried on, although it has to be admitted that I would have had difficulty in accepting defeat in a vote for the chair if I had stood and it had come to that. But: that again is something I shall never know.

'On the assumption that I stood successfully, there remained the overriding need to change the board. It would have required head-on measures that I would have found easy in my normal business, but in the football club I was dealing with some who met outside the club and whose combined opposition could easily defeat my intentions. To repeat; it was not that I wanted absolute power (one in the history of the club was one too many) but there were changes of such magnitude in the offing that I would have been unable to move effectively without them. In essence I needed to reform the board, but as nothing was ever the fault of "us", so the answer to that one was clear enough for anyone to guess.

'Wrongly, I now believe, I let my resignation go through and left the boardroom for the last time with words of real regret, embellished by an unnecessary lambasting of John Jackson. David Iven was gracious enough to express his regret at my decision while others looked on in silence. John said words to the effect of "speak for yourself Doc", and that was that. Or it would have been at a normal place.

'But: it then dawned on me that without my assistance they could not process the wages. After a football lifetime of being

Burnley FC gopher, I must have found it difficult to stop and having left the board and the club, I allowed my business to continue to process these wages for many more weeks while they got their act together. I really must have been soft in the head and I remember telling a football friend weeks later that the BFC wages were still going through our computer. He thought that my mental state was worse than paranoid, and that I really did need to have my bumps felt.

'In the summer I had some time to reflect on what I had done and had many mixed emotions over this time. The following season soon came round and if I needed confirmation of the kind of place I had left behind, it came in a way in which I would never have expected it. Stephen, my youngest son, was in the school sixth form and I like to think that none of my children had been spoiled, or brought up to expect the silver spoon treatment. Generally hard-up, Stephen had supplemented his pocket money by acting as gatekeeper at Turf Moor on home matchdays. The fiver for this function was more than welcome to him and he carried out his job effectively and never once missed turning up without giving notice, and neither was he ever one penny wrong in his takings. At the start of the season, he turned up as usual to be told that his services were not required and I know to my certain knowledge that it was difficult to get reliable gatemen. Were these people now having a go at my schoolboy son?

'Teasdale purported not to know about it when I questioned him. Maybe he did not know, but I can guarantee that in his place I would have known, not just Stephen, but every employee whose job was being terminated. At least, it provided to me some justification that I was better off out of the place.

'When the new season started with the first ever Fourth Division fixture, I just could not bring myself to attend and spent the afternoon walking with my wife and granddaughter. But I could not take my mind away from Turf Moor and for the first time in my life I experienced mixed feelings when the result came through. Absenteeism did not apply to my sons and sons-in-law and inevitably I was soon back at the Turf, except now I was paying my money at the turnstiles. Sometimes I entered the sanctuary with the very occasional guest ticket supplied by David Iven, and now and again as a guest of the match sponsors. I always found it hard, however, and uncomfortable, with me the often-unwitting focal point for discontent and general moaning. In fact, old Grumpy Town at its most vocal. My very being ached for involvement and it was more than I could stand to see the club struggle both on and off the field.

'The directors eventually got round to processing the club wages and I was relieved of that function. But here were still frequent enquiries to me from board members who were now realising that if they left everything to one member, and that one member departed, then there had to be an awful lot of matters about which they had not bothered to be informed. I do not try to be confrontational for the fun of it and much prefer to make progress by consent and sharing of knowledge and forward planning; but when colleagues show no interest in day-to-day running and just "leave it to Derek and he will sort it out" then they should not be surprised to be struggling when Derek packed his bags.

'None of this stopped them ringing or sometimes writing to me to ask what had been done or agreed on club matters. There were two particular issues which stick in my mind and each in its own way betrays the extent to which I had been left holding the baby and how little interest, much less involvement, had been shown by other directors.

'One of Alan Hutchinson's hotels had been used for accommodation for new players in the area before they moved houses and Alan had provided this service for the club. His hotel naturally kept records of accommodation and Alan would accept costs against his own business. Some months after I had left, the club sent me a copy of charges from Alan's hotel and asked what I knew about it. These Burnley directors did not even know what arrangements had been made for their own players and the copy they sent to me actually included the name of one of them who had signed for expenditure on the hotel account. I could have told them what it was but, in my disgust, which I was finding ever harder to conceal, I did not bother to do so.

'Even more incredibly, in June 1986, 13 months after I had left the club, I got a letter enquiring about the employment terms of John Doherty who had joined the club at the same time as John Bond. Some people might think it strange that 13 months should elapse before getting round to establishing the terms of employment of a senior manager. Better late than never might run the argument. But hold on: the only reason that the enquiry was made at all was because John Doherty had been sacked. For reasons that now escape me I weakened on this one and advised the club where to find the written evidence, but could not resist the final barb. "May I have the temerity to suggest that next time you sack an employee, you establish his terms of employment first."

'When responding to requests for information in writing, I found it difficult indeed not to remind directors that everything had been available to them if they had shown sufficient interest to participate at the appropriate times. It is one of my greatest regrets that I have been unable to rid myself completely of a degree of irritation towards some of them. I know it does no good and I am not proud of it but it would take a better man than me to turn the other cheek.

'I had slaved to keep the shop open, always been available for the unglamorous jobs, been there at ground safety meetings, represented the club at times of trouble, provided bottles of port out of my own pocket for sponsors at Christmas, left my family on New Year's Eve for club reasons, got my son to give up his house for three months for a new player, transferred shares to Frank Teasdale to enable him to take his place as a director. My time at Turf Moor ended as such an unhappy experience and I belatedly came to the conclusion I was better off without it. But: a part of me died when I walked out of that boardroom for the last time.'

In the *Burnley Express* of 17 May 1985, Granville Shackleton went to town in his report of proceedings. Gill's resignation was headed as a 'sensation'. Shackleton described it as the most dramatic week ever at the club and if anything, Gill's diaries do not fully portray the full shock and turmoil of what was going on behind the scenes. Shackleton was scathing:

'Sort out the boardroom, decide who is going to manage the club and start TODAY the colossal task of building a new Burnley Football Club from the ashes of the old. This is a shattering day for the Clarets. Certainly, it WILL be if the Swansea-Bristol City game this evening sentences our cherished club to the Football League basement of the Fourth Division[55].

'It is shattering in any case, as the troubles and divisions that have for so long affected teamwork in the boardroom come right to the surface. The managing director, Mr Derek Gill, has resigned from the board. Mr John Jackson says he has resigned from the chairmanship but intends to carry on until a successor is appointed. Morale throughout the club is extremely low. The players that have taken us through a disappointing season to the verge of the dreaded drop have mostly been retained.

'Mr John Benson, not knowing whether or not he will be the manager next season, can hardly be expected to go after new men, even if finances were available. He knows it would be totally unfair to his successor should the board decide to replace him as

55 Yes, they were relegated despite winning two of the last three games. There was a tortured six-day wait until the match in South Wales ended the season and the 0-0 draw consigned Burnley to the Fourth Division. Had Swansea lost, they would have stayed up. Football is filled with ironies. Swansea were managed by John Bond.

manager. Yet this week, clubs throughout the Football League announce their retained lists, and it seems logical to assume that Burnley should waste no time in looking at who is available to boost the Clarets' cause.

'So where do we go from here? It is God help us if we have to wait until the second week in June for the next development in unravelling this dreadful tangle. The boardroom battle, for that is what it is, must be resolved speedily and satisfactorily. The position of the manager must be clarified urgently. And the major task of rebuilding for next season, only 14 weeks away, must start at once.

'We urge the board to bear firmly in mind the words of Mr Basil Dearing when he was appointed a director last August. "Burnley Football Club belongs to the people of the town. It is not there for the aggrandisement of the directors, or indeed the players."'

How ironic that in the same edition of the *Burnley Express* there was a fulsome article and reminder that exactly 25 years earlier Burnley had paraded with the First Division championship trophy.

17

Four days from receivership

THERE WERE an astonishing 62 applicants for the vacant managership when John Benson was dismissed. Player of the Year had been Tommy Hutchison and his name was top of the list. Derek Gill was an admirer of his but Gill was no longer a director. Instead, the board in its wisdom appointed Martin Buchan, the former Manchester United defender. Hutchison, snubbed, was asked about being assistant manager. He said no and chose to leave. Thus, the board saddled the club with Buchan who left after just four months, honest enough to admit that he couldn't cope and that management was just not for him. Frank Teasdale was now chairman and asked assistant manager Tommy Cavanagh to take over, which he duly did.

The club had no money, stalwart Derek Scott left, and Michael Phelan was sold along with Wayne Biggins. The season limped along, literally; Joe Gallagher was still there with his gammy leg, and Cavanagh too had a leg that limped. The boardroom limped along; this was an ailing club, with no progress in the Milk Cup or the FA Cup. Gates were minimal at under 4,000, commercial income paltry, and the bank was worried.

Somehow, after eight games the team was in eighth place but then an abysmal performance at Chester made up Buchan's mind. He had had enough, after a performance he described as 'suicidal'.

Presumably he thought that if he saw any more like this, he too would be suicidal. He was Burnley's fifth manager in just two and a half years. This was a shambles of a club.

Cavanagh had a spell of five wins and one defeat in a run of nine games. The future might have looked claret but off the field there was financial gloom. The annual balance sheet showed losses of over £250,000, debts of £410,000 and another £240,000 owed to creditors. Fans had begun a 'Save Our Club' group. Somehow, a couple of victories lifted Burnley to ninth in the new year but then the next nine games gleaned just five points.

In February of 1986, John Jackson, still a director, sold his shares to Frank Teasdale and resigned from the board, tired of the abuse and the fingers that pointed at him for ever having appointed John Bond, not that long ago. After the euphoric promotion of 1981/82 over which he had presided, it had been downhill all the way. He could take no more. 'Jackson quits Burnley Board' was the headline in bold black as Granville Shackleton reported on the sorry tale:

'John Jackson, former chairman of Burnley Football Club, dropped a soccer bombshell yesterday afternoon when he announced that he had resigned from the Turf Moor board of directors. Mr Jackson told me, "I made my decision to resign at the weekend and I have written to the chairman, Mr Frank Teasdale, explaining my reasons. I do not intend to enter into any discussions as to my reasons and I have nothing to say except that I am, and always will remain, the most ardent Burnley supporter."

'Mr Teasdale, who had still to receive the letter when I contacted him, will not make a statement until he has been able to read it.

'Former Burnley director Derek Gill said, "I do not know why John Jackson has resigned but I have to say that the level of personal abuse to which he has been subjected has exceeded all the bounds of decency and civilised behaviour. For his own good

I am glad that he has made the decision and I hope he is able to enjoy his football much more in the future."

'There have been constant calls for John Jackson to resign, both while he served as chairman and since his resignation from that post just over a year ago. He took over following the resignation of Bob Lord[56]. His appointment was seen by many as the beginning of a new era at Turf Moor. Sadly, things have turned sour and the controversial appointment of John Bond and then the dismissal of John Bond as manager have seen him "fall from grace" with a lot of people.

'It is only last month that he sold the majority of his shares to Mr Teasdale, who took over as chairman in May 1985. He has faced the brunt of supporter anger during demonstrations both inside and outside the ground over the last two years.

'One of his most public opponents was university administrator Harry Brooks who, prior to yesterday's resignation, had offered £1,000 to the Clarets' *Burnley Express* appeal, on condition that Mr Jackson quit the board. Mr Brooks said yesterday, "I am absolutely delighted with the news and I can guarantee that I will now follow through with my pledge. I am sure his resignation will be greeted with delight and relief by a great many supporters and I am confident that the club can now make real progress. The recovery can begin in earnest."'

Harry Brooks's forecast of recovery was sadly inaccurate as things went from bad to worse. Teasdale warned of liquidation and to combat this, there was a new share issue. But an icy winter blew through Turf Moor and the place was heading only one way, towards insolvency. Fewer than 2,000 spectators bothered to watch a home game against Crewe in April. Few people wanted the new shares and Teasdale warned the club was just days away from folding. There were genuine fears that the last home game

---

56 It is a myth that Lord resigned. He was replaced as chairman in his absence.

really would be the last one ever, and with that in mind extra programmes were printed to be sold as souvenirs. Somehow the club survived, as the Derek Gill diaries will shortly describe.

It had been the worst season in Burnley's history both on and off the field, with a boardroom and set of directors that was simply not fit for purpose. Granville predicted that if the next season was as bad, then the club was heading for the Gola League (as the Conference, now the National League, was known at the time). He must surely have written it never even dreaming that it would very nearly come true.

Towards the back end of the season, Gill began to formulate his rescue package. His diaries bring more detail:

'I have made no secret of my mixed feelings during the latter part of my directorship and they were probably even more mixed in the year or two thereafter. I had precious little regard for my successors who had been prepared to criticise, and who had sacked my schoolboy son from his Saturday job as a gateman, never late, never a penny out in his take. The board I left behind were more wind than action and yet from time to time had no hesitation in coming back to me when they did not know their own business. I once wrote that there were directors here whom I would not consider for employment. One day I will wake up and realise it was all just a silly dream.

'Escapism by walking out with my wife and granddaughter on match afternoons was never going to last long and I was soon back, but now it was sitting quietly in the Butcher's Stand[57], doing my best to keep my thoughts to myself. Not always successfully it has to be admitted, but always under the cloak of anonymity when joining in the normal match chatter and "expert" opinion.

---

57 Bob Lord of course, aka Owld Bob, Lord Bob, Bob Chop, Old Bollock Chops, Sir Loin of Beef.

'On one occasion I found myself in the directors' box at Bury, having been offered a pass by the home secretary. It was the strangest experience to be sat behind the Burnley board and one which I did not try to repeat for a very long time. I am afraid that I spent more time watching them and ear-wigging than concentrating on the match but the one good aspect of the experience was the reminder to me that I was not missing much by being deprived of their company. Burnley lost by the way and the match was the second leg of the first round of the League Cup. Burnley had won the first leg by 2-1 and under the rules of the competition, the away goals counted double in the event of the aggregate scores being level.

'Losing the second leg by 2-1, Burnley scored a second goal thus requiring Bury to score twice more to win on aggregate. It was most interesting to hear my erstwhile colleagues discuss the implications of this startling arithmetic. It brought back to mind a game at Wimbledon during my first season and Wimbledon were heading for relegation and we were pushing for promotion and it was goalless. Martin Dobson played most of the season in his sweeper role and in the way of things often wore the number seven shirt. Even in his sweeper role, Martin would break forward from time to time and happened to break up the right flank just in front of the directors' box. One of my illustrious colleagues thereupon noted with evident surprise that he did not think that Dobson would make much of an outside-right. Now then, what did Len Shackleton say?

'Now that I was outside the sphere of influence, I actually began to feel more guilt relating to the state of affairs than I had ever done while I was involved, and despite my hard feelings towards Frank Teasdale resulting from what I considered to be his betrayal, I was all too aware of how difficult a time he must be having with his lack of experience and knowledge. All that, piled on top of being thrust into such a difficult situation. I also accepted that he had not actively sought the chair, rather had the job found him as the best available alternative to John Jackson. Despite all the reservations, I think if he had come forward with a peace offering, I would have rejoined and done my best again, as I had to accept in my own mind some responsibility for the shambles. Of course, no such possibility ever became a realistic option and the stage was set for seven long years in the Fourth Division.

'Far from any peace offerings, and let me make it abundantly clear that I made no moves to take any initiatives, all I seemed to get was more criticism, rarely directly, but there just the same by attempts to shift responsibility in my direction. In anticipation of all this, I retained some copy correspondence that has gathered dust in my files until now, but which, once reopened, enables me to speak with some authority that comes only from possession of the facts, plus a memory indelibly marked by those hurtful and unhappy events of so long ago.

'Tempted to speak out before now, I have always resisted as far as I could, as I would not have taken any action liable to do damage to the club. Now that there is no such possibility of causing any such harm, I am free to put the truth on record and, in doing it, put the unheard side of the case. Of course, I wish to vindicate myself and others who have been wrongly or excessively accused of mismanagement, but at no stage will I ever pretend that my part was totally blameless. Unlike my previous colleagues, I can produce and recall financial figures that prove the case, and has been put so many times, it was never reckless spending that caused heavy losses, it was the mistakes in judgements in the signing of players who reduced, not improved, team performances, and this in turn led to the disastrous fall in gate and sponsorship receipts.

'Then a funny thing happened in February 1986, just nine months after my own departure. John Jackson threw in his hand and left the board. And this did make me sit up and take notice. I could hardly have made it clearer that although he and I had our differences, I would still venture the opinion that his knowledge of league procedures and personalities outstripped the combined knowledge of the other four by a proverbial mile.

'It was then put to me that the final item that led to John leaving concerned payments to two former players that in turn were due to a loyalty provision in earlier contracts. If this were true it was remarkable to say the least and was just another chicken coming home to roost, as a result of directors taking too little interest in the running of the club involving the unseen, unglamourous side, which, more often than not, has more bearing on the state of play than the upfront posturing so beloved by some.

'There had been in place, since the heady days of the First Division, a playing bonus scheme that was completely unsustainable in the lower reaches of the league and it posed a mammoth problem when considered in the context of the retention of the better players. Put simply, there were contractual obligations of a very onerous nature for every match won, or even drawn in away fixtures. Without going into detail which would be unfair, and in any event not entirely necessary, it is sufficient to relate that a home win, even in a run-of-the mill mid-table or end-of-season fixture, had the effect of activating bonus payments that exceeded the net gate receipts. To get out of this problem I had to go through countless meetings with many players. Much goodwill needed to be in place to achieve the desired objective, which was to get universal agreement to new contracts, which would incorporate different bonus terms, more in keeping with the status of the club.

'Evidently, when the original contracts were drawn up, it had not crossed the mind of anybody that the club might one day be relegated from the First Division. The obligations had followed right through to the Third Division despite the devastating effects on revenue. The problem in correcting this exceptionally onerous commitment was twofold. In the first place was the desperately hard ruling that where a new contract offered to a player did not match his previous agreement in every respect, and the words "in every respect" were the killers, then the player became a free agent and could move on without transfer compensation to the club. The secondary problem lay in the clear realisation that it was not thought possible to allow the bonus scheme to evaporate by neglect on new contracts, as it had been reasoned that it was impossible to run a team containing players on different incentives.

'On later reflection, I am not sure that we were correct in that supposition and with hindsight it might have been better to put the facts on the table to newcomers and remunerate them on different rates. But hindsight was not on tap and we did not do that. Consequently, new agreements were needed and I regard it as one of the best achievements of my time that they were put in place without the loss of one single player and with no discernible discontent.

'This exercise went through the club at a budgeted cost of £40,000, all of which was debited to the Gill era and naturally too late to relate to the old back-of-an-envelope regime that caused me the problem[58]. The new bonus scheme without doubt saved the club many thousands of pounds. But that's life I suppose.

'Why it should suddenly become relevant was that the resignation of John Jackson was apparently related to the payments to two departed players of a proportion of the "loyalty bonus". Now, that if true is so stupid that words fail me except to add that this is a part of the whirlwind reaped as a result of long neglect. I know that Teasdale was still relatively new but as I reminded him on another matter, he took on the job and should not have run to me when he did not know what to do. Or at least if he was going to do that, then he might have kindly offered me some sort of accommodation at the times when I was needed. How people act towards others when there is no imminent gain from the occasional

---

58 So, it was Gill who was criticised for the £40,000 costs.

2017, reunion of groundsman Roy Oldfield and Brian Flynn. Both of them there during the Bond season, both of them highly regarded by director Derek Gill. Picture by the author.

Bond welcomes Daley. Picture courtesy of Burnley Civic Trust

Gill presents a memento for Dobson's 400th appearance for the club. Courtesy of Gill family collection.

Pre-season with John Bond, training run full of optimism.

Left to right, Bond, Vince Overson, Billy Hamilton, John Benson and John Sainty. Picture courtesy of Burnley Civic Society.

The full Bond squad. Picture by Howard Talbut.

Roger Hansbury leads and Tommy Hutchison in second place. Picture courtesy Burnley Civic Trust

Derek Gill courtesy of the Gill Family

Derek Gill receives the National and Provincial cheque. Picture courtesy of Gill family collection.

Steve Taylor in action in Milk Cup game at Spurs. Picture courtesy of Burnley Civic Trust

Lee Dixon sold. Picture courtesy of Howard Talbut

Brian Flynn. Picture courtesy of Howard Talbut

Vince Overson. Picture courtesy of Howard Talbut

Michael Phelan, sold. Picture courtesy of Burnley Express

Ray Deakin leads out the team for the Orient game

Manager Miller waits for the final whistle. Burnley's problems began with the relegation season of 1982/83. They accelerated with the Bond season. Financial problems multiplied after that, and the Orient season was the climax to all this. Both pictures courtesy of Burnley Express.

good gesture tells you who your real friends are. However, there was a further twist when the funds eventually started to run out altogether.

'Nothing should now attempt to minimise the extent of the difficulties that were faced by Teasdale and his board when they took on the responsibility in May 1985, and this should be accepted when examining the history of the first year under their control. They were hamstrung by a lack of finance, exacerbated by an even greater lack of knowledge of how to handle this new-found responsibility. A horrendous combination if ever there was one. As sure as night follows day they were set to struggle and struggle they did as the records show.

'This is not to infer that I think I could have done anything which would have removed the losses incurred in season 1985/86, as they were inevitable until increased revenues through match takings and sponsorship were in place. The crucial question therefore is whether or not more could have been done to enhance this much needed increase in revenue. I have set out elsewhere the three elements of revenue available to clubs like Burnley and these comprise takings at the gate, commercial income and thirdly profit on transfers. In that first season under the new chairmanships there were two outgoing transfers for which there is good reason to suppose that the club did not get remotely close to their market value. These were Michael Phelan and Wayne Biggins. A later examination of the financial accounts for the year ended 31 May 1986 discloses a profit on them, but no or negligible spending on transfers in. I know for certain that both Phelan and Biggins could have commanded better fees. Without doubt, Phelan was sold for far less than his real value and there had been an enquiry for him during the latter part of my own time. It would have resulted in a much higher fee if it had been known and handled differently. As one of Frank Teasdale's first actions had been to dismiss John Benson, it is more probable that he was never aware of the full picture. Thus, the club consequently received but a fraction of Phelan's worth. Speaking to John Benson later he was able to confirm my suspicions. One more chicken come home to roost I'm afraid.

'If the year brought any positive changes, then I for one was unable to detect them. Once or twice, I had hit out in my continuing frustration with it getting the better of me, and I knew that in my heart I was a long way from getting over the disappointment, regret and anger that I still felt in more or less equal proportions. Consequently, towards the back end of the season, when I attended a meeting of some seven local businessmen along with representatives from the board, I was more prepared to state my requirements before I would commit myself to a further spell in the madhouse.

'Certainly, I still missed a part of the involvement but time was adding its own perspective and I was able to draw a balance between what I might be missing and what I might be landed with, if I returned. Frank painted a very pessimistic picture and looked for financial commitments from prospective new board members. At that meeting two men promised a financial commitment and were co-opted. I agreed to continue discussions but made it clear that I would prefer to remain on the outside and would wish to return to the board only if, by doing so, it ensured continuity of the club, which was now being put into question by the present incumbents.

'These men can protest until doomsday but there was never any question of Burnley Football Club going out of existence. The nightmare scenario was for the then board to bring in an administrator or a receiver, whose first duty would have been to find a new buyer. Let there be no semblance of doubt that a buyer was there, ready, willing and able to fulfil all the essential conditions of a rescue. It would of course have resulted in a completely revamped board. Perhaps that is why it never happened.

'After this long year on the sidelines, I found myself attending a meeting at the Manchester headquarters of the club's bankers. This was in May 1986, very near the season's end. John Jackson had departed taking with him the best brain on the board and seriously reducing the experience available to extricate themselves from the mess that was expanding by the day. Roosting chickens had been replaced by the headless variety. I met Frank Teasdale on a couple of occasions and it was impossible not to feel some human sympathy for him, and I had a feeling of guilt at having left him to pick up the pieces. I had always known that the job would be exceptionally difficult for him coming into it as he did with virtually no background. Many people outside football imagine that it is all too easy, and that all is needed is for themselves to get hold of the reigns to demonstrate how it should be done. There is also some cogency in the argument that I too fell into the category once of a day, but that is a theory for others to advance. The point I would wish to make is that there are no magic solutions and as John Jackson used to say, even in a league containing the best 20 teams in the world, one of them would finish at the bottom. And no doubt they would sack the manager.

'The meeting at the bank was sandwiched between exploratory talks which I held with members of the board and for a time it seemed that déjà vu was on the cards, so that I was back with the mental gyrations of trying to straighten out my own attitudes towards it all. Frankly, I was still torn between a desire to do all that I could to help the club, but not to the extent of tearing apart my own lifestyle, and undergoing all the old traumas once more. I was in the fortunate position of knowing that I could immediately introduce new cash into the club, and amounts were mentioned that would have removed the immediate pressure on the club, as long as the bank would undertake to maintain the existing levels of financial support. My proposal to them was to ask that new funds introduced would not be used to reduce the overdraft facility and I further proposed that the overdraft be converted to a loan account, with regular repayments. These would systematically reduce the exposure of the bank, while giving the club the certainty of budgeting, which I regarded as essential while reconstruction was effected.

'The bank was unimpressed by my suggestion of a loan account to replace the overdraft and for my part I recalled the farce of the Billy Hamilton transfer negotiations when we were squeezed between the bank and Robert Maxwell, thus being compelled to settle for a most unsatisfactory transfer fee. Not a good start one might think and I was filled with foreboding for the outcome of the bank talks. Much nearer home I realised that it was no idle threat by the board to call in a receiver and I confirmed to the bank that I could guarantee a sum that was five times the relatively modest sum being asked of prospective directors. This was not nearly enough to take the club out of its borrowings but would easily finance the close season and give time to get into the real job. I also made it clear that I was willing to come in, only on my own terms.

'My home telephone number was red hot with calls from interested parties and others, just eager to know what was going on. I was flattered to be contacted by more than one capable investor stating that if I were to return to the club, they would be interested in providing finance and support. In every case I told the truth that I would be returning to Burnley only on my own terms and these would obviously be unacceptable to most of the board, unless they were left with no alternative. In fairness it has to be said that I would have taken the same attitude in their position. But in a nutshell, I knew that there was no possibility of Burnley going under as had been asserted by those eager to amplify their own "knowledge".

'On the day after the TSB meeting, Frank wrote an odd sort of letter to me asking where the money was coming from and mentioning one other person who had let it be known that he would be interested in joining me, but not the existing board. I replied to this letter from Frank confirming that the money was honestly earned and legal. I thought that I had put everything as clearly as possible, confirming in my letter my willingness and ability to carry the commitment through. The main conditions that I laid down were: I rejoined the board as chairman for a minimum three-year period; Frank remained as vice-chairman; the bank agreed to give their support at existing levels; I handled all financial matters; I handled the appointment of a team manager, probably Martin Dobson.

'A further meeting then took place in the offices of Basil Dearing on a Monday night which I attended at very short notice breaking another appointment in order to attend.

'Now I will be the first to admit that the conditions that I laid down could be interpreted as asking to be the second Bob Lord except I will argue that I did not insist upon being the majority shareholder, this making it possible for me to be removed by the others if I showed tendencies to emulate the great man, absolute power and all that. However, I was quite firm in my mind that there was no other way that I was going to return. There would be a board not exactly to my taste but acceptable on the whole and undoubtedly containing more workers than the one I had left. I was therefore very disappointed to hear Frank say that he would resign if this package went through. By now his paranoid jibe had no relevance in the context of the urgency of the situation[59].

'At the meeting in Dearing's offices, David Iven seemed keen to see me back and Basil took an eminently practical line, without displaying any personal preferences and gave me the impression that a company liquidation was a real possibility. We discussed the question of meeting the wages bill, due the following Wednesday,

---

59 At this point the club was four days away from receivership.

and I confirmed my willingness to do just that, having learned that the directors had themselves been in the position of having to put money into the club, during the year.

'It was necessary for me to leave them at nine o'clock and as sure as makes no difference, that I was returning to the club and that I would be persuading Frank to stay once the dust had settled. At this stage I should add that Frank went out of his way to say that he would not be taking his bat home and would continue to give the club his support as always. I was told that Frank would ring me the next day to continue the talks and finalise the details. I told nobody other than my wife whose reaction was that the description of "paranoid" flattered me if we were to go through all that again.

'In view of what happened, it is a good job that I told no one and I said nothing, as to my utter amazement I heard absolutely nothing from the directors until the Thursday afternoon of that week, when Frank rang me to say they had been able to arrange a package without me. As Wednesday had gone by in silence, arrangements must have been made to pay the wages. I was not at all surprised by the call but surely somebody could have kept me in the picture for those few days. Maybe leopards do not change their spots after all.

'During these talks, I had indicated a willingness to provide some limited sponsorship as it has never rested easily with me to be at loggerheads with anyone. I simply do not see any point in it and, like every other person I have met, I have preferences in the company I keep and those with who I am obliged to work or associate. The other sort is best left to get on with their own devices and as far as possible, live and let live. But the next development caused me to go back on the promise, if that is what it was, regarding the sponsorship that I offered.

'There followed in rapid succession two outrageous statements through the press which gave me every right to demand retraction and more, had I been of a mind to press them to the limit.

Incredibly, a local paper carried an article headed "Gill Takeover Bid Fails". To have my offer of help so gruesomely distorted made me thoroughly sick and left me with a strong loathing of others, more than I had ever thought myself capable of developing.

'The club also issued a long and garbled statement through both the *Burnley Express* and the *Evening Telegraph*, in which there was great reference to the "consortium" supposedly led by myself which was imagined to be lurking around every dark corner waiting to remove, by fair means or foul, the custodians of all that was good and proper at Burnley Football Club. I wrote to Teasdale asking for an equally prominent withdrawal but of course it got me nowhere. I had promised David Iven that finance existed to retrieve the club's misfortunes, and for the avoidance of any lingering doubt wrote to Teasdale to say that the offer of the safety net was now withdrawn.

'It was not until the accounts of the club for the year to 31 May 1987 were published some 18 months later that I could deduce how the initial finance was secured and it was much to the credit of the main sponsors, who had evidently paid two years in advance, to give the first chink of light and breathing space in the absence of permanent capital. Allied to the issue of new shares, there at least existed a basis for continuation.

'To this day I have never fully forgiven the last episode and I would have to be the biggest fool under the sun to fail now to accept where I stood with some members of the board. Yet within the next month I was to get another letter asking me to be of assistance in the case of the John Doherty dismissal. The letter in question came in June 1986 and I replied stroppily. Soft-headed mug that I am, I then had second thoughts and rang to give the details that were needed and by the admission of the club saved them another few thousand pounds.

'A year or two had passed and I had left the club and had attended some but by no means all the home games, always paying my way, never asking nor receiving any favours. The club reached a Wembley final against Wolverhampton Wanderers, and the game was attended by more than 80,000 spectators. My wife and I were among the crowd and had also been to the Preston semi-final tie when Burnley won to get to the final. I was as pleased as the next guy and made sure I had a free weekend for the final. After all, I was still a major shareholder. I asked for tickets for the final for which I would be happy to pay as always, but was told I could go and queue for them like anyone else. A gratuitous insult. From that day, Burnley Football Club has never had a penny from me apart from admission money.'

* * *

In the *Burnley Express*, Jimmy McIlroy and Granville Shackleton summed up the events of the final few weeks. Shackleton had headlined one piece with 'Four Days to Sink or Swim', when he reported that there had been threats to turn off the gas and electricity at the club because of unpaid bills. The grim warning had come from director Basil Dearing following a poor response to the 42,000 new shares issued that were for sale. 'Grim,' said Dearing with four days to fold or survive. 'Triple Blow for Clarets' wrote Shackleton next:

'A move to bring former managing director Derek Gill back to the board of Burnley Football Club has failed and another shock development has been the resignation of promotions manager, Neville Neville. And now I am told that the Burnley Football Supporters' Club which is holding its committee meeting tomorrow night will be discussing a resolution that says some members are "very disgruntled with what is going on at Turf Moor at the moment".

'Clarets chairman Frank Teasdale was not available for comment yesterday. But Mr Gill, who resigned from the board of directors last May, confirmed that a move to inject money into the club had been turned down in the past week. In a brief statement yesterday he said, "There was never any question of a takeover. Substantial money was available subject to conditions which were not acceptable to the board of directors and I am no longer interested."

'I understand that one of the conditions was to have been that now the bank has guaranteed to back the club until the end of next season, Mr Gill should have become chairman. I also understand that the group backing Mr Gill would also have wanted Martin Dobson to return to Turf Moor as player-manager.

'With the move to get Mr Gill back having failed, the Bury player-manager will probably sign a new two-year contract at Gigg Lane and will also be keen to sign freed Clarets Kevin Hird and Alan Taylor. As expected, Burnley have not asked for re-election to the Central League next season. Shortage of players and lack of cash to cover several longer trips gave them little option.'

McIlroy, by now quite heartbroken and aghast at the state the club was in, and in his role as a reporter for the *Burnley Express*, wrote about the lifeline given to the club by the Trustee Savings Bank:

'Burnley Football Club yesterday received the green light and speculative rumours that it was about to fold were dispelled. Following a meeting between club directors and bank officials it was announced that league soccer would still be played at Turf Moor next season. Chairman Frank Teasdale, along with Dr David Iven and third director Basil Dearing, met officials of the TSB in Manchester where the club's financial plight was discussed, resulting in the bank securing the future of the club for the next 12 months.

'Mr Teasdale said, "Naturally I'm pleased we can still carry on, but I must emphasise that although we have got the bank's backing there is no need for complacency from anyone."

'The board presented cash flow projections to the bankers that led to an agreement of financial support until the end of 1986/87.

By then it is hoped that all the outstanding liabilities that the club has to meet will have been extinguished. Coupled with further stringent economies and a better use of the club's resources, the board and the bank are confident that the future can be faced with confidence.

'Chairman Teasdale said, "There is still a lot of work to be done but I am convinced that if we get the continued support of the Burnley public, we can start getting this club on the right road again."'

The right road again? If only Teasdale had known what was in store during the next season. If the club at the back end of 1985/86 had been within four days of insolvency and receivership, by the end of the next they would be just 90 minutes away from oblivion. The madness of the John Bond season and its lingering effects was not quite over.

18

Saved from the brink

MAY 1987 and, as Burnley faced the most crucial game in their history, his name was still bandied around as the sole cause of all of the club's misfortunes. There are those even today who cannot forgive John Bond for the consequences of the season he spent at Turf Moor.

Shortly after his appointment, he forecast, 'A year from now, they'll know I've been around.' Whoever 'they' were certainly did know. More than 25 years down the line 'they' still know. His prophecy reverberates around Lancashire for all the wrong reasons. Bond spoke about his 'proven flair' and said he was the one who could make things happen. Alas, he made the wrong things happen. 'I will have my finger in many pies,' he added. 'I have charge of Burnley, lock, stock and barrel.' On his departure, the Burnley board were staring down at the bottom of the barrel.

Martin Buchan had gone, Tommy Cavanagh was gone and with supreme irony in came Brian Miller, the man removed by John Jackson and the directors. Derek Gill was no longer on the board; Jackson was gone and Frank Teasdale was chairman. A new man had arrived, Clive Holt, and Basil Dearing had also departed. The critics were out in force, both in the local press and at the stormy AGM where Harry Brooks was the scourge of them all.

The club remained penniless, the team cobbled together with young kids, old pros and Joe Gallagher. Joe was in the final year of his four-year contract, the living reminder of John Bond's season. Leighton James was back. 'We won't be promoted,' said Miller, ever the realist. Burnley had no chance of going up, but how close they were by the season's end to going down and out – nobody could have predicted that. It was the first season of the new rule that the bottom club in the Fourth Division would exit the Football League. And three years along the line, John Bond continued to cop the blame.

It was his fault that there was no money. It was his fault that it was all spent. The accusations of recklessness, poor signings and lack of identity with the club and town would not go away. At the beginning of his tenure, there had been money in the bank and a team that simply needed a couple of astute additions. Instead, he had come in and turned the place upside down, 'they' said. Bond had been honest enough to admit that he tried to change things too fast and should have retained Frank Casper, but had not Jackson told him he wanted success and a promotion? He admitted to making poor signings, but was it his fault that Joe Gallagher was deemed fit to be bought, by the medics?

Seven years in the Fourth Division, 'they' said, was the price the club paid for this rash manager and his policies. But Gill knew it was not solely John Bond. If the season had been a mess, he was not the only culprit. There were others in the boardroom. And the sheer, rotten bad luck of the Kevin Reeves injury; you could not ignore that.

And was it his fault that those same directors had appointed John Benson as his successor and not Tommy Hutchison? And then even after that, was it his fault that Frank Teasdale and his board had appointed the doomed Martin Buchan, and again not considered Hutchison?

And maybe most crucial of all, why did Jackson, Gill et al, not dismiss Bond on the night they sat in the boardroom until the early hours after the League Cup defeat to Crewe, when they knew there and then he was the wrong appointment, so early in the season, and debated whether to pay him off or not? They chose to keep him, they chose to fund his new players, they chose to stick with him.

With those decisions, they effectively changed the course of Burnley history, consigning the club to failure and the Fourth Division for far too long.

What a heavy price both Gill and Jackson paid in terms of their personal well-being. Gill's foray into the world of the football boardroom left him dissatisfied for years, hugely hurt by the 'paranoid' accusation, deeply scarred by the rejection of his bid to support and help the club when it seemed it was down and out. He retired to his business, his family and his music interests, occasionally dipping into his diaries, adding to them in 2005, and thinking of what might have been.

Jackson's marriage broke down around the same time that he stepped down as chairman, and it is reasonable to think that the chairmanship had undermined his marriage. The red top newspapers had made him a target when *The Sun* featured him at a London game, under the headline 'Football Chief's Away Days', with a picture of him and his then lady friend, who later became his second wife.

An impossible relationship with Gill, abuse from fans, fractious AGMs, media criticisms, all distracted from his work as a barrister; who can blame him for thinking that it was just all too much? He was well respected for representing Liverpool fans at the Hillsborough inquiry and was the prosecuting barrister in the Peter Adamson trial. Adamson, a star of *Coronation Street*, had been accused of sexual impropriety and when the actor wore his Burnley FC tie at Burnley Crown Court, maybe as a way of identifying with the club and former chairman and prosecutor, it did not go down too well in judicial quarters. Jackson continued his unquestioned support for the club until the day he died in 2008 aged only 68.

Bond, too, was damaged by the whole experience. He managed at Swansea, relegated in the season that he left, then Birmingham and Shrewsbury, the latter going down under his management. When Shrewsbury were due to play at Burnley, the police advised him not to attend, fearing retribution from the home fans. He died in September 2012, after involvement with radio, and assisting John Benson at Wigan Athletic.

Brian Miller returned to the club at the beginning of the 'Orient Season', inviting Arthur Bellamy back as assistant manager and to the coaching staff, from his position as Gawthorpe groundsman, the post he had been offered by Bond with the story, apocryphal most likely, that Bond simply asked him, 'Do you know how to drive the tractor?' Gill, on the sidelines, used the local press to blame Bob Lord for the mess the club was in. Bond retorted with the rebuke that it was wrong of Gill to be blaming Lord, no longer there to defend himself. The Bond name just would not go away.

It is not the purpose of this book to go into graphic detail about the 'Orient Season'; it is already there in *No Nay Never Volume One* and the Roy Oldfield book *Mud, Sweat and Shears.* But if football is like a jigsaw puzzle, then you might say that the first piece of this particular puzzle was Bond's season. Nobody knew at the beginning of the 'Orient Season' what lay in store, but all these years down the line and with Burnley having clawed their way back over the years and established in the Premier League at the time of writing, what this book can do is remind people of how close they came to demotion from the Football League under the new rule that the bottom club would join non-league football. By the final game the football world looked on agog as one of the founder members was about to spend 90 minutes playing for its very existence.

This wasn't supposed to happen, said the media and Burnley supporters, and indeed the board of directors who tried in vain to have the decision overturned. The stark reality was that while the trap was designed to weed out the weak clubs, the ones that regularly ended up at the bottom, here was something totally unforeseen. This was the club that had been champions, played in Europe, produced a galaxy of star players and had a formidable history. Just over ten years earlier they had been a First Division club with players like Martin Dobson, Dave Thomas and Leighton James.

In a town of dereliction, depression and dilapidation, the ailing Clarets only added to the general gloom, mirroring the economic plight of the area; thousands in fact were past caring, something reflected in the attendances. At the beginning of the Bond season, the club had been awash with money. But now, a 'Save the Clarets' fund was started to try and do something to help reduce the £800,000 debt and the losses of £10,000 a week.

'Never again will the players earn the ridiculous wages of the Bond era,' the local press announced. Not quite a fair statement perhaps, as there had been a £300 a week limit, although all the new players Bond signed were put straight on that figure. Chairman Teasdale, at the beginning of the season, had once again been to the bank, cap in hand, to plead for funds. Fine, they said, but scrap the reserve side in the Central League. At one point manager Miller had just 13 professional players.

A new face had joined the board, Clive Holt, who was still there 30 years later until 'ousted' by new American owners in 2021. Holt well remembers that first year and the first meeting he attended.

He said, 'I remember the first meeting. It was some meeting. Basil Dearing announced that the club was insolvent and was trading illegally. I sat there thinking what have I joined. What have I let myself in for? What am I doing here? But we got round that problem by having the ground revalued at a higher figure and in a stroke, we were no longer insolvent. Frank Teasdale was excellent at holding off creditors and even sent flowers to the tax lady. He was excellent at finding sponsors who would pay upfront rather than spreading their money over a season. At the beginning of the season, I went to watch a friendly at Wigan and I began to question my sanity as to why I had joined the board, we had so few players that day.

'Near the end of the season there was a game at Scunthorpe that we lost and directors from Lincoln were there to watch and see us lose. Afterwards they gloated that they would be safe. How wrong they were. It was Lincoln who went down. I remember there were four clubs that could have gone down on that final day. But if Burnley won, I was sure that one of the others would lose. And that's how it turned out, and the money from the Orient game and the huge crowd allowed us to get through the summer.

'At one point when it did look like we would go out of the league we had this tongue-in-cheek plan to take over struggling Cardiff City, a club then about to collapse. The idea was to relocate them to Burnley and rename them. We even spoke to the Football League about it. So, Wimbledon becoming MK Dons and moving to Milton Keynes was not a new idea.'

Ironically, there was no hint in the first few weeks of what was to come. But then the rot began. A 6-0 defeat at home to Hereford United was played in front of fewer than 2,000 spectators. The local radio station reported, 'Oh, what a sad story here at Turf Moor, the crowd leaving the stadium fully 15 minutes before the end. To go down narrowly at home may cause some questions but to be thrashed 6-0 is beyond any questions, isn't it? The crowd are gathered outside the offices right now and they are chanting "rubbish, rubbish," and "we want our money back, we want football." I can't say anything that would add to Burnley's misery. The players know it. The management know it and all I can repeat is the sad, final score of Burnley 0 Hereford 6.'

In late April, Jimmy McIlroy in his *Burnley Express* column wrote a piece that was filled with anguish. It was a lengthy article in which he wrote about the club being on the brink of extinction, the mountain of apathy in the town, the unbelievable mistakes that had been made, the money wasted, that the club was close to folding and if they finished 92nd it would be the end. He urged the town to rally round and to support the Clarets Survival Fund, to keep the name of the town on the map and that the club was the town's greatest ambassador.

When the final game approached, there were fears that there would be riots if the worst happened. One supporter planned to run on the pitch and chain himself to the posts if they were losing with 20 minutes to go. There was a bomb scare and the ground was searched. The queues were huge and the game kicked off late. The tension was indescribable as reporters flooded into the stand to write their final obituaries.

Suffice it to say here that the match was won, tears were shed, the celebrations lasted long into the night and everyone vowed that this must never happen again. It had been an unthinkable, unimaginable situation the club had been in and the origins, fans insisted, were in the John Bond season and the squandered money.

And Joe Gallagher: it was his last game for the club but after the game, in the shower, he realised that his wedding ring was missing from his finger. Groundsman Roy Oldfield remembered that he was mortified and came to see him to ask if he would look out for it while he was repairing the pitch. The pitch was churned up and littered with divots and mud in places. Find a ring on a football pitch? Roy agreed to do what he could. An impossible task, he thought to himself, but kit man George Bray came up with a solution:

'Tell Joe to offer the apprentice who finds it a tenner.'

On the following Monday, when the apprentices came in to work on the pitch, they were organised in a line to walk up and down and look for it. To everyone's amazement, it was found. Joe left the club a hero for his part in the Orient win, and delighted he had his ring.

For reporter Keith McNee, however, there was tragedy. He had reported on the Clarets for years, was a manic supporter, utterly devoted to the club, but the Orient match was one game too many. He fell ill during the game and had to leave before the end. It must have broken his heart to do this and maybe he didn't realise that this was a warning sign of another more serious heart attack to come some weeks later. At half-time another reporter had found him leaning against a pillar looking dreadful. He had declined the offer of a doctor and said he'd be okay. Sadly, he wasn't. It was his last game reporting on the club, and since the promotion of 1981/82 and then the cup games of the following season, there had been little that was good to report.

19

More from the press

PETER HIGGS, in a *Burnley Express* article, outlined the arrival of John Bond, 'John Bond will retain his outspoken image in his new role as manager of Burnley Football Club. But whatever headlines the Clarets make in the coming Third Division campaign, the new boss will demand a down-to-earth approach from the players. These were two of the aspects of the Bond style of management to emerge within 24 hours of him taking over at Turf Moor.

'He arrived amid a blaze of publicity at a pre-arranged press conference on Tuesday, a tall, tanned, confident man in a grey suit to match his Mercedes parked outside the club entrance. The club had made no formal announcement in advance about the identity of the new manager but it was no surprise when Mr Bond walked through the door of the Executive Club in the Bob Lord Stand to face the cameras and reporters, and to be warmly greeted by his friends from the media. In his two years at Manchester City, the one-time West Ham full-back got to know the Manchester press pretty well. And even though he was joining a new club he was totally at home among this gathering.

'One national newspaper man summed up the new manager when he told me, "John Bond is the best soccer manager for publicity I've ever worked with."

'The style will not change even though Mr Bond has moved from the big city to homespun Burnley. "I expect Burnley to get as much publicity as Manchester United or City next season," Bond said. "If I can make my voice heard on something that I believe in then I shall do it. I believe it is important for the club. It is important for everyone."

'The need to promote the Clarets (in more ways than one) was also stressed by chairman John Jackson as he told reporters why Mr Bond had been selected from more than 30 applicants for the post[60]. As he said of the board's choice, "He has experience at all levels of football and has the qualities we are looking for in a manager to take us not just back to the Second Division, but right up to the First Division."

'Praising the calibre of men on the shortlist, Mr Jackson added, "We were so impressed that we would have been happy to employ any of the six men on the shortlist."

'Mr Bond had created a favourable impression when, as Manchester City manager, he brought a team to play in the Alan Stevenson testimonial match at Turf Moor 18 months ago and this said Mr Jackson had stood him in good stead as a possible successor to caretaker boss Frank Casper. In accepting the job, at a salary understood to be in the region of £20,000, Mr Bond said that there were many clubs in the Second and Third Division he would not have considered, even if they had offered him £40,000 a year.

'He will work at Turf Moor without a contract, by mutual agreement. Assessing the job, he said, "I know Burnley's financial position, they don't owe anyone a penny; and the level at which they can live. I've got to manipulate staff and get fresh players in. If my record at other clubs is anything to go by, it shouldn't take long to put things right and I'm not using Burnley as a stepping

---

60 It is worth reminding ourselves again that Bond had already been offered the job and told to stay quiet. Any interviews that took place with other candidates were simply cosmetic.

stone. They are not a big club but they could attain gates of 20,000 and the status of Coventry and Ipswich."

'As he set about the task of sorting out the players and coaching staff to his own requirements, Mr Bond promised that special attention will be given to rebuilding the youth policy. "It was something I built up at Norwich and now they have as good a youth scheme as anyone in the country. It's not simply the only way forward for Burnley but for all clubs."

'Looking ahead to the Third Division campaign he said, "People, even within the club, are saying that we have no right to be there and it should not be too hard to get out. I agree with the first part of that statement but anyone who thinks it will be easy is making a big mistake. You have to be working at proving you are the best and that is achieved only by good attitude and good discipline. The players will be left in no doubt about that."

'Mr Bond will be a tracksuit manager, sharing the coaching duties with assistant manager John Benson. The exact make-up of the backroom staff had, up to yesterday, still to be decided, while the new manager carried out a review of the situation. Another of his early tasks was to have talks with the players who have been offered new contracts but have yet to sign them. The six are Martin Dobson, Willie Donachie, Lee Dixon, Derek Scott, David Miller and Billy O'Rourke. And I understand that all six are prepared to accept the terms offered to them and will be re-signing for another season.

'Above all, Mr Bond plans to act quickly. "Any changes we make in the running of the club will be sorted out soon so that we can get on with the job. It's likely to be a busy few weeks."

'A revolution began at Turf Moor this week and the old club will never be quite the same again. Whether it proves successful only time will tell. But one thing is certain. It will be fascinating to find out.'

* * *

In September 1983, Higgs again wrote in the *Burnley Express*, this time about a 'Meet the Manager' evening at the club, 'Burnley boss John Bond was in typically outspoken form when he faced more than 350 fans in a "Meet the Manager" evening at a packed Centre Spot last Thursday night.

'Making it clear from the outset that he would not get into a slanging match with anyone over his policies or actions, he still produced some remarkably candid answers that kept the audience fascinated for two hours. Although adopting a serious stance on most topics he was ever prepared to enliven the evening with a joke or a wisecrack and set the mood with one of his first remarks by saying, "I am tempted to say that there's more here tonight than there are at the matches. But I was afraid you'd come back at me and say it's more interesting here than it is on the pitch."

'In answer to some pointed questions his replies covered subjects ranging from transfer policy, his signings so far, his opinions on the role of directors, what he thinks is the future of Burnley Football Club, why he left Manchester City, his attitude to the press, and his thoughts on the reaction of Burnley officials and supporters to him so far. Asked about the reasons for Burnley's decline, Mr Bond referred briefly to the past, taking up the theme that Burnley still had a great tradition to build on.

'"But it is too delicate for me to answer why the club is in its present position because it involves too much of the past. But one thing I would say is that the person who was responsible for leaving such an outstanding ground and creating a club of substance, perhaps stayed on too long. You can't have one single person running a football club. You cannot have a dictatorship and there has got to be a democratically run board of directors.

'"It seems to me that this club has been in decline for ten or 15 years but you are lucky it still has a status in football. Ron

Greenwood who was born here still loves the area and thinks this is a magic club. I was talking to Lawrie McMenemy only yesterday and he was saying what a good club Burnley is. You still have that status to build on, which a lot of clubs have lost. But if you don't do something about it soon, Burnley will lose it too. That's why it is important to get back to the Second and then the First Division as quickly as possible and that's what I am here to help you do."

'In seeking that aim, Mr Bond stressed that it would not be overnight and called for a degree of patience from the fans. "Even if you had Brian Clough and Bob Paisley in charge it could not be sorted out straightaway," he added. "But I've said that I will get things sorted by the end of September and from that point onwards I will take full responsibility for what happens. In order to get the team that I want and we need, in order to have a good chance of promotion, we have got to bring in new players and you can't pick up good players for £10,000 or £15,000. That is why we have to spend. It is important that we have a go at getting this club in the right direction again. We can do that without putting it into any sort of stupid debt. Then if we do that, we will have a chance. You don't have to fight these battles. I will fight them for you."

'Questioned on the signings he had made so far, Mr Bond admitted that some of them had not played up to his expectations. But he refused to concede that age was a factor. "Half the teams in the First Division would take Tommy Hutchison right now, so there's no argument about him. He's a good player. Gerry Gow was peanuts at £15,000. He may not play all the games but he is a very good influence to have about the club, make no mistake about that."

'He refused to be drawn into an argument with some fans who challenged him on the decision to sell Brian Laws to Huddersfield. But he restated his opinion that he did not believe that Brian Laws was a good defender and added, "I have not come here to destroy Burnley Football Club or to be a failure as a manager. I have never been sacked as a manager and I don't intend to start at Burnley. Nothing would give me greater pleasure than to get this club back to the First Division and the only way I'll do it is by getting what I believe to be the best team together. I don't want to sell the players that you like but if I have to in order to get the best team, then so be it."

'Asked whether he would sell Billy Hamilton to Newcastle he said, "I will fight tooth and nail to keep him because I believe players don't come more honest than Billy and he can be a tremendous asset to us. But if a club comes along with a silly offer, then I believe it is only fair and in the interests of the player and the football club to put that offer to them and for the player and club to make a decision."

'He recalled the £1m sale of Kevin Reeves from Norwich to Manchester City while he was manager, after Reeves had been bought from Bournemouth for £50,000. "I didn't want to sell him, but it was good business for the football club."

'On transfer dealings Mr Bond was asked why so much came out in the press in advance when it had been club policy to keep deals secret in the past, until they had been settled, or virtually done. "It's a situation in which you can't win. Dave Sexton got sacked at Manchester United not on his results, but because he did not speak to the press enough. Alf Ramsey was one of the most successful managers of all time yet never really got on with the press. All I can say is that I'm sure Burnley supporters are glad when they pick up newspapers and there's so often something about the club in them. And I promise that by the end of the season, this club will be one of the most talked about in the country[61]."

'On the subject of directors, Mr Bond told the audience that he believed their job was to control the finances and to control the

---

61 And so it was, but for all the wrong reasons, when he was sacked.

manager[62]. After earlier saying that the reasons for his departure from Maine Road was because he got too much interference, he said, "I don't believe that directors should get involved in the playing side at all."

'In answer to a questioner, Mr Bond said that he would have come to Burnley even if there had been no money to spend on players and also told the audience that there was no other club in the area that he would have joined. But he shocked listeners when he revealed, "I have felt less wanted at this club than at any other club I've been at. And that disappoints me. All I want is a chance. But when I hear some of the remarks that are made, I realise that these people would destroy life rather than make it. I want to be part of you and I want to help you. If you give me your support, I will work like stink to make this club great again. But make us feel welcome and make us feel as if we are needed."

'The occasion was also attended by assistant John Benson and players Billy Hamilton, Brian Flynn, Derek Scott and Vince Overson. But the player to whom Mr Bond awarded the highest praise was Michael Phelan. Asked why Phelan had not yet represented the England under-21s, he said, "Perhaps because Bobby Robson has not seen Burnley play latterly. If ever I have seen a certainty to play for England it is Michael Phelan. He's quality right the way through and I hope he goes all the way to the top because he deserves to."

'The night ended with possibly the most encouraging statement of all from Brian Flynn. As one of Burnley's longest-serving players in two spells at Turf Moor, he was asked to comment on the remark of Brian Laws that he was joining a club in Huddersfield that was friendly like Burnley used to be. Flynn said, "Burnley will always be a friendly club because it is such a friendly town. At

---

62 Surely by this he meant they should only control the manager's spending. He had made it quite clear he wanted no interference on anything else.

the moment the manager and the players are just getting to know each other. But we will sort things out and we'll be up there near the top of the league at the end of the season."'

* * *

Jimmy McIlroy, in a *Burnley Express* article in October 1983, had a simple prediction, 'Sorry Bondy, it's not promotion year.' He wrote, 'Having watched Burnley in their last two home games and assuming I had seen the best and the worst of them, I am forced to predict that they won't win promotion this season, but neither will they be relegated.

'On Saturday, the Clarets' performance against Gillingham matched the weather, abysmal. But on Tuesday they gave a much better display in similar nasty conditions, to go a long way to winning back the fans by beating a toothless Southend side. Tuesday night's 3-0 victory was absolutely vital for the team and manager John Bond because of the "stick" they have taken from the crowd when going down 3-2 on Saturday.

'My mission was to take stock of the current Burnley side and the progress, if any, made by manager John Bond since he took over in the close season amidst a great deal of controversy among Turf Moor followers. In all honesty, in these two games, it is difficult to see any improvement on the side that was relegated last year. But at the same time two swallows do not make a summer. Bondy has said he hasn't completed his team building yet and has admitted it is not a balanced 11. It is certainly lop-sided with only Tommy Hutchison providing any width or wing threat and the midfield badly need a ball winner.

'It is a bad sign for a team to play with a sweeper at home as was the case on Saturday. It means there isn't a great deal of confidence in the defence, because no matter what any advocate of this system may argue to the contrary, it is simply and purely defence orientated. Yet playing this way, Burnley lost. Thankfully caution was thrown to the wind on Tuesday and Martin Dobson played in midfield instead of being wasted at the back.

'It wasn't surprising to hear some of Bond's outbursts early in the season that he understood why Burnley had been relegated, because the squad lacked enough good players. I too was of the same opinion, even when Brian Miller was manager and promotion was obtained. Even when those unbelievable scalps such as Spurs, Liverpool, Coventry and Birmingham City were being obtained, the side failed to convince me it was a good one by the standards I apply.

'John Bond has been involved at First Division level for some years and naturally this was his measuring stick and not surprisingly in a matter of days he realised the squad he had inherited fell far short of what he had been used to. I believe it is impossible for a manager to lower his sights appreciably in a short time, and that the former City boss was just a shade hasty in writing off some of the players, which is why he set about bringing in his own men. That tag unfortunately definitely applies at the moment and will do until results get better and the side plays consistently well. If not, then scenes like last Saturday's boos when Vince Overson was brought off, instead of one of his own signings, will be heard a lot.

'Bond has now had time to take a good long look at the Third Division and he must be aware that it doesn't take an exceptionally good squad to win promotion. Last season I felt better players were needed to stave off relegation; right now, I'm not so sure if any marked improvements have been made, although it would seem more signings are on their way. In all fairness, when the buying spree has ended this side should be allowed time to settle.

'Besides Tuesday night's result, another pleasing aspect was the debut of 19-year-old David Miller. He fitted in nicely and confidently to be rewarded with the all-important second goal and it wouldn't surprise me if David one day develops into a first-class full-back. Tommy Hutchison may have lost a bit of pace and the youthfulness to get to the byline but he is still a beautiful crosser of the ball. He is a player ever since he came to me as a 19-year-old trialist at Oldham, but I couldn't raise the cash to take on another wage, so dropped a huge clanger. If he were three years younger, Billy Hamilton's goal tally would benefit tremendously. Tommy would be finding him with perfect centres from the line, the kind of player on whom the Northern Ireland international thrives.

'Kevin Reeves is a neat, skilful player, to my mind the type best suited to playing just behind the main strikers creating chances for them. Watching Martin Dobson closely on Tuesday, I couldn't help feeling he could do a superb job as a striking partner to Hamilton. He has enough know-how to stay out of trouble; he could hold up the ball long enough upfield until support arrives and he is a good header and striker of the ball. I bet he could be a revelation up front.

'Bond bought Gerry Gow no doubt to add bite to the midfield. On Saturday he was way below form and out of the side on Tuesday. If he cannot do the job then this type of player must figure high on the manager's shopping list. I am a little bit puzzled that Derek Scott cannot keep his place in the side because his all-out enthusiasm on the right side of midfield often impressed me and he would provide more of a balance.

'The middle of the defence looked ruffled on Saturday against a couple of big strikers. But Southend fielded a power-puff attack, so neither Overson nor Phelan were ever seriously troubled. Perhaps when Mal Waldron is freed from full-back duties he will add experience to this department. So, there we are: a poor display followed by a much improved one, leaving me feeling that some more improvement is necessary to not only win promotion, but also to justify the spending spree.'

* * *

Following the departure of Bond, the resignation of Gill as a director, the relegation at the end of the John Benson season and all the subsequent criticism of the board, widespread dissatisfaction grew. The AGM became a scene of heated and personal debate, tempers were high, and anger was undisguised. The local press was bombarded with irate supporters' letters and journalists were never short of material. One of the club's biggest supporters and sponsors was John Gilbraith, who, in an impassioned letter during the early days of the Teasdale chairmanship, highlighted the way that the club was now in the doldrums, but asked who was responsible and what the disagreements were during the Gill/Jackson period.

When Bond was manager, players who had Burnley at heart, left the club and were replaced by players only interested in the size of the wage packet. Who allowed this to happen, he asked. But what he deplored was the constant knocking of the club by armchair supporters in its hour of need. And as for the consortium of businessmen now interested in taking over, where were they when the club needed sponsors?

Clive Holt, who would himself soon become a director and remain so for 30 years, replied:

'May I reply to John Gilbraith's letter of Wednesday, 6 November. Firstly, all supporters must commend Mr Gilbraith and his company, Gilbraith Commercials, for the financial support that he has given Burnley FC. I also believe that one of his company directors, Mr Frank Teasdale, is working very hard for the betterment of the club. The correspondence that has appeared in the press over the past few weeks has not been penned by armchair supporters, but from a genuine desire to prevent a further downward spiral of a great club into a position that cannot be rectified.

'Unfortunately, confidence in the board, by the majority of supporters and shareholders, is poor, particularly with regard to Mr John Jackson and Dr David Iven. The board is answerable to shareholders but has additional responsibilities to its supporters and one expects a standard of honour equivalent to that of directors of a large public company. It would appear that many of the supporters and shareholders feel that this standard has not been maintained during the most disastrous period of the club's history. The policies pursued have failed the club both financially and on the field of play.

'All staff, including Mr Bond, were responsible to the board with the two above named gentlemen being leading members. But, to endeavour to place all the blame for the unfortunate situation which now exists on to the previous board and Mr Bond would appear to be a classic example of taking the easy option. The point must be made that the constitution of the current board has altered very little.

'I believe that the feeling of many potential sponsors is that they are not prepared for further money to be given to the club with no guarantee that it will not be wasted while the board formation remains unaltered. Unfortunately, the board still remains uncommunicative with the supporters and the normal answer to any request for information is "no comment".'

Holt wrote more, pointing to areas where money was wasted and that the board should communicate more clearly the problems of the club. It was clear he would have liked fresh faces on the board and that Jackson and Iven should resign.

Gill, no longer a director and by now no longer part of any group looking to take over the club, also responded to Gilbraith:

'The letter from John Gilbraith obliges me to reply. I had no intention of joining in the debate about the present plight of Burnley FC and can state that the so-called consortium of businessmen has nothing to do with me.

'Burnley have no better supporter than John Gilbraith, who in his position as employer of the club chairman cannot engage in public speculation without his words carrying substantial implicit authority. However, he commits the elementary error of equating support for the club with support for the board. For as long as the running of the club is believed to be unsatisfactory, and the running of the club must be the responsibility of the board, supporters will react in the only way open to them and stay away and withhold financial support.

'Since I resigned on 16 May 1985, there have been no boardroom changes and the letter implies that prior to my resignation, the reforming zeal of the present five was held in check by me. If I had carried that sort of weight things would have been very different. For example:

'Martin Dobson would have been appointed manager. He was approached for the job in March but refused to take it while Mr Jackson remained on the board. Frank Casper could not be approached without consent from Bury but I have his permission to say he was of the same mind.

'Shareholdings would have been equalised among the directors.

'Regular board meetings would have been held and team managers and staff would have known and understood their responsibilities and authority levels.

'The board would have accepted its responsibility for the running of the club and would not have treated the employees with a lack of respect and indifference that destroyed their enthusiasm.

'Now let us see what has happened since the present five had a clear field. Two managers have gone and the latest appointment has taken place in circumstances almost beyond belief. First-team players have left and even the club captain is on a week-by-week contract. Experienced and invaluable staff are reduced to despair. The secretary walked out, to be persuaded to return a few days later. The general manager has resigned. A celebration dinner to mark the 1959/60 championship was held which I attended and my company supported. Only two directors were present, Dr Iven and Jack Simmons. The chairman had been in London and was needed there the next day. Had I been chairman, I would have walked back before I would have missed it. How the hell can you expect public support if you do not lead from the front?

'I love Burnley FC, and it hurt me deeply to resign and leave, never dreaming that one day I would find myself unwelcome at the club. But it remains my opinion that the board lacks the ability and credibility to put things right. I leave others to judge whether or not it has improved since I left.'

Accusations and letters flew back and forth. There was no question that this was a club in a mess both on and off the field with a hapless board. The inimitable Harry Brooks pulled no punches. Chairman Teasdale gave as good as he got.

'AT A STORMY ANNUAL GENERAL MEETING last night, Burnley's former chairman John Jackson was accused of dragging the club into the Fourth Division,' wrote Keith McNee in his report of the 1985 Annual General Meeting. 'Loughborough University registrar Harry Brooks asked chairman Frank Teasdale to comment on former managing director Derek Gill's statement that Martin Dobson would not return to Turf Moor as manager because Mr Jackson was still on the board. Mr Brooks added, "Will you say whether in view of the depth of feeling against Mr Jackson among many supporters, you feel it is in the best interests of the club for him to continue as a director?"

'Mr Teasdale said, "We find ourselves being pulled into the mud. This question is not relevant at this meeting. I don't see any point at all in bringing up things like that, although you obviously feel strongly."

'Mr Brooks hit back. "If Mr Jackson went, support for this club would increase. More than any other person he was responsible for dragging Burnley into the Fourth Division. I give up in disgust at the cynicism."

'Mr Jackson's only comment was, "Is that a promise?"

'The board had earlier been faced with a barrage of questions about the state of the club, many of them put by Mr Brooks and businessman Clive Holt. And when manager Tommy Cavanagh was asked to address the meeting, he said, "Some terrible things have been said tonight. Everybody in football knows that Burnley once had a spirit that could not be matched. I just don't know where that spirit went.

'"You are not on a winner at this club the way you are going on now. It is horrendous. I know you are frustrated but the club will be destroyed if things don't change. It is easy to throw insults and I would not want to be a director in this atmosphere because I could not take it. The first few weeks after I took over, all I saw was demonstrations and petitions. That shows up the weaknesses. We need to pull together and not let all this aggro reflect on the players."

'After vice-chairman David Iven was re-elected to the board, he said he wanted to reply to those who had criticised him publicly and called for his resignation, especially Mr Brooks. "I have been associated with Burnley FC for a long time and for most of it we were in the First Division. I will not run away now and I will not be driven away."

'Mr Brooks moved on to the attack again and said, "There is a tradition in public life that people who fail should go. It is the height of cynicism and affrontery for Dr Iven to offer himself again for re-election. I speak for the man on the Turf Moor terraces when I say there is no belief in this town that Dr Iven is competent to be a director."

'Another shareholder, Bernard Rothwell, told the board that he would not want to be a director of a club that had presented such abysmal financial figures. Burnley lost nearly £5,000 a week during the last financial year and were more than £600,000 in the red. "We are nowhere near in the league," he said, "and the balance sheet is a disgrace. Don't the directors feel any shame?"

'Mr Teasdale answered, "I don't feel any shame. But I am a new boy on the board. My colleagues will have to examine their own consciences."

'Despite pressure from shareholders, the board refused to reveal how much money had been paid as a settlement to former manager John Bond. Director Basil Dearing said that part of the agreement with Mr Bond was that the sum would not be disclosed by either side. Former managing director Mr Derek Gill then said to Mr Dearing from the microphone, "You suggested to me that John Bond should get £5,000 to keep quiet. The final figure was probably twice that much."

'Mr Dearing replied that the settlement had been made at less than the amount that Mr Bond had claimed in the first place, and was in the best interests of the club.'

Clive Holt as good as had the last words at this stormy AGM, 'A lot of people in the town think that the board stink.' Nothing could ever have been blunter than that.

The saga continued when Jackson sold the majority of his shares to Teasdale but remained on the board. Gill continued to criticise the board, saying that it engendered an atmosphere of mistrust and non-cooperation and stated he would never accept the post of chairman with the current members. Brooks and Holt continued their campaign to rid the board of Jackson and Iven, but failed in attempts to buy their shares. Four hundred demonstrators bayed their anger outside the ground before a home defeat to Swindon Town.

Despite his unhappiness with the board, Gill did in fact go out of his way in the press to say that the level of personal abuse to which Jackson had been subjected in the preceding months had been intolerable. He made a telling comment to journalist Keith McNee:

'It is no secret that he and I had different views on how the club should be run. In retrospect it is obvious that our chairman/

managing director relationship was flawed from the start and doomed to failure.'

Brooks continued to bombard the local press with his letters in which he said the situation was just a nightmare. Holt invited Basil to dinner at which they might discuss the club's position. The invitation was rejected. And then Keith Meadows in the *Daily Mirror* wrote, under the headline 'BOND BLASTED, BURNLEY SACKED HIM TOO LATE', 'John Bond's judgement in the signing and selling of players was branded as catastrophic yesterday. That warning to Birmingham City, the latest club to employ John Bond as manager, came from the man who partly blames the flamboyant boss for leading Burnley towards Fourth Division oblivion. Derek Gill, Burnley's managing director during the ill-fated latter part of John Bond's reign, says, "He inherited a healthy financial situation and left the club struggling to make ends meet."

'Bond fanned the flames of his controversy-packed 14-month stay at Burnley when he slagged the Lancashire club in a TV interview. He said it was one of the worst-run clubs he'd seen and he was never going to be welcome when the fans booed him at his first home game. But Gill, a director at that time, rapped back.

'"He was booed because of what had happened before his first home match. We'd just lost 4-1 to a newly promoted side and then at Crewe in a Milk Cup tie. But the main reasons the supporters were not exactly jumping with joy was that he'd bombed out Brian Laws without seeing him play a competitive game and had tried to humiliate Martin Dobson, the club captain. He referred to Martin as "Colin" Dobson and appointed Tommy Hutchison as captain without telling Dobson. Martin, at 37, is a better player NOW than Bond ever was. Bond discarded good players for has-beens. He was certainly the worst manager I've ever worked with in terms of his transfer dealings which seriously weakened our team. Every club he has been to have been relegated within 12 months of John Bond leaving. Swansea is the one exception so far."

'But Gill admits, "Bond is right in saying Burnley were a badly run club. He was never the right man for the job and I couldn't believe it when I read of his appointment while on holiday."

'Gill clearly believes that John Jackson, who picked Bond as manager while he was chairman, shares the blame. "The directors write the cheques and I take my part of the responsibility as well, but I was appointed managing director after the damage was done. After that, there was a profit on transfers in my time. But the board could not handle Bond. They wouldn't work with him, yet hadn't the courage to sack him until it was too late."'

Jackson had stepped down as chairman in May of 1985. He resigned from the board in February 1986. It seems appropriate to end this very small chapter of reports with Keith McNee's account of that resignation. He had been on the board for just under ten years; no mean feat.

McNee wrote, 'Burnley FC's former chairman, John Jackson, has sensationally quit as a director. Only weeks after selling the majority of his shares, barrister John Jackson has sent his resignation letter to chairman Frank Teasdale and says he won't change his mind.

'"The reasons for my resignation are a matter for the directors and myself and nobody else. I will not be divulging the contents of my letter to Mr Teasdale at any stage. My resignation will take effect in a month's time and I will, as always, continue to support Burnley."

'Mr Teasdale said, "In my opinion it is a sad day for the club. He has done a great deal of work for our club and his knowledge will be missed. I cannot comment on his letter because I have not yet seen it but Mr Jackson has informed me that he is resigning. It is too early to say if the board will be strengthened but the situation will be reviewed."

'My view is that Mr Jackson has taken an intolerable amount of personal abuse both before and after stepping down as chairman last May while remaining as a director. Only last month he sold 850 of his shares to Mr Teasdale, leaving himself with just 100. Almost certainly he has not found the transition from being the chairman to merely a board member an easy one to adjust to. The deal between Mr Teasdale and Mr Jackson left the chairman holding 1,150 shares followed by Dr Iven with 922.

'Mr Jackson, 46, insisted that his decision to go was not taken because of the hate campaign against him by some supporters, although his critics claim otherwise. One of them, businessman Clive Holt, said, "The pressure of public opinion has at last forced him out. He has finally realised that Burnley FC was divided with him as a director. I just wonder why his resignation has taken so long. There can't be much fun in the personal abuse that has gone his way for months. But now, everyone can pull together for the sake of the club."

'Another critic, Harry Brooks, said, "It has finally dawned on Mr Jackson that he had to go. I had pledged £1,000 to the club's new fundraising scheme over the next year and I will now certainly honour that offer."

'In addition to Mr Teasdale, Burnley's other directors will be vice-chairman David Iven, solicitor Basil Dearing and Lancashire cricketer, Jack Simmons.'

* * *

In truth, Jackson had simply had enough, tired of the abuse, criticism and the fingers pointing at him. He was drained by the heated exchanges at Annual General Meetings and the frequent attacks from two people in particular, Brooks and Holt, plus various supporter groups. The effects on his personal and professional life were intense. In addition, he genuinely thought that by stepping down completely it would assist Frank Teasdale and make his task easier. He has served for nearly ten years with only one of them truly enjoyable.

Bond had been Jackson's appointment but he could argue that it was so close to being a success. A gamble it may have been, but Jackson saw in him a man who could sweep away the cobwebs and bring new thinking to an entrenched club. They say that one man does not make a team, but the sad case of striker Kevin Reeves might disprove that. After his premature and untimely retirement in mid-season, the season unravelled and there are more than just a few supporters that will argue that, but for that, the season might have been an eventual triumph. Football is filled with the 'if' word, but if Reeves had continued with that magical partnership with Hamilton, if Bond had succeeded, then promotion would have been a personal triumph for John Jackson and there would have been no slide into the mire of the Fourth Division.

Jackson referred to the two seasons after promotion as a 'nightmare'. If such things are bad enough for supporters, then for a chairman they are doubly so. One thing remained undiminished: his love for the club. Success for him was confined to just the one promotion season and after that, he suffered the slings and arrows that come when you are chairman of a club like Burnley, when supporters who had seen all the years of greatness, now saw a club on the brink of disaster.

This chapter could go on and on with the innumerable reports, letters, confrontations, arguments and accusations concerning the sad state of Burnley Football Club in the years following the John Bond season. There were seven years in the Fourth Division following the Benson relegation, seven years in the football wilderness with Teasdale at the helm. No one could ever accuse him of lack of courage and that courage was rewarded in 1991/92 when Jimmy Mullen's team at last won promotion from the Fourth to the Third Division with a brand of exciting football that was a joy to watch.

But even then, club troubles were still far from over; and other Burnley history books relate all those years of strife. In 2022, the club is a proud member of the Premier League, battling above its weight, and hugely successful in comparison to the years that we have looked at in this book.

For the rest of the story, may I recommend *From Orient to the Emirates* by Tim Quelch. Publication of this Bond/Gill/Jackson book sees the 30th anniversary of the promotion at York in 1992, the promotion that is seen as the end of the wilderness years and the beginning of the long road to the Premier League.

20
Recollections

FORMER REFEREE Keith Hackett was familiar with both John Bond and Burnley Football Club in the 1980s. He wrote:

'One of the major occasions in my refereeing career was to be appointed to referee the 100th FA Cup Final in 1981 between Tottenham Hotspur and Manchester City. Bond had become the manager of City at the start of the season and with a reputation of having been a West Ham player, he clearly tried to get the team to play a short passing game rather than long balls. The first game saw Tommy Hutchison score both goals to earn a 1-1 draw. The replay, the following Thursday, became a classic, made famous by Ricky Villa scoring the winning goal to give Tottenham the 3-2 win.

'Shortly after I blew the final whistle, I was approached by John Bond who clutched my hand and gave it a warm handshake, congratulating me for my contribution to the game. For a losing manager, hoping for his team to lift one of the most cherished trophies in English football, it was a magnanimous gesture.

'I would go on to referee one of Bond's teams again when he was boss at Burnley but his side at that time was not performing well and he was clearly in a stressful situation. After one game at Turf Moor, he knocked on the changing room door to seek clarification on a couple of decisions. I explained to him how I had come to my decision and had a job to do. He left the dressing room giving me a handshake and thanking me for my contribution.'

It is clear from Hackett's testimony that Bond was measured, courteous and fair. It takes a lot for a man who has just lost an FA Cup Final to thank the referee. To say he was in a stressful situation at Burnley is putting it mildly and that must have been clear to Hackett.

* * *

Kevin Bond was good enough to respond to the email I sent him about his father. While not wishing to be drawn too much into the story he did pay tribute to John as a football man, saying that it is why he should be remembered, 'At one point he was one of the highest profile managers in the country and you do not get to that level without being a man of substance. My father built a good team at Burnley and played exciting football. He did the very best he could at all times professionally and certainly at Burnley.'

The newspaper reference he sent contained this tribute from Steve Daley, 'There aren't many icons in the game but John Bond was definitely one of them. I didn't always see eye to eye with him but I always had the utmost respect for him, I really did. Looking back now, I realise he was a fabulous manager and a fabulous man, too. He was doing his job at Burnley, and he always wanted the best for every football club that he was at. He was passionate about football, and we were both passionate about football, and sometimes that's why we disagreed. But at the end of the day, he would always have a beer with you.

'He was a character, along with the likes of Malcolm Allison, Ron Atkinson and Harry Redknapp. At Burnley he wanted to bring in experience, Brian Flynn, Billy Hamilton and Dobbo were already there. But you can't legislate for injuries. When he signed me for Burnley, I was playing in America and he flew all the way to America with the chairman John Jackson. We talked for a couple of hours at the airport and after everything had been agreed, he said, "Let's have a beer to celebrate." He loved his football and he loved the five-a-sides and if you didn't pass to him there was hell to pay. He would always listen though; it wasn't just that we were doing it his way and that was it, although we often did do it his way. But, if you gave him 100 per cent in games, he would pull you through.'

* * *

It is certainly true that the Gerry Gow signing was not one of Bond's finest moments, a sentiment that the manager himself acknowledged. There is a book waiting to be written about great players who, just like a boxer always looks for one last fight when he really shouldn't, sign for one club too many when their legs are gone and their bodies are past their sell-by date. Gow was just such a player at Burnley and was heckled for two reasons: firstly, he was a Bond signing, and secondly, he just wasn't very good at that stage of his career.

Neil Palmer's fine book, *He's Here, He's There: The Gerry Gow Story*, calls Gow's Burnley chapter 'A Club Too Far', and that is exactly what it was. He was no longer the all-action hardman of Bristol City and Manchester City, but a player who confessed his body was wracked with pain after every game. Gow later confessed that it was a signing that should never have happened. At Bristol City he had been outstanding and remains a legend – talented, fierce, competitive, inspirational and the playmaker. That was very much the case at Manchester City; but in truth even by then his knees were in a poor state. By the time he came to Burnley they were totally shot. One might surmise that Bond must have known that but hoped for one last hurrah.

'I hated my time at Burnley,' Gow said. 'It was a club too far for me and the fans didn't like me either. I remember playing Gillingham at home and I was barracked during the game as usual. Just before the final whistle I'd had enough of this one particular bloke giving me stick all game, so when I got the chance, I went over to see him and looked him in the eye and pointed to the players' bar and said, "After the match, you and me." He agreed.

'"We lost the game 3-2 so I went to the players' bar and I was seething and couldn't wait to see the guy. I thought, well, he's my size so if it kicks off, I can handle him. As I walked into the bar, I saw him and he was 6ft 6in at least. What I didn't know was that the area of the enclosure where he was standing dips down over a foot. So, when we were staring eye to eye, he was standing in a two-foot hole. Well, I took a deep breath."'

Like all classic football stories like this it ended with them having a pint. In later years, Gow confessed that he was simply not fit enough to do himself justice at Burnley, and, in fact, felt he had let Bond down.

* * *

In a *Burnley Express* interview with Peter Higgs, Kevin Reeves spoke of why he had joined Burnley. 'Scoop of the year,' Higgs had called the signing, a player at the peak of his career and a full England international. One of the reasons behind the move, Higgs felt, was the personal magnetism of manager Bond. The flamboyant Bond behind the scenes most definitely inspired a fierce loyalty from his players.

'I've played my best football under John Bond's guidance,' said Reeves. 'His ideas are very much based on attacking football which is great for me. In training, for example, far more work is done on attack than defence. If I thought it was a permanent move to the Third Division, I would not have considered it. But from everything I've heard and seen, this club will not be in Division Three for long[63]. Promotion to Division Two is just a start and then we can go on from there.'

63. But for his career-ending injury he might well have been right.

Reeves saw a strong similarity between Burnley and his former club Norwich City. 'They are both soccer outposts where visiting teams don't like playing, and they've both been successful in the past. They are football towns whose success seems to lift everyone in the area. If I can help bring that back to Burnley over the next few years, I'll be very happy. It should be quite an exciting time.'

* * *

Supporter Martyn Helm had a very surprising experience in Manchester at the time of the Bond question and answer session at Granada TV's studios, after he had left the club. 'I was working in Manchester and thought the meeting would be at Granada studios, so after work I ambled down with my non-footy work-mate. We were told at reception we should be with the audience in Burnley. However, I told them I couldn't get back to Burnley in time so we were invited to watch the programme from the directors' lounge, cups of tea provided. After the programme finished, in walked John Bond, very flustered and sweating, with host Elton Welsby. They didn't see us and someone said to Bond, "Oh, there are a couple of Burnley fans to meet you, John."

'He spun round very quickly looking agitated. I shook his hand, explained why we were there; he calmed down and then I recall blurting out some questions about his signings, Gerry Gow and Mal Waldron, if I recall correctly. He said he had bought players that he knew and thought they would do a job for him.

'After about ten minutes chatting, the programme director interrupted to say they had to leave to go to a meeting to go over the programme. We gave our thanks and left. To this day, I will never forget the look on John Bond's face when he turned round to see me.'

* * *

In Tubbs restaurant in Colne near Burnley, I met up with two of Derek Gill's sons, David and Stephen, David being the eldest of all of Derek's children. David was the first of the family to be taken to Turf Moor by his father. Both Stephen and David are involved in the business that their father expanded, Lupton and Place Ltd, which now employs 130 people. Stephen is the managing director and David the financial director. The company specialises in aluminium die casting. It is one of the leading European firms, if not the leading one, in the field.

It was an emotional meeting; the love and respect they still have for Derek is clear to see and their admiration for him remains unbounded. He was a man of principle, they said, had no time for the 'establishment', had no hesitation in speaking his mind, and couldn't tolerate fools and frauds. Stephen is the son who once memorably told Robert Maxwell one Sunday morning when he telephoned to speak to Derek, what to do with himself, less than politely.

His father's blunt speaking was best illustrated in a newspaper that David brought along. In 1987, director Basil Dearing came under much criticism for defending a local football hooligan at a time when there had been a club campaign against such hooliganism. Mr Dearing was 'not fit to be a director', Gill said. 'It is the height of foolishness for a director of this club to defend someone in that situation.'

It was David who became the confidante that Derek talked to about everything. In the early days it was just David, being the oldest, who Derek took to Turf Moor. Eventually, he bought five season tickets for himself and four sons in the Cricket Field Stand, paying his way at all times. David was the son who gave up his house so that Steve Daley had somewhere for himself and family to live when he signed.

The family history of Burnley support went back 100 years; David's great-grandfather had been to the 1914 FA Cup Final and on one occasion had actually walked from Burnley to Blackburn to see a game. Burnley Football Club was in his father's blood, said David, and never was he prouder than when asked to serve the club by John Jackson. And yes, he did get to a point when he wanted to be chairman, not out of vanity or personal glory, but because he was convinced that he could do a better job than the efforts he was witnessing.

The 'night of the long knives', as he called it, was well remembered; the night of the home defeat against Crewe in the League Cup under Bond with the cracks showing and the appointment already clearly a poor one. Ironically, it was also the moment when Bond wanted clarification of his role and spending range. Without it, he was threatening to walk away. It was the night that Doc Iven was to relinquish his place on the board and become president. Derek would become chairman, backed by Colin Sanderson and Alan Hutchinson. Except Iven did not resign from the board and Sanderson abstained from the vote, in effect supporting Jackson. Sanderson, Iven and Jackson were all Freemasons, said David, and Derek wasn't.

And Derek was so angry, added David. He was livid at what he felt was just such a huge let-down. It was the night when he believed he would become chairman, but instead became managing director.

I asked at what point did Derek realise that he would not be able to work comfortably with the chairman. Maybe it was the away game at Chelsea, suggested David, when Burnley lost and John Jackson arrived with friends and asked Ken Bates for free tickets. Bates said no and an angry Jackson had written a cheque with something rude on the back. Derek was so angry at the chairman's behaviour, said David, who was there at the time, adding that this was probably the point (Miller was the manager and it was the relegation season) when Derek sensed that this was an unworkable relationship, they were so different.

Who were the people he admired and respected, I asked. Clement Attlee, his long-time hero, and Roy Jenkins. In football,

Bill Fox at Blackburn, Jimmy Adamson and Brian Clough. They'd met Clough at Forest reserve games and remembered one of his one-liners, 'I have no A-levels, my qualifications are my trophies.'

Both David and Stephen underlined how the hurt that Derek felt lasted 20 years and more. 'Heartbroken' and 'unfulfilled' were two of the words used. But there developed what became a long-running family joke. Another brother, Peter, would say to his father that the new fixtures were out.

'I have no interest in any new Burnley fixtures,' Derek replied. Then there was a slight pause before he asked, 'But who do we play on Boxing Day?' You can take the man out of the football club, but you can't take the football club out of the man.

* * *

Derek Scott made nearly 350 league and cup appearances for Burnley, scoring 29 goals. He made his debut in 1975 and left in 1985. He was there for the four critical seasons of the Gill period.

'A great coach but poor man-management,' he said of working under John Bond. 'He had clear ideas about how the game should be played and believed we should have the freedom to play, much as they did in his time at West Ham.

'We'd looked forward to John Bond coming. It was no surprise really; we knew that John Jackson wanted a big name. It was no surprise when he was sacked either. Once it was clear with a few games to go that there would be no promotion, we never saw him after that.

'He arrived at Gawthorpe for his first meeting with us and told us we'd just been relegated so therefore we must be crap, except it was an even stronger word than that. After the first game at Hull, that we lost 4-1, he came into the dressing room and told various players that they'd never play for him again. Joe Gallagher was one and Lee Dixon another. What Bond did to Martin Dobson was diabolical, having a go at him in training, belittling him. A lot of us were shocked and taken aback. You just don't do this. Anyway, Dobbo went back at him and gave as good as he got[64].

'He'd only just signed Joe Gallagher. He banned Joe from training and wanted rid of him. At one stage they tried to pay him off but Joe was having none of it and stood his ground. So, he'd run down from his home in Padiham, through the trees, and join the training ground on his own and run round the track for half an hour every day and then he'd run back home. That way he knew they could never sack him and say he was unfit.

'When a new manager comes, all you want is a chance to show him what you can do. But too many players never got that chance. He brought his own players in and made a definite us and them situation. But Kevin Reeves and Hutchison were two class players.

'It was John Benson who was the arm round the shoulder guy. Bond's man-management was poor and there were some people he treated terribly. But Benson was a nice guy, too nice to be a manager and it was when he was manager that we were relegated. The promotion before Bond probably came a year too soon. We had a lot of young kids in that team, Brian Laws, Andy Wharton and Kevin Young, good players but Bond didn't want them. Laws went to Huddersfield and I learned later that Mick Buxton the manager wanted me. But Bond wanted to keep me so sold him Brian instead.

'John Sainty used to slaughter some of those young players. What was funny when I was an apprentice was that when we cleaned the terraces after a game, I could find more money than I got paid.'

* * *

Mention the name of Bond on any Burnley fan website and the responses will come thick and fast. One of the great stories is that

---

64 I asked Dobbo about this for this book. Dobbo chuckled and said he was saving that for his own book. Fair enough. Memo, look out for Dobbo's book.

when the Clarets played Shrewsbury Town some years after he had been at Burnley, in the replayed game he had stood at the back of the stand disguised as a steward, still fearing the wrath of local people. Bear in mind that several years had gone by. In one newspaper next day there was a grainy picture of what was said to be him. To this day nobody is absolutely sure if it was Bond or if the story is apocryphal.

The first match at Turf Moor was a 1-1 draw in December 1992. Burnley won the replay 2-1 at Gay Meadow. Bond hadn't attended the game in Burnley. Even all these years later in the eyes of the Burnley fans it was still a grudge match with a mood that was far from sporting. At half-time there was trouble when one of the food huts was closed. One fan recalled that it became known as the 'Shrewsbury Pie War' when the hut couldn't cope with the number of Burnley fans and closed the shutters. Bedlam broke out and the local constabulary arrived en masse, shoving and thumping anyone who got in their way. Another fan described it as one of the nastiest atmospheres he had experienced, especially in the second half when a few decisions went against Burnley.

Tension increased when Shrewsbury took the lead and there was a real worry that if that scoreline had remained, there would have been mayhem after the game.

'I honestly believe,' wrote another fan, 'that if we had lost 1-0 there would have been a lot of trouble and damage in and outside the ground. As it turned out, the two late goals changed the atmosphere completely and the match ended with scenes of wild jubilation.'

Roger Eli was a substitute in the game at Shrewsbury. 'I remember being roundly booed by the Shrewsbury fans when I came on,' he remembered. 'But then I was instrumental in getting the Shrewsbury centre-back being sent off at Turf Moor.'

The subject of the Shrewsbury game prompted this summary of Bond on a fan site, 'With the benefit of time and reflection,

Bond became unjustifiably the scapegoat for the state of the club in the mid-to-late 1980s. He was a convenient figurehead to direct anger towards. When he arrived the weight of expectation was like a millstone round his neck and he appeared to exude the attitude that just by being there and lending his name to things, success at this lowly level would simply follow. Therefore, in following years, he has definitely become a scapegoat. But there were so many other factors involved. As a larger-than-life character, never shy to court the media, or give a printable quote or opinion, he was always going to fall short if ultimately you cannot deliver the goods.'

* * *

Frank Casper arrived in Burnley in the late 1960s, the first player to be bought by Bob Lord. A wonderfully deft and skilful striker, he was a fixture in the side until a severe knee injury ended his career in the mid-1970s. He stayed at the club fulfilling many roles from coach to manager, eventually making way for John Bond, and then later returning. Today, he still lives in Burnley. He had little time for John Jackson and remembers an early conversation with Bond when he was asked by Jackson to go and see him at the club. Bond had just arrived and Jackson indicated to Casper that Bond in the next room would like to speak with him. If it was at this meeting that Bond told Casper that he would not be keeping him at the club, it was something that Bond later regretted and admitted publicly.

Casper recalled that he told Bond to be careful of Jackson, 'He'll screw you.' 'No, he won't,' replied Bond, 'I'll screw him.'

In the sense that Bond went on an immediate spending spree, it could be said that this did happen, especially with extravagant expense claims. Within a year, however, Jackson had sacked Casper and for good reasons.

But there was certainly no love lost between Casper (and Miller for that matter) and Jackson. Even after promotion Casper suspects that Jackson was keen to be rid of him and Miller but was hardly in a position to sack them. At an end-of-season trip to Majorca, Casper let Miller know that they were to be offered a miserly £7.50-a-week pay rise. They considered telling Jackson what he could do with the offer, and walking out, but then thought it was what Jackson possibly wanted them to do. They stayed, but Casper was sure neither would be at the club within a year.

When they asked about a transfer budget after promotion, they were told free transfers only, there was no money. Relegation followed but Casper to this day feels that without the Overson injury they would have stayed up. The whole successful system was affected. Promotion had been won with Phelan and Overson as centre-backs with Dobson behind playing sweeper. It allowed Brian Laws and Andy Wharton to bomb forward at every opportunity as wing-backs. With Overson missing, Dobson had to play centre-back in a system that was never as effective.

'It was the cup run that season that kept Brian going,' said Casper. 'And on the day that he was sacked, Jackson never thought we would win the game that night, nobody actually told me he had been sacked. I was simply told I was in charge that night for the Tottenham cup game. There were no mobile phones back then so Brian couldn't contact me. After that, and the win, I was never actually told I was manager. We won more games and Jackson would simply tell the press, "Frank's in charge." Winning games, he was hardly likely to sack me but at the end of the season with the defeat at Crystal Palace, he was able to do that.

'I got on well with Derek Gill. We talked a lot. But it was a boardroom where too many people just didn't like each other. He was a droll guy but with a knowing twinkle in his eye. He'd say something and smile, letting you take in what he'd said. We became quite close and he'd tell me what he thought was going to happen. More often than not, he was right. He hinted that we would be sacked. I used to talk to him about John Jackson.

'"Am I talking out of turn?" I'd ask him. "No, you're not," he'd tell me with a smile. He'd have made a good chairman. It was just not a happy time.'

* * *

If ever anyone wonders exactly where the money went so quickly at Burnley after Gill had turned things round, and more than £300,000 had been received for Trevor Steven plus the insurance money for Kevin Reeves and the resale of Mal Waldron, it didn't help that Bond certainly had some extravagant tastes. Huge phone bills, expense claims[65], and what amounted to free petrol for both himself and his wife nibbled away at the reserves.

Long-time supporter Allen Rycroft was able to confirm the petrol story, although, to be fair, Bond was certainly not the first or the last manager to make use of a club's money. And before him, Bob Lord had certainly propped up his lifestyle with claims to the club for a whole range of things.

Allen got on well with John Jackson, he said. 'I was the first chairman of the supporters' club that Jackson initiated. And someone I knew well was club kit man George Bray. He was like an uncle to me; he lived very nearby and I played with his son all the time. John Bond used to give George his old suits that he'd finished with. So, there was George in these expensive suits and he thought he was royalty.'

* * *

Tim Quelch pulled no punches in his account of the signing of Joe Gallagher, 'The £30,000 fee that Burnley shelled out to West Ham in the summer of 1983 for Joe Gallagher was a calamitous error. He had once been a conscientious, commanding and composed centre-half for First Division Birmingham, but no longer had the mobility

65 Frank Casper had also referred to these.

or pace to fulfil that role. In fairness to Bond and Gallagher, not even a medical specialist from Manchester could find anything wrong with Gallagher's knee other than a degree of retraction.

'What the medical personnel overlooked was Gallagher's limited capacity to twist and turn. This was brutally exposed in his first truly competitive game at Hull. Whenever Joe needed to shift direction suddenly, stress was placed on his damaged knee, causing him to hobble. The Burnley fans recognised this, quickly dubbing him Galloping Joe. Gallagher did not play another game for Bond.'

* * *

Joe Gallagher was delighted to talk about his time at Burnley and harboured not an ounce of ill feeling or any bad memories.

'Derek Gill was an absolute gentleman,' he recalled. 'He was with all the players.'

He had slightly different views on John Bond. He recalled that he had been impressed that in a game between Norwich and Birmingham, Bond, then the Norwich manager, came down to the touchline from the stand to see if he was okay after he was injured in a tackle. 'It helped me see John Bond in a good light, years later when he wanted to sign me for Burnley. But in fact, once I was there, I never really took to him.'

In our long phone call, we both acknowledged that all this took place over 25 years ago and clear memories fade and become hazy. It meant that Joe had no recollection of the club making determined attempts to pay him off, or of lapping the fields alone to keep fit. But he did remember the header that Ian Britton scored against Orient in the game that saved Burnley. 'I was behind him and coming in for the header myself, but he got in front of me and scored. If I'd headed it maybe it would have gone over the bar, but thank goodness Ian scored.' There's that word 'if' again. It could well be that Joe not getting the header saved Burnley.

'After the Hull game I was just dropped. But Bond never said a word to me. For weeks he never spoke to me, not even hello, he just ignored me. He was never rude and never swore, but I could pass him in a corridor and there wasn't even an acknowledgement. I just stayed out of his way, trained with the reserves with John Benson and played some reserve games. I just tried to keep fit and stay cheerful. Home was in Padiham, a little estate near the training ground where I lived with my wife and daughter, and she attended the local high school. We were very happy there, especially in the final season of my contract when I got back to playing.

'Yes, I did have a bad knee and couldn't fully bend it, it was always a problem and it did affect me. It may sound odd but I never suffered from injuries. Testing it on the terrace steps was correct, but that was commonplace back then and I passed the medical with flying colours. But for team photos when the front row players sometimes squat, I couldn't do that.

'I thoroughly enjoyed my four years there at a great club with some great players; Billy Hamilton, Martin Dobson, Derek Scott for example, and Tommy Hutchison. Yes, I was well paid, £300 a week, and if you ask where did all the money go, Bond brought six players in, I was one, all of us on maximum wage of £300 and bonuses. Not that I got many bonuses.

'Yes, I remember the incident with Martin Dobson. It was common practice for Bond, and any manager for that matter, to stop any practice game and gather us all round him so he could explain something or have a go at somebody. And on this occasion, it was Martin he decided to have a go at telling him he wanted him to do this, and do that, run here and run there. Well Martin just looked furious and answered back, Bond was being so aggressive with him.

'After Burnley I worked for 14 years for the PFA and then several years at Birmingham City in a sort of ambassador/host role. Covid ended that but fingers crossed we can get back to normality soon.'

When I told Joe that supporters called him 'Galloping Joe', he laughed. 'I like that, yes,' he chuckled. Football is filled with ironies, and Joe, who barely played a game for three years, then became a hero after the Orient season and the final game.

* * *

Vince Overson speaks highly of John Bond even though the early days consisted of endless abuse and animosity. 'We felt trepidation when we heard he was the new manager,' said Overson. 'I started with Harry Potts and then Brian Miller and Arthur Bellamy. The family atmosphere was so important. Then there was Frank Casper to continue that tradition. Harry Potts used to collect me from the hotel and drive me to training. His driving terrified me.

'How our life was about to change when Bond arrived. Here was this brash, confident, larger-than-life figure that was never out of the papers. This is the unknown, I thought. And I was injured, the abductor tendon in the groin. I'd played through the injury at the end of the promotion season in 1982/83, we thought it would settle in the summer but it didn't and I missed most of the next season. I had cortisone injections instead of surgery. And I was still out of action when Bond arrived, struggling with pre-season but trying to get back. He gave me absolute hell, slaughtering me in front of the others. He offered no sympathy. I felt like packing things in, the pain was bad, I felt just so low at rock bottom. Then came the key moment.

'Again, in front of everybody he set into me telling everyone I wanted HIM to persuade me to carry on. On and on he went and said that it was ME that needed to make the decision. How could HE do it, he hardly knew me. There was a lot of effing and blinding. Why don't you just eff off, I told him. He laughed, turned away and walked off. I'm sick of you, I shouted as he carried on walking. I was absolutely fuming and in the next training game smashed into him and took him out. That felt good, I said, as he lay on the floor. And still he laughed. In that session I clattered everyone I was so angry and worked up. Even little Brian Flynn as nice a guy as you could meet. Everyone got a kicking. And after that session he wanted to see me.

'I'm thinking to myself that's it, I'm done, finished. But no. "You scared the shit out of us all today," he said. "This is the Overson I wanted to see. You do the business for me and I'll look after you."

'It was the turning point. And he was as good as his word. I was physically getting better and I was picked ahead of Joe Gallagher and Mal Waldron. I got a new contract and a pay rise and never looked back. Was all this just brilliant man-management on his part? Some players need an arm round the shoulder, others a good kick up the arse. The latter was what I got. Mind you the young players were terrified of him because they felt so intimidated but I got to see the warmer side. He'd bring piles of suits in and throw them on the table and say help yourselves. Groundsman Roy Oldfield got warm sweaters.

'Chairman John Jackson I couldn't stand, I found him just so condescending. I had no time for him. On an away trip I overheard him and John Bond having a real argument in the corridor one night. Voices were raised and I said to room-mate Derek Scott, hey come and listen to this. It was about Joe Gallagher and Bondy was screaming at Jackson to get rid of him. It was a real set-to. I got the feeling they didn't like each other.

'Derek Gill, I did like. He was a pleasant man and a fair man. Always had a smile on his face. You could always talk to him.

'Training with Bond was so enjoyable and every day I couldn't wait to get into Gawthorpe, said Vince Overson. 'He wanted me to bring the ball out and play it, not just to be a centre-back smashing people. He wanted his centre-backs to be able to move out wide and get crosses over. We worked on that. Kevin Reeves was so good to play with. He was a joy, the way he brought others into play and the way he made himself available for me to find making my job so much easier. Maybe it was a turning point when he had to retire. Who knows what might have happened if he had been able to carry on; he was such a great link with Billy Hamilton.

'It was no surprise really when Bondy left. The fans had turned against him and during a game you could feel the atmosphere. In the final games we'd be thinking this doesn't feel right, where is he? It's funny, I bumped into his son Kevin Bond some time again and he expected me to be slagging his father off about the time at Burnley. But no, I told him he was the best coach I knew.'

* * *

If a supporter can be a legend, then perhaps that description fits Dave Burnley, who until the Covid pandemic had not missed a game since the early 1970s. Without a car and living 75 miles from Turf Moor, somehow this unique man had seen every match until events dictated that fans were locked out of stadiums.

His first book, *Got to Be There*, devotes several pages to the Bond season. A few paragraphs are worth including here:

'In June 1983, for the first time in 30 years, a manager was enrolled who had no previous connection with the Burnley Football Club, either socially or professionally. His name was Bond … John Bond! One of the most familiar figures in football at the time, Bond had recently resigned from Manchester City.

'The epitome of swank, he strutted into town like a football version of Arthur Daley. And just like the character in the *Minder* TV series, he too was recognisable by his camel-coloured Abercrombie overcoat and ridiculous sausage-sized cigar. His luxuriant mane of carefully coiffured hair looked to have absorbed the thick plumes of cigar smoke from below, such was its silver consistency. He came across as a big-time Charlie in small-town Burnley. From the start there was no common denominator between such a diverse pairing, and the partnership did not lie easily.

'I could see what "old silver head" was trying to achieve. He was looking for instant success from footballers that had performed in the top flight. "Had" being the critical word and now resembled a Dad's Army, with Bond himself representing the ill-fated Captain Mainwaring.

'Amidst a run of insufficient victories, a mood of ever-increasing impatience was directed at Bond and his managerial team. And after a terribly demoralising 1-0 defeat at lowly Newport County in early April, the scale of popular discontent became critical. With no sign of a return from our major investments, the realisation dawned that the good ship Burnley was sinking fast.

'John Bond had tried to bankroll Burnley up the divisions but had failed miserably. When he tried to counter these accusations with the insensitive claim that, "Burnley fans must realise that they are a small-town club and cannot compete with the big teams," he might as well have handed in his notice there and then.

'Any lingering respect for Bond soon dissipated and the vitriol became ever more personal.'

Much of it may be undeserved; the loss of Kevin Reeves was pivotal, but that vitriol has continued to this day, 40 years on.

Postscript

IF YOU had to pick two items from among the many available, two items that in a nutshell might sum up the broken relationship between Derek Gill and John Jackson, two items that might best illustrate the opinions they held, they might be Derek Gill's 1985 resignation letter and John Jackson's earlier statement in the 1984 directors' report. The latter came at the end of the Bond season.

Jackson wrote, 'In the summer of 1983, a policy decision was implemented by our manager on behalf of the board. That it failed, and failed dismally is a matter of record, and it is only with the benefit of hindsight that I am able to maintain that the greater part of the disaster was due to lack of judgement in its implementation, rather than an inherent fault in the policy.

'The year saw the problems off the field reflect badly on the field, and my urgent plea to those whom the cap fits is to either stop their behind-the-scenes manoeuvrings, or seek fresh pastures. The club and board need all the genuine support possible. Although most of our problems were self-induced, the unfortunate injury suffered by Kevin Reeves was the biggest single blow to our playing strength. I wish him the very best of luck in his new role at the club.

'As you are no doubt aware, we have organised our team management staff by appointing John Benson as manager, and

I am pleased to welcome Ian McFarlane as his chief coach. I ask on their behalf that they be given a fair chance to carry out their duties in a supportive atmosphere.

'In addition, I welcome Mr Basil Dearing to the board, confident that he will prove to be a great asset.

'As is apparent, I have not dwelt at length on matters set out elsewhere in these accounts. I hope that my underlying message is clear, if it is not, I will spell it out in simple terms. We need the continued support of everyone. We welcome constructive criticisms of interested parties, but neither our manager, our players, our staff or our directors should have to suffer from the petty jealousies which regrettably have been all too common in the last 12 months.'

I asked David Gill if the remarks about behind-the-scenes manoeuvrings in the second paragraph, and the petty jealousies, in the final paragraph, were a reference to his father Derek.

'It's definitely dad,' he replied. With that as the background, Jackson and Gill worked together for another year until Gill handed in his resignation letter, dated 16 May 1985.

It read, 'The correction of the present plight of Burnley Football Club requires total dedication, honesty and business sense and there is no time to be lost. I know that the present board is incapable of rectifying the situation. It has been widely speculated that I would assume the chairmanship of the club when the present incumbent stands down. I have to state that I would not accept the position of chairman of a board comprising the present members.

'Fundamental changes are required and any question of personal loyalties must now be set aside in the interests of the club. It is the club that matters and there is a solemn duty to ensure its survival long after individuals are gone. The board of which I am a member has made serious errors of judgement but worst of all has engendered an atmosphere of mistrust and non-cooperation within the club. The board must take responsibility and my own worst error has been to hold on too long in a vain attempt to keep things stable.

'Before this club can recover, failed and incompetent individuals must be removed. I love Burnley Football Club and to have been part of its decline will haunt me for the rest of my days. I have neglected my wife, family, friends and my business to try to help the club, but the job has failed and I must submit my resignation. At one stage I imagined I could put matters right but now I realise I could not do so, carrying board members that would not get a job in my own business.

'The club is desperate for an influx of Claret and Blue-eyed businessmen who will put the interests of the club first. I would dearly loved to have served on such a board, but my loss will be of no consequence if the club succeeds.'

It was a bombshell of a letter, which was made public, not just for the fact that he had resigned, but for its blunt portrayal of the situation and his reference to failed and incompetent individuals who would not get a job in his own business.

Both Gill and Jackson were gone. But the worst was still to come and it would take another seven years before the situation was rectified, seven more years of penny-pinching, begging bowls, struggle, poor results, disappointments, let-downs, near-disaster and demonstrations against chairman and board.

As this book was nearing completion and the deadline approached for submission to the publisher, I was given a recording of the infamous Granada interview with John Bond when he was asked blunt questions from audience members via a live feed from Turf Moor. He came across as smart, assured, articulate and confidently ready with every answer. He admitted he had made mistakes but he didn't feel guilty about anything.

When asked about where had all the money gone his answer was defiant. He had spent £308,000 on bringing players in, he said. But he had brought in £575,000 taking into account the Kevin Reeves insurance money[66].

'You ask me why they have got into so much debt. I don't know the answer. I'll ask you the same question.'

Bearing in mind the successful income generated by Gill's sponsorship deals, the return to a healthy bank balance, and then the £575,000 that Bond had referred to, it is a pertinent question. Just where did all the money go? At the end of the season the club posted a loss of £227,015.

Maybe that, in itself, is another story.

---

66 There had been the £300,000-plus from the Trevor Steven transfer, plus the resale of Mal Waldron.

TAYLOR
DATSUN